BLIND FAITH

The Miraculous Journey of
Lula Hardaway,
Stevie Wonder's Mother

AN AUTHORIZED BIOGRAPHY
OF LULA HARDAWAY

DENNIS LOVE AND STACY BROWN

SIMON & SCHUSTER

New York London Toronto Sydney Singapore

SIMON & SCHUSTER
Rockefeller Center
1230 Avenue of the Americas
New York, NY 10020

SIMON & SCHUSTER and colophon are registered trademarks
of Simon & Schuster Inc.

For information regarding special discounts for bulk purchases,
please contact Simon & Schuster Special Sales at 1-800-456-6798
or business@simonandschuster.com

Book design by Ellen R. Sasahara

Manufactured in the United States of America

Permissions appear on page 263.

1 3 5 7 9 10 8 6 4 2

Library of Congress Cataloging-in-Publication Data

Love, Dennis, 1954–
Blind faith, the miraculous journey of Lula Hardaway, Stevie
Wonder's mother : An authorized biography of Lula Hardaway /
Dennis Love and Stacy Brown.
p. cm.
1. Wonder, Stevie. 2. Rock musicians—United States—Biography. 3.
Hardaway, Lula. 4. African American Women—Biography. I. Brown,
Stacy, 1968– II. Title.
ML410.W836 L68 2002
782.421644'092'2—dc21
[B]
2002021634

ISBN 0-684-86979-9

ACKNOWLEDGMENTS

WE ARE GRATEFUL beyond measure for the opportunity to write this book, and for those who were gracious enough to help see us through.

It all starts with Cindy Hansen, who built the first bridge. Without the generous and unerring insights of Tom Kunkel, not to mention his unflagging faith in the authors, this project would have expired long ago. Clint Williams exhorted, challenged, and believed.

Our agent, the marvelous and steadfast Flip Brophy, took up our cause and kept us between the ditches. It was our great fortune to join forces with our editor and champion at Simon & Schuster, Chuck Adams, who shared our vision and exercised extraordinary patience. Patty Romanowski copyedited the manuscript with formidable savvy and genuine care, and saved us a thousand embarrassments.

Among the many who contributed their time and/or assistance, we would like to particularly thank Barrett Strong, the Four Tops, Berry Gordy Jr., the folks at Motown past and present, the *Detroit Free Press,* and the staffs at the Library of Congress and the Los Angeles Central Public Library. Many works by other writers influenced what appears here, especially Suzanne Smith's absorbing *Dancing in the Streets: Motown and the Cultural Politics of Detroit*; John Swenson's benchmark 1986 biography, *Stevie Wonder*; Nicholas

Lemann's *The Promised Land: The Great Black Migration and How It Changed America*, simply a great book; and Gordy's strikingly candid *To Be Loved: The Music, the Magic, the Memories of Motown*.

The dedication for this book speaks for itself, but others who aided, abetted, vetted, advised, encouraged, and sustained include a slew of Loves (especially Bill, Jennifer, and Barry and them); Rikki and Jordan Brown; Samantha Brown; Nathaniel and Maureen Brown; Yashi and Austin Brown; the fabulous Valerie Smith; DD Despard; Cheryl Weinstein; Leslie Jones; Emily Remes; Jay and Anne Tingle; Mary Pols; Stacy Finz; Jaxon Van Derbeken; Dorothy Korber; Kimberly Kindy; Rex and Kathleen Babin; Aurelio Rojas; John Hogan; Beth Fhaner; Keith Marder; Lynette Rice; Larry and Joanne Kent; George and Jean Price; Carolyn Kjer; Dan Weintraub; the Gonsalvi; Nicole McDaniel-Smith; Rex and Stacy Salas; Jeannette Branch; Jason Zimmerman; Tony Strothers; Ken Curry; Reggie (Cuzin') McKeiver; Arlette Stewart; Jon Dolphin; Tracy Campbell; Marilyn Shaw; the Mahmud-Bey family; Herman Hardaway and the Hurtsboro gang; Hardaways Calvin, Larry, Tim, and Renee; the people of Detroit; and Bunny the Cat.

And, lastly, the holy trinity:

Although this book has not been authorized or endorsed by Stevie Wonder, we thank him for making himself available for interviews. We owe Lula Hardaway a debt we can never repay—her astonishing courage was our fount, our wellspring, our mighty Mississippi. Above all, eternal gratitude to the lovely, talented, and resolute Terri Hardy, aka Mrs. Dennis Love, who stood firm amid all the tumult and the shouting, the victories and the stumbles, and by God's grace is still here.

FOR OUR MOTHERS
VIRGINIA LOVE AND BERTIE MCDANIEL-SMITH

CONTENTS

"At another time she asked, 'What is a soul?'
'No one knows,' I replied; 'but we know it is
not the body, and it is that part of us which
thinks and loves and hopes . . . (and) is
invisible.' . . . 'But if I write what my soul
thinks,' she said, 'then it will be visible,
and the words will be its body.'"

—Annie Sullivan, 1891, recounting a conversation
    with Helen Keller

Well, son, I'll tell you
Life for me ain't been no crystal stair.

—"From Mother to Son," by Langston Hughes

BLIND FAITH

PROLOGUE

Saginaw, Michigan, 1952

*Y*ou *need a miracle. God bless you and your baby boy, but there is nothing we can do. I am so sorry.*

It was the last doctor—the best doctor, the Mayo Clinic doctor—who said that. She had waited in his private office, the wriggling two-year-old in her lap, with all those impressive-looking diplomas on the wall, and then he had come in to talk to her. He was tall and intense, wearing a long, starched, white lab coat, a pair of half-moon spectacles teetering on the end of his nose. He had peered down through those spectacles at the clipboard in his hands for a great long while, and then he took the spectacles off and looked at her and the uncomprehending boy, and told her. Straight and honest. You need a miracle. God bless you and your baby boy, but there is nothing we can do. I am so sorry.

You need a miracle. Lula had taken those words home with her to Saginaw, which wasn't home at all. Not for an Alabama girl raised on a sharecropper's farm in the hot and humid middle of nowhere in the Black Belt, near a tattered little village called Hurtsboro, about a day's mule wagon ride from Montgomery in those days. That was home to her. But that was such a long time ago, eleven years now since her life crumbled around her and she made her way to this godforsaken place.

But not so long ago that she couldn't remember how it felt, then, to be back there. In times like these, with the winter cold starting to settle in, another whip-cold Michigan winter with the chill wafting into her bones like a ghost, Lula would remember what it was like back then in Alabama, where it never seemed to get cold and where children grew up strong and healthy and could see forever.

It never occurred to her, back then, that she would live anywhere else. Because when you are a child, Lula had decided, even a poor child, you don't ever really think that your world will change. You can't even picture it. You don't even know that any other world is out there. Even when times are hard and there isn't enough to eat and your back hurts so bad from picking cotton that you wonder if you'll ever stand upright again, a child will tell herself that everything is okay, because she doesn't know any better.

A little girl like that back in old Alabama . . . it would never enter her mind that one day she would be waiting on a platform at the train station in Columbus, Georgia, just across the state line from Eufaula, barely eleven years old, her planet in pieces, with no one to care for her but some man who called himself her daddy, a man who lived somewhere up in the grim reaches of Indiana at the distant end of the tracks. She couldn't have predicted that long, swaying, clacking train ride north and the very different world that awaited her there, gray and snowy and hardscrabble and without love. She couldn't have foretold the cruelties she would endure at the hands of ice-hearted men reeking of whiskey, men who would spend their money and their nights next to a warm stove in a gambling house rather than buy coal for their women and children shivering in a drafty, freezing stand of sticks back home. Those cold nights! Those nights when you sit there wrapped in some threadbare blanket and flimsy shawl, fighting off the ghost chill, thinking about that breadwinner who might come with money or who might not, but will sure enough come home sooner or later with anger in his soul.

That little girl chasing her favorite cat down a dusty dirt road near dark couldn't imagine any of that. Not when the sun is almost gone and the air is like a wondrous warm liquid and the crickets begin to rumble and the fireflies are darting and fluttering, their tiny yellow lamps flickering as if there is nothing amazing or spectacular about it at all. And there isn't, not when you're a little girl and you believe the world is a place where things are good and constant and make sense. You could never see yourself in a bitter-cold, crazy-dark tenement hallway with the knife in your hand, your jaw throbbing from the balled fist, a flash of blade and blood, the howling, the crimson tracks across the dirty, moonlit snow.

No, that little girl couldn't see any of that, not on a hot, savage-bright Sunday morning alongside a red-clay dirt road, with the church windows flung open to catch even the promise of salvation or a breeze, handheld paper funeral-home fans foaming back and forth like white-caps on a choppy sea, the sound of the choir filling up the little white building as if it would burst. Not when the preacher, looming like an apparition, is up there bellowing and frothing at Satan in a voice that surely reached into the bowels of Hell, a voice strong and pure enough to make Satan think twice before attempting to deliver his evil into the hearts of this solid-rock congregation. A little girl wrapped in that much love and faith couldn't possibly envision a life where the Devil runs unchecked, where wind and hearts and blood run cold.

That young girl couldn't peer into the future and see that baby, her third child, born too soon, destined to spend fifty-two days in an incubator. She couldn't envision the day when that precious baby boy, the one with a special spark even as a tiny thing, the special spark that stopped people on the street—*Look at that child!*—she couldn't foretell the day when that doctor would take off his half-moon spec-

3

tacles and tell her, straight and honest: *You need a miracle. There is nothing we can do. I am so sorry.* Or how people would stop her in the street; *Look at that child!* they would say. *That child has the spark, the spark of something I've never seen!* A little girl couldn't see that, not when she dreams of her own grown-up life, of some fine husband and their fine children and their life together, a life full of warm-liquid evenings and rumbling crickets and fluttering lightning bugs and churches and choirs and bellowing sermons and Sunday fried chicken and white tablecloths, a life of being wrapped in a man's love, in God's love.

The doctor's words stayed with her: *You need a miracle.* Little Stevie's affliction would have to be in the hands of the Lord now. But what kind of God would take from a helpless child the power of sight? Lula had seen them on the streets, the blind beggars and panhandlers, selling their pencils and gum and asking for handouts, dirty and pathetic and lost. In night terrors she saw Stevie huddled on the pavement, his mother dead and gone, and the panic would well up within her again, panic and desperation, the desperation that builds in a mother's heart when she has given up on the doctors and the hospitals and the clinics, and wonders what else she can do.

And then, on the radio: hope.

The radio preacher, the one who heals the sick and lame and—*Yes, Lord*—the blind, the one who exhorts demons from sinners, makes the drunks put their bottles down, brings the unconscious and near-dead to life, that preacher is telling his listeners about an upcoming trip to the Midwest. St. Louis and Topeka and Kansas City and Gary and Detroit and Saginaw and . . . Saginaw! At the fairgrounds. The hope rises in her heart, and she prays her thanks to God, and she mails in an offering of three hard-won dollars. The name of the preacher's radio program is *Healing Waters.* The lame and the halt and the blind have been restored by this man of God, and if God wills it, her little boy might see.

4

And so weeks later she wrapped the boy, walking good now, in his warmest clothes and begged a ride to the fairgrounds pressed hard against the outskirts of that cold and forbidding town, where the big revival tent loomed like the Promised Land bathed in torchlight. Admission is free, dear Sister, just remember the Lord when the plate is passed. It was warm inside, hundreds of people already there, black and white, clapping in time to the gospel singers onstage. Little Stevie was perched on her hip, mesmerized.

Shortly the singing stopped and the Reverend Oral Roberts took the stage, throwing a bolt of electricity through the still-growing, jostling crowd. The preacher, his stallion-black mane of hair glistening, started slow and quiet and stealthy and then began to pummel the crowd with his piercing taunts of their unworthiness before God, taunts punctuated by *amen*s and dramatic chords from the piano. Finally, he sent out the call: "Who among ye would be healed? Who among ye would be healed before God?"

Dozens surged toward the stage. Lula gripped the boy tightly and began to force her way to the front, like a determined fullback swimming for the goal line. At the foot of the stage, amid the swirling tumult, men in suits were choosing who would be allowed onstage and turning others away; Lula still was at least fifteen feet away when one of the men began to bark, No more! No more! She bulled closer and somehow hoisted Stevie in the air. My baby is blind! she yelled. My baby is blind! A thickset white man beside her took up the chant: Her baby is blind! Her baby is blind! And suddenly the crowd just seemed to part, and she was there, the boy bawling, the men hustling her up onto the stage.

It seemed like something out of the New Testament, the braying multitude, the cursed and the afflicted before them, an old crippled man next to Lula speaking in tongues. Another elderly man in front of her shook uncontrollably, his body racked by palsy. Behind her, a young woman's face was marred by a spidery lesion. And Stevie, his opaque eyes rolling back into his head, but not crying now, instead quiet, rigid, instinctively transfixed by the moment. One by one, the preacher began to minister to them, laying his hands on tormented bodies, beseeching God to heal them, to stop the Devil's work, to allow this gentleman to walk unaided, to stop this elderly brother's tremors, to restore beauty to this young woman's face. One by one, he challenged God to invoke His mercy. And, one by one, the afflicted responded. The blathering old man fell silent, reason suddenly reflected in his face, and then he abruptly let his crutches fall away, standing gingerly yet unaided. "Praise God!" someone shouted, and the crowd cheered. The palsied gentleman ceased shaking; the crowd thundered. Roberts placed his hands on the young woman's face, then swept them away; the blight was gone. She gaped in astonishment as someone held a mirror before her. The stage fairly shook with the crowd's seismic roar of approval.

Stevie and Lula were last.

That little girl in long-ago-and-faraway Alabama could never have imagined a time when she would crumple to her knees before a crowd on fire, clutching her precious child as if he might suddenly ascend to heaven on wings, tears of terror and joy plummeting down her face, the radio preacher placing his hands over the boy's eyes and yelling time and again, "I command you to see! In the name of Almighty God, I command you to see!" and the doctor's words echoing in her head, in her heart, and on her lips:

You need a miracle!
You need a miracle!
You need a miracle!

Part One

LULA

One

PARADISE

S HE WAS THE FIRST to arrive, the sister in the powder-blue suit from the Sunday school class, standing in the foyer, rigid, tentative, like a statue with a pocketbook. She was *exactly* on time. Lula figured the sister must have driven around the lush hills south of Ventura Boulevard in the winter rain for fifteen minutes before finally parking and knocking on the door, not wanting to be early but not willing to wait a second longer than she had to.

She stood there in the foyer and took it all in: the white-and-gold French Provincial furniture, the sparkling chandelier that made the late-afternoon light dance, the lush white rugs, the mahogany dining room table dense with food and wine, the white baby grand in the center of the room. She had that hungry look, the look Lula had seen before, hungry for whatever she could see.

And there was plenty to see. No question about that.

Can I take your coat, Sister? Lula asked.

Why, sure, she replied, snapping awake. Lula slipped the raincoat from her shoulders and gave it to the maid, who had drifted in from the kitchen along with the heady smell of baking bread.

Lula took the sister by the arm and led her into the living room with the soaring ceilings, toward the table. Let me pour you some champagne, Lula said. Sit down over here, and I'll get you something to drink. We'll visit until the others get here.

Well then, I don't mind if I do. The sister giggled slightly, then caught herself. She took the crystal flute proffered by Lula and smiled warmly. Sister Hardaway, she said, this is a fine and lovely place you have here. Just fine and lovely.

Well, thank you, Sister. I've been blessed.

An awkward silence. The sister took a long, greedy pull of champagne, and then another. The hungry eyes rested on the snow-white baby grand.

Will Stevie be—

The doorbell sounded. Excuse me, Lula said. Let me get that.

The other ladies from the Sunday school class began to spill through the door, laughing and chattering and shaking off the rain, and the social was underway. They gathered first in the living room, sporadically gawking about, as if in Manhattan for the first time. Then, at Lula's nudging, they began to graze along the well-appointed table and sip champagne. After a while they began to scatter about the house, several settling in the den, the walls spangled with framed gold records and the shelves dotted with framed pictures—Stevie with Coretta Scott King, Stevie with President Nixon, Stevie with Everybody.

The talk was of the church, the preacher, the preacher's wife, of Brother This and Sister That. Didn't the choir sound good last Sunday? Will you be here on Easter Sunday, or visiting your children? No one spoke of the invisible yet overwhelming presence in the room, the omniscient superstar ghost of the great Stevie Wonder. It would be rude, after all. This was Lula's party, Lula's house. They would have loved to have asked a thousand questions—What's your boy doing now? Tell us about that boy!—but they did not. Not even the sister in the powder-blue suit, even though she now had the too-quick laugh and the unmistakable glow of someone unaccustomed to alcohol before the sun goes down, if at all.

Soon enough things began to break up. One by one or in small clumps, the guests paid their respects to Lula in the foyer and began to make their way out the door. The last was Sister Powder Blue, listing slightly in her tracks.

I appreciate your coming, Sister, Lula said.

Honey, it was my pleasure, she replied, gazing about one last time. I just love your home, your lovely home. And you treated us so nice.

Well, thank you. We'll do it again sometime.

So lovely. The sister smiled and shook her head. I'll tell you one thing—

What's that, Sister?

You must have been a praying ass to get all this.

Lula stared hard for a moment. Then, slowly, she gave the sister a diplomatic smile. Thank you for coming, she said again, and gently closed the door.

Lula walked back into the heart of the house, taking in the white-and-gold French Provincial furniture, the sparkling chandelier that made the late-afternoon light dance, the lush white rugs, the mahogany dining room table still dense with food and wine, the white baby grand in the center of the room, the baking-bread smell. She poured half a glass of champagne and sat down on the sectional sofa and felt the old anger rise like bile.

A praying ass?

I must have been a praying ass?

Sister, you have no idea.

You best believe I was a praying ass.

Lula sat in the darkening silence of the room, her son's famous countenance radiating from every wall and shelf, and felt the hot tears of memory come.

• • •

To get to where it all began:

You float down out of the Southern haze until the Birmingham skyline materializes amid the rolling, tree-peppered hills, which, depending on the season and the drought, are a lush green or a desultory brown. The plane bumps and brakes and rushes to a halt, and before long you are in the car working your way out of Birmingham, which is modern and prosperous and new-seeming, down Interstate 65 toward Montgomery, which is not.

Montgomery, as if frozen in time, still looks as if it could serve as a movie set for the quintessential redneck capital city in the 1930s. The bone-white statehouse gleams dully above the two-storey, brick-and-mortar downtown façades, plain but rigidly resolute in their resistance to the linear desires of contemporary architecture. You half-expect, if you hang around long enough, to catch sight of a rotund, broad-faced, string-tied, porkpie-hatted caricature of some good-ole-boy legislator, his white Palm Beach suit mottled with two great flowering patches of sweat from beneath each armpit, ambling up the avenue toward the capitol after a languid, mostly liquid lunch at the Elite (pronounced "E-light" among the locals), a lunch provided for by, let's say, the cattlemen's association or the teachers' union. The city still has that air about it.

But Montgomery is not only the capital of the state but is also the nexus of the Black Belt, Alabama's still-rural middle swath, so named for the rich soil that has dry-spit out a living for those who have farmed it for two hundred years. But the Black Belt carries another connotation. Once you leave Montgomery behind, be it to travel east, west, or south, Alabama's African-American population is at its most predominant. Some counties—like Lowndes, or Wilcox, or Bullock—are 70 percent black or more, and, unlike rural areas anywhere else in the country, have power structures that are almost exclusively black:

black commissioners, black school boards, black mayors, black sheriffs. Whites, meanwhile, have voted with their feet. They are gone.

The irony is obvious and overwhelming. Blacks, transplanted here two centuries ago as slave labor to prop up the great antebellum plantation mansions that glistened like fine ships on a dark, loamy ocean, have ended up with the land as a sort of rueful inheritance. These are some of the poorest counties in America, and—if you take the time to stop along the wandering two-lane blacktop and talk to any of the polite yet suspicious old-timers, who are legion—you'll be told that while the color of the man wearing the local badge may have changed, not much else has. People is still poor and grabblen for whatever they can get, said one old man in overalls and clodhoppers, who introduced himself as Harvey, watering a modest garden behind a small white frame house with the obligatory swing on the front porch. People is poor and always will be.

So the plantations are gone from around here, as is just about every other sign of economic activity. That is abundantly clear as you drive east out of Montgomery into the country, where tarpaper shacks and dust-streaked double-wides and stooped, rust-flecked farm equipment fly by in a never-ending blur. And there certainly are no plantations in Hurtsboro, Alabama, population five hundred and ninety-two, which is where you will find yourself after about an hour of watching the blur fly by and availing yourself of the passing lane every chance you get to make your way around the sputtering hay truck going thirty-five or the postal carrier in the old Buick station wagon who lurches to a stop at every forlorn, weed-constricted mailbox with the name stenciled in spray paint on the side.

Except you don't stop in Hurtsboro proper, which is three blocks of tattered small town that still looks like an artist's depiction of the Depression at its nadir. No, you keep going along the two-lane for another mile or so, then make a hard right and leave the asphalt behind for a red-clay road, its shoulders draped in kudzu. You barrel along for about a mile, past shacks and barns and sagging houses that make the highway's window dressing back there look like Glitter Gulch. Then, finally, the church—the little Baptist church, redbrick now, with the original white cinder-block building resigned to the rear, with the cemetery just beyond. The church appears, you hang a left, and you know you are almost there.

The road, lined with barbed wire, is little more than a turkey trot. Big branches hang low. You take it slow . . . and round a bend and break back out into the open sunlight where the dirt lane slips through an expanse of pastureland. Another fifty yards and the road suddenly expires as though it just got weary and quit. It is stone silent. You are utterly alone. If this is not the end of the earth, it is a fine rendering of it.

And then you realize that straight ahead, in the short distance among the sagging pines and the tall, dusty broom sage swaying in the slight afternoon breeze, is the rubble of the old home place. By all appearances, most of the house that once stood here burned many years ago. The only thing left erect with any notion of pride or poise is an old, crumbling brick chimney. The rest is charred debris and what used to be.

IT HAS BEEN nearly sixty years since Lula Hardaway lived among the pines and swaying broom sage here on the outskirts of Hurtsboro, just beyond the reach of the small-town tatter. Stevie Wonder never lived here, nor has he ever visited this place. But it is the place where his mother came into consciousness, where her legs took root and steadied beneath her, only to fling her northward toward the strange and cruel and wonderful destiny that became places like East Chicago and Saginaw and Detroit and Los Angeles.

Here, at this particular end of the earth in 1932, a young, unmarried, pregnant woman named Mary Ellie Pitts, still in her teens, came in a lurching, mule-drawn wagon from Eufaula—a thriving river city, further east near the Georgia line—to bear a child with the assistance of her uncle, Henry Wright, and his wife, Virge. Henry and Virge were sharecroppers on what is now the expanse of pastureland but, back then, was a billowing field of cotton that was planted, tended, and harvested by several black families, with Henry acting as sort of a patriarchal overseer for the white planter.

Henry Wright was a big, strapping, authoritarian man who knew farming and understood people, both black and white. Little is known about his background or ancestry, but to the handful of those in Hurtsboro who vaguely recall him, Henry was emblematic of— and yet a departure from—the black men who played principal roles in the sharecropping economy of the rural South in the late 1800s and well into the 1900s. He was a gruff opinion leader within the community and an absolutely dedicated family man with a brood of children who worked on the land just as diligently as he did. He handled the finances for the sharecropping collective, acting as middleman between the families and the landowner, at once field boss, banker, and mayor.

That made Henry a very unusual sharecropper, according to the ways of the Black Belt, for blacks almost without exception were placed at a great disadvantage. Sharecroppers essentially were economic prisoners within the self-contained fiefdoms that were the plantations. They were issued scrip, rather than real money, redeemable only at the plantation store. As late as 1965, Martin Luther King Jr. encountered Alabama sharecroppers who had never laid eyes on U.S. currency. Sharecropping families worshiped at plantation churches and their children attended grossly substandard plantation schools.

Each sharecropping family farmed a plot of land, as much as forty acres depending on the sharecropper's reputation for hard work and the number of able bodies at his disposal. While the crop was brought to fruition the families relied on the "furnish," a monthly payment by the landowner meant to cover expenses until harvest time. The furnish rarely was adequate, even for the standard of poverty prevalent then, and most sharecroppers were forced to purchase items from the plantation store on credit. The final accounting came at the "settle," which occurred after the sharecropper had delivered his cotton to the plantation gin. In November each sharecropper would be called to the plantation office, where he would learn how much money he had cleared from his crop—if any—and get paid.

For most sharecroppers—black and white—the settle was a crushing ritual. Rarely did they come away with more than a few dollars. More likely, the planter's arithmetic—which included charges for store purchases and other, sometimes murky, fees—would show that the sharecropper had broken even or, worse, still owed the plantation money. That deficit would be carried over to the next planting year, ensuring that the sharecropper started the new year in the hole.

(One old sharecropper told of the blatant lengths to which one owner would go to avoid paying what was due. At one settle, the sharecropper purposefully held back twenty-five dollars worth of scrip, which ordinarily would have been turned over to the owner for credit toward cash. The owner did his computations and determined that the sharecropper owed a few dollars. The sharecropper then pulled the hidden scrip from his pocket, which would have covered the "debt" and brought him some real cash besides. Undeterred, the owner blatantly "refigured" the settle yet again and determined the sharecropper still owed money.) If a planter chose to shortchange a sharecropper by lowering the weight of his cotton, the sharecropper's hands were tied. If a planter chose to layer a sharecropper's account with suspect equipment repairs and the like, so be it. The sharecropper was powerless.

The sharecropper had little or no recourse. Legal action was out of the question. To even question the settle was risky business in the

Depression-era South. Legends abound here of sharecroppers shot by owners as a result of arguments over the settle. Punishment in such cases usually was nonexistent; the big plantations were above the law. When troubles arose on their land, the planters handled it themselves. The local authorities would stay clear.

Inevitably, the end of the year presented a sharecropper who had come up short with few options. Finally, there was the decision at which most sharecropping families inevitably arrived: sharecropping elsewhere. Some were forced to sneak away to escape a burdensome obligation to the planter. There was a great annual redistribution of black families throughout the plantation South that strained both the families and the social structure of the entire black community. Rarely did a move do much good for a sharecropping family's circumstances. The relatively few plantations where sharecroppers regularly cleared money rarely had openings, so the families that moved usually wound up at another dishonest place where they would once again end the year in debt.

It was a cruel and distressing system, one that in many ways worked against the planters as well as the sharecroppers. It certainly couldn't have been good business for the landowners to have to deal with the constant churn of field labor, but the more unscrupulous and shortsighted planters shrugged it off as just the way of getting business done. In the 1930s, slavery was a reality only six decades in the past, an experience and time well within the memory of many, many people, white and black. Sharecropping was undeniably viewed—by the white planters, anyway—as an evolutionary step removed from the slave days, while most sharecroppers certainly saw it as simply another, albeit more complicated, manifestation of forced servitude.

Those few sharecroppers who were able to find a plantation that was run in an aboveboard fashion and where their families were treated with a modicum of respect considered themselves lucky indeed.

• • •

AND SO IT WAS with Henry Wright, who was diplomatic and wily and commanded respect from the planters he dealt with, in no small measure because he also commanded respect from the sharecropping families he partnered with. Dealing with Henry meant that you dealt with the chieftain of about five or six families. Henry guaranteed the quality of each family's work and deportment. In return, Henry guaranteed the families that he would ensure that they were dealt with as equitably as could be hoped for. Henry oversaw the food purchases, negotiated the settles, and generally served as a buffer between the planters and the families.

This was a rarity, indeed. Henry's interlocution with the planter meant that there was a prized, if relative, stability among what amounted to the farming commune he headed. And so, for a number of years, Henry and Virge and their brood of children lived in the clapboard house amid the broom sage and not-yet sagging pines, enduring poor and desperate lives that were, at the same time, more secure than any of them could have ever hoped.

So it was natural, then, that Mary Ellie Pitts, her belly beginning to swell, would hitch a jostling wagon ride with a relative and finally make her way down the turkey trot to the clapboard farmhouse amid the billowing cotton. She needed help, and care, and a good roof over her head. The father of her child, Noble Hardaway—a fine-looking man, knowledgeable and glib—had disappeared as quickly as he had appeared, visiting his family from up North. But when Mary Ellie's condition had become apparent, he had vanished. There would be neither love nor aid from him, which was fine with Mary Ellie. Her mother and father, tired of her contrary and independent ways in matters of men and everything else, had given Mary Ellie her unconditional release into the world years ago. But now she needed help, and she wasn't about to go back to Mama and Papa, who were dirt poor anyway, and old. So it was Henry and Virge who willingly pulled the short straw, who took in their blood because there simply wasn't anyone else who would.

Two months later, Lula Mae Hardaway was born in the teeth of one of the poorest corners of one of the poorest states in the most poverty-stricken chapter of American history. But her birth was greeted as a blessed occasion, a gift. She came into the world healthy and grinning, with a dusting of reddish hair. They named her Lula, but they called her Little Red.

Mary Ellie stayed for about six months. But then the contrarian, independent part of her breached, like a whale leaping clear of the water, and she made her apologies and excuses and promises and left. She didn't come back. And Henry and Virge became Papa and Mama, and Little Red wouldn't know anything different, not for a long time.

TO THINK OF Hurtsboro as idyllic in any sense of the word—particularly during the Depression and World War II, when Lula lived there—seems almost ludicrous. The way of life there, even today, would be a shock to the system of most Americans. Yes, today there is some subsidized housing, and there is a local pizza delivery outfit, and a couple of gas stations that stand sentry out on the main highway that blazes through the town in a tremendous hurry to just keep going somewhere else. Some of the people who live there now commute to jobs in Montgomery, or Eufaula, or Columbus, Georgia. Downtown there is a struggling drugstore and some people, white and black, milling about. Mostly, though, it is a typical small Southern town that, like its inhabitants, is barely getting by. Its young people leave at first light, if they have a glimmer of ambition. It is dying a slow, not very complicated death, a death that is being repeated throughout the rural South as the big cities and their suburbs steal away the lifeblood of Hurtsboros everywhere.

But for Lula Hardaway, Hurtsboro was a happy place, even in those punitive times. There wasn't always enough to eat, despite Henry's assiduous efforts. The work was hard and long, and Lula herself was no stranger to the fields (as a small child she was dragged up and down the cotton rows in a wooden crate attached to a rope; at age six she was expected to do fieldwork herself). But for one of the precious few times in her early life, she was surrounded by a nuclear family, complete with father and mother, and an extended network of family and friends comprised of the other sharecropping families who lived nearby. As the youngest child—and as one who was there under special circumstances—Lula was doted on. There were playmates, lots of them, and there were golden afternoons when the children all gathered and ran and shrieked and played as children do, trappings be damned.

In the evenings, after the smokehouse ham and black-eyed peas and cornbread had all been cleared away, the family would settle in next to the stove and the singing would begin. Some of the songs were gospel hymns, others old slave songs passed down through the years. Henry would rumble deep and low, while Virge had a sweet tenor that cut through all the voices that filled the house. The songs were punctuated by Henry's ruminations on Jesus and the family's forebears, spliced with interrogations of the children about the various ways in which they spent their days. He spoke of a time, long ago, when black men were kings. Sometimes, the children would ask if Henry believed that black men would ever be kings again.

I don't know, child, he would say.

But we are all kings and queens on the inside, if we choose to carry ourselves that way.

We are all kings and queens, he would say, though we may not have a throne or a kingdom. Riches come from within.

And then Virge's pure voice would start up, and the little congregation joined in and the clapboard house bulged with the sound.

Sometimes at those moments, in the summer, Lula would slip outside—for she was the baby, and special—and spin and career among the fireflies that appeared from some secret firefly-hiding place (she could never figure out where) at dusk. Then suddenly she would stop, turn toward the house, and stand motionless and steady. The song—maybe it would be "Bound for Canaan Land" or "In the Sweet By-and-By"—poured from the house, filling the sky. It sounded different, better, from out there, pent-up and cascading from the open windows. And the fireflies, swarms of them, blinking-blinking, swirled about her in a vortex as she stood motionless, listening, watching, feeling as if she were the absolute, inarguable center of a knowable and fathomable universe. The lightning bugs would swirl about her, and she felt that if she stood still enough, long enough, the fireflies would pick her up, gently and carefully, light as a feather, and carry their special friend to the secret firefly-hiding place. She imagined that it was a cave in some distant, as yet undiscovered woods. It would be a place of sheer happiness; a dark, cool place where the lightning bugs flitted and blinked and sparkled all day long, impervious to the withering sun outside.

But they never took Lula there. So she would stand there motionless and steady as the song bulged until the darkness was complete and the lightning bugs seemed to evaporate into the night, conceding to the stars. And then Lula would slip back inside, sitting on the floor next to Papa, nestling up against his oaken shins and taking in the glory of melding voices and talk of kings.

Two

THE SWEET BY-AND-BY

Life's evening sun is sinking low,
A few more days and I must go,
To meet the deeds that I have done,
Where there will be no setting sun.

—Old field song, "A Beautiful Life,"
William Golden, 1918

WHEN PAPA DIED, it was as if someone had blocked the sun. He loomed that large, not just in Lula's young life but for the entire sharecropping community he considered his own. Driven by some tireless spirit that left others in awe, he could outwork, out-think and, while he was at it, out-smile anybody. He was a constant who seemed indestructible, even immortal. His death, for those who depended on him for leadership and their very livelihoods, was like waking up one morning to discover that the sun no longer rose in the east. It had seemed as if Henry Wright, who was nearly seventy but could undoubtedly whip any man half his age, would live forever. Certainly, Lula never considered the possibility that Papa would, or even *could*, die.

• • •

IT CAME SUDDENLY.

He was chopping cotton on a shimmering June morning, the sun already massive in the sky. It was warm, to be sure, and humid, but the summer had yet to take on the oppressive, almost hallucinogenic swelter of July and August. Henry was steadily working down his row, setting the pace for the others. Lula was about three rows over, and back a good thirty yards or so. But she saw him clearly as he inexplicably stopped hoeing—inexplicably, for Henry never stopped in the middle of a row without very good reason, usually resting only between rows—and straightened up to his full considerable height and looked quizzically toward the house, as if it had struck him at that moment that he had forgotten to tell Virge something important. Then his legs seemed to give way and he sat down, hard, dazed, in the dirt-clod jumble. Then he slumped back, disappearing below the green stalks. And everyone began to run toward him, thrashing through the cotton.

Odd, the images that stay with you from childhood, the snapshots the brain chooses to take, often bypassing the big picture for some smaller detail. Lula was ten years old when Henry Wright, her Papa, rose up ramrod-straight among the green stalks in the yellow sunshine and then gave way in a collapse that brought his world down with him, the way dishes tumble from shelves during an earthquake. Indeed, that image, shocking in its abrupt purity, burned itself into Lula's memory for eternity. But the strongest image—a picture with sound, actually—was the *whack!* of the screen door slamming behind Virge as she catapulted from the house, apron flapping, an anguished terror contorting her face, her legs digging against the soft soil as she ran toward the clump of stooped bodies hovering over her lifeless husband.

Whack!

The sharp report of the screen door slamming suddenly, violently. Years later, the sound would come to her in the night. That sound, and then the image of Virge running, desperate, hoping but somehow already knowing that life had just changed beyond all measure. Lula watched Papa slump, heard the *whack!,* and spun around in time to see Virge hurtle from the house and the porch and begin to churn through the soft dirt. And that was what stayed with Lula, for she could not connect to Papa, motionless on the ground, as if struck down by God himself. He was already in some other place, a place Lula could not even fathom. But she instantly connected to the lightning bolt that had passed through Mama Virge, propelling her forward; she, too, had felt the piercing, jagged jolt sear through her body. And she knew the terror that contorted Virge's face, for she felt her own terror, for the first time in her life—that unique and singular terror of not knowing what will happen next.

Whack!

So loud, so sudden, so final.

The closing of a door.

HENRY HELD ON for a few days, bedridden, weak, and incoherent. Old Doctor Malone from town paid a call, checked Henry over, and the look on his face let everyone know that Papa wasn't going to get any better. Lula watched as the doctor pulled a long needle from his bag, fussed with it, and then stuck it in Henry's hip. That will help him rest, sure enough, the doctor said.

Henry died that night. Lula always wondered what was in that needle and trembled at the sight of one for the rest of her life.

The funeral was held in the little white church up at the intersection of the dirt road and the turkey trot. Lula sat next to Virge—her Mama—snug up against her as the funeral-home fans undulated and the preacher thundered about how good men and women all go on one day to receive their reward. Virge told everyone who came by the house to pay their respects in the days after it happened about how God, at the last critical moment, told her to look out the window:

I was fixing some dinner (for in those days lunch was dinner, and dinner was supper) and God said to me, Virge, your man out there needs you.

And I said, Lord God, that man don't need nobody. He never needed nobody his whole life.

But God said again, Your man needs you. And I looked out the window, and I saw Henry Wright stand up straight and strong and proud and look right at me. He looked right into my eyes from across that field. And God said to me, I'm taking him now.

Praise Jesus, someone would mutter respectfully.

I ran out there because I wanted to tell Henry Wright that he was the best man God ever put on this earth. But he was already gone.

Praise Jesus.

At the funeral, they sang:

In the sweet by-and-by
We will meet on that beautiful shore

And:

Swing low, sweet chariot
Comin' for to carry me home.

Then they took Papa and buried him in the church cemetery. Lula stood there as the dirt showered down on the rough-hewn pine box, made by hand by Henry's fellow sharecroppers, and wished that she could be in the dark place with the lightning bugs, blinking, blinking.

LIFE RESUMED, in a manner of speaking.

Henry Wright's oldest son, James—no spring chicken himself—took nominal charge of the sharecroppers' activities. But for a long while, there was a listlessness to the entire enterprise, as Lula and the rest came to grips with Henry's sudden death. They all returned to the fields, each with a little more work to do to take up the slack. Every last one of us could die, Lula thought, and this cotton would still be standing here, swaying under the massive sun, demanding to be tended.

Virge seemed lost; Lula was too young to understand the persistent longevity of grief. She found solace in her playmates, the cousins and the others who still had energy, somehow, to run and play and fight and argue after a day in the field. Their romps and explorations continued. There was one "play sister" who was especially close—her name was Annabelle, but everyone called her Goop—who was older than Lula, in her late teens. They were close in the way that only big girls and little girls can be, sharing secrets, inseparable. And it is those friends—the closest friends—who can hurt you the most, wound most mortally.

It happened late one afternoon. There was a small ditch that ran among the sharecroppers' houses where strawberries grew wild, and Lula and Goop often played along its banks, tossing rocks, picking berries, or just watching the afternoon blend into evening.

On this day, amid the strawberries, there was an argument.

No one remembers how it started, just that there were words, jealous words that tumbled out and became hurtful. And the moment came when Goop, angry, digging for the words that would be true enough to sting the most, found them.

You're so high and mighty, she told Lula, for a bastard child.

Lula stared at her, uncomprehending.

Yeah, that's right, Goop said, twisting the knife with relish. You don't even know, do you, you ninny?

Know what—

You don't even know who your father is.

Yes I do, it's—

Or your mother. You ninny.

And then there was silence, that moment when the assailant

draws back, bloody knife in hand, to look at his handiwork before racing away into the darkness. It was just a heated exchange between playmates that escalated into the hurt that only the sheer, unvarnished facts can provide. And Lula, even at that moment, knew deep within herself, instinctively, that it all had the awful, undeniable ring of truth.

It was too awful not to be true.

Goop, horrified at just how successful her assault had been, turned and ran. Lula, cloaked in the daze of sudden revelation, turned and walked toward the house, the only home she had ever known, toward Virge. Her Mama, wasn't that right? And maybe what Goop said sounded true, somehow, but Mama will put it right. Just like she puts everything else right. Or used to, before Papa died.

Virge, sewing, sat in the old straw rocking chair that always was reserved for Papa. It was his favorite chair. Virge said she liked to sit in it because it made her feel close to Papa, even though he was gone now. There are little ways we can still feel close to the dearly departed, she liked to say.

Lula walked up to Virge as if in a dream. Mama, she said, don't I know who my Papa is?

What did you say?

Don't I know who my Papa is? Somebody said—and my Mama, too. Somebody said.

Lula waited for the immediate reassurance that it was all a lie: Well, of *course* I'm your Mama! And, what, you don't think Henry Wright was your daddy? What kind of foolishness has gotten into you?

Lula waited for it, but it didn't come.

Virge just looked at her in a funny way, a look Lula had never seen before. It was a look full of fatigue and love and pity. The other truth that Lula knew deep down within herself was that Virge surely cared for her as much as any child that came from her own loins, just as Lula loved her as much as she could love any natural mother. But on that day, the truth just seemed to stand there between them, ticking. For a long time, it seemed, Virge just sat there and rocked, looked at Lula, and said nothing. Finally she spoke, in a small voice that seemed to say everything:

Who told you that, child?

VIRGE DIED NOT long after, having never really regained her footing after Henry Wright's death. Lula was taken in by James, and that act of kindness bought her a little more time in the only world she had ever known, but James was ailing, too, plagued by a weak heart brought on by a life of working in the unforgiving fields. Now it was his job to lead, to work harder than anyone else. It was his job to provide his best impression of Henry Wright, which everyone agreed was an awesome challenge for any man.

James would come home from the fields, dragging himself in like a dog that had been beaten and kicked around all day. And everyone reckoned he had been. James was like Lula and the rest of the extended family—he had never envisioned life without Henry at the helm of it. He wasn't a natural diplomat. He wasn't a shrewd negotiator. No matter how hard he tried, he was just James.

Sometimes he would have pains in his chest, sharp, shooting pains, and he would tell Lula to rub him there, right over his heart. *Rub a little harder, Red, rub a little harder,* he would say, his tired face ratcheted up in an awful grimace. On one blazing-hot afternoon, he came home, sat down heavily, and called for Lula to minister to him again.

Make it go away, Red. It hurts so bad.

I'm working, James. I'm trying.

And then James released a big, breezy sigh, and said: Come on and get me, God.

He folded in on top of himself in the chair like he was asleep. And that was that. He died right in front of Lula, her hand on his heart.

Everything repeated itself: the mournful coming and going in the night, the sound of the pine box being hammered together, the hand-held fans swimming in the thick hot air of the little church, the sweet by-and-by.

But there was something different this time, too; Lula could see it in the way everyone looked at her. She saw the furtive glances cast in her direction by the relatives she didn't know, she heard the quiet current of conversation and the shaking of heads. Finally, one of the older cousins sat down with Lula and told her: It was all over. The farm would have to be given up. And Little Red would have to go somewhere else.

Relatives she had never known convened and decided her fate: She would go to East Chicago, Indiana, and live with her biological father, a man she had never met—a man she did not know even existed until that day of truth and reckoning down by the stream.

And so, a few days later, Lula packed her meager belongings into a small wooden crate. There were hugs and tears, but it all seemed as empty as Lula's soul. An aunt she did not know took her to the train station in Columbus, where she boarded for Indiana and a new life. It was to be a new life considerably different and more brutal than she had ever envisioned.

Three

INTO THE COLD

I T WAS JUST a train ride, but certain journeys in life are filled with portent.

Even at age thirteen, Lula Hardaway knew that her clacking, swaying, twelve-hour trip into the unknown North was a life-changing, even life-shattering, development. Don't worry, her aunt had told her at the cracker-box train station in Columbus, which to Lula may as well have been cavernous Grand Central Station. You'll be with your daddy. Not much comfort, really. Lula didn't even know what her father looked like. *If he never cared in all the years before,* Lula mused to herself, *why should he care now?*

Yet Lula's portent—terror, actually—involved much more than that. She was a young girl fresh off a sharecroppers' farm, battered with loss, casually educated, in an age when people did not travel widely. She had no frame of reference about the world she was clacking and swaying toward. Horizon-expanding tools like radio and movies had not touched her world. She had seen no newsreels of big northern cities, the bustling streets, the monolithic smokestack factories. She had never seen snow.

Lula knew she would see all these things, and more. She didn't know it in a specific way, but in the way that you know that you don't want to walk around that dark corner at that late hour. You can't really see anything to be worried about . . . but, still, you stay on the lighted path.

The move north would prove to be the most influential wrinkle in the story of Stevie Wonder. Without it, events take a different course that no one will, of course, ever know. Without it, Lula remains in the socially oppressed and culturally detached Black Belt. She bears children by other men. Maybe one of those children is born with once-in-a-generation talent. Maybe that child finds his way into the Motown studios, a thousand miles away, or some other, closer, music test tube where he can flourish and mutate into what he is destined to become.

Maybe.

Probably not.

And so Lula Hardaway hurtled north toward her destiny and the destiny of those not even born.

THE FIRST THING she noticed was the chill.

It wasn't just the night air that already carried the threat of winter, far removed from the warm thickness that still enveloped the Alabama countryside. There also was the dead cold radiating from her stepmother, who met her at the train station, and regarded her like an unwelcome stray.

Well, come on, then, said Vera. I guess you're his, all right. Look just like him. You probably got a hard head just like him, too.

So much for the red carpet. Lula and Vera caught the bus to the small tenement apartment where the Noble Hardaway family resided, already crowded with two other children.

The teeming city pushed in on all sides. East Chicago was a typically bleak Midwestern industrial city of the period, dominated by steel works and the still-germinating automobile industry. Noble Hardaway made his living as a steelworker, barely making ends meet, if at all. It suddenly dawned on Lula that she was an afterthought, unwanted and superfluous.

Her growing fears were confirmed when her father came home later that evening. He was a handsome man with Irish blood and a scowl. A draft of cold entered the house with him and didn't seem to leave as long as he was there. He regarded Lula with a half-grimace. No hello, no hug, no pleasantries about her trip. Certainly there were no inquiries about her life so far or about her welfare.

You do what Miss Vera tells you, he said coarsely. And no back talk.

And with that, he sat down to the sparse dinner set out on the kitchen table. When he finished, the others crowded around and got their share. Lula ate last. It was a custom she would follow as long as she lived there.

Which wasn't long.

Lula enrolled in school, but it immediately became apparent that it was a meaningless exercise. She essentially was uneducated. The sporadic schooling she had received in Alabama had taken its toll; she could barely read. Anything other than basic, simple math was beyond her reach. And while the mostly black classrooms of the day in East Chicago afforded instruction that was far inferior to the education being offered white children in the better neighborhoods, to Lula it all seemed incomprehensibly advanced and impenetrable.

She attended school for one semester. After that, she never went back.

THAT DEVELOPMENT WAS greeted with outright hostility in Noble and Vera's household. It wasn't that a premium was placed on getting a good education. But the Hardaway children were expected to go to school, at least until they were old enough to work. Then they were expected to have a job. If they wanted to continue school as well, fine. In any event, Miss Vera opposed the idea of Lula hanging sullenly around the house; and Lula, already resentful of the Cinderella treatment she was receiving, didn't like the idea herself.

So, at first, she didn't tell anyone that she had quit going to school, spending her days walking aimlessly about the gritty smoke-stack neighborhoods. The ruse lasted about a week, until word circulated back that Lula wasn't in school. (She should have known better; black folks were as thick as thieves in East Chicago. Everyone seemed to know each other. Lula's neighborhood was referred to as "Alabama North," because everyone there seemed to have migrated from Alabama.) Upon receiving the news, Vera immediately took her case to Noble, pouncing on him right away as he shuffled in from work that evening.

That child ain't even goin' to school, she said. Just out runnin' around all day. You gonna put up with that?

Noble Hardaway seemed to swell up with bile. Get in here, he told Lula. That right? What you doin' all day, then?

Lula, fear-frozen, said nothing.

I knew you was gonna be nothin' but trouble. This hangs it. We ain't gonna feed this mouth and put up with this.

Still Lula said nothing. She didn't want to go to school. She didn't want to stay here, at this house. She didn't want to do anything.

Noble Hardaway was storming about in the kitchen. Go see Ilona, he told his wife. Go see Ilona and tell her that she can take this child in, or we can just send her back. Tell her we tried. We tried.

Ilona Morris was Lula's great aunt in what was known as New Edition, a suburb of Gary, Indiana, about a thirty-minute drive from East Chicago. Her husband, Robert, was a prominent deacon in a growing African Methodist Episcopal congregation in Gary's unfolding black community on the city's West Side. Aunt Ilona, as it turned out, was the one who had orchestrated Lula's move from Alabama to East Chicago. That child needs to be with her kin, she had told Noble when the news of Henry's death filtered north. You take that child in. It's your obligation. It's your dues.

Noble resisted. I got a house full of children now, he said. I can't bring another one in. This house is busting at the seams now.

But he relented, once Ilona assured him that she would take Lula in if it didn't work out somehow. But you make it work, she told Noble. That child needs to be with her daddy.

But now, two weeks into the experiment, it wasn't working. Tell Ilona it's her turn now, Noble thundered. I knew she would be nothin' but trouble.

And so a week later, on a biting-cold afternoon with fat, gray-black clouds hanging low, Lula packed a small cardboard box with all her clothes and possessions. Ilona was to drive her Buick from New Edition and collect Lula and her belongings. Lula and Vera waited in silence for Ilona to arrive. Finally the Buick rolled into view, and Ilona emerged with a big smile on her face, like a saving angel.

Well, now, you go on and mind your Aunt Ilona, Miss Vera said. 'Cause I don't know what you'll do if that don't work out.

Everything will be *fine*, Aunt Ilona said.

A few minutes later the Buick rumbled to life and slowly began to roll. Lula looked out the window to where Miss Vera stood, her arms folded tight against her overcoat. For a split second, their eyes locked; for a split-split second, Lula thought she saw a flicker of some-thing . . . she thought she might have seen pity. Whatever it was, it was gone in an instant, replaced by the familiar look that said, *I got mine. You have to go get yours somewhere else.*

Lula realized she knew nothing about this woman and that this woman really knew nothing about her. She wondered if Miss Vera had ever been truly loved. *I've* been loved, Lula thought. Maybe not now, but once upon a time.

She turned her gaze away from Miss Vera and thought fleetingly of old Mama Virge. Mama Virge used to sit in Papa's old straw rocking chair. *There are little ways we can still feel close to the dearly departed.* The Buick began to surge more powerfully now, and Lula looked out the window. Miss Vera was out of view now, gone.

Suddenly, the air outside began to fill with white, swirling spits of ice. Lula was transfixed. The spits then began to morph into big white flakes, flying about like some sort of powdery rain. Law', here it comes, Ilona said, here it comes. With her tattered glove, Lula wiped the fog from the window and pressed her nose up against it.

She had never seen snow.

IT WAS DIFFERENT at Aunt Ilona's house, for a while.

Aunt Ilona and the Deacon, as he was known, were an older couple; their children were raised and gone. Unlike Miss Vera, Aunt Ilona seemed pleased to have a young girl in her home. Lula had her own room, all neat and squared away. There was no pecking order for food. The three of them sat down for dinner together every evening at the appointed time, except for the nights when Brother Robert was off on visitation or other church business, which was often. Even then, Lula and Ilona would have dinner all the same. Ilona bought Lula some new clothes and seemed to take a genuine interest in her life and well-being.

Ilona agreed that school probably was a lost enterprise for Lula. I suppose you can always go back to school, she said. In the meantime, we'll find you a job. I'm sure a smart, fine-looking young lady like you can find some work.

And there *was* work. The war was on and had taken many of the community's men away, which meant that there actually were considerable work opportunities for women. A whole new generation of black working women was discovering that there were alternatives to domestic work. The factories not only provided significant income but also a tangible sense of independence.

And so the word went out, and in about a week or so another deacon in the church passed along the news that a seamstress position at one of the local textile mills had opened up. Lula knew her way around a needle and thread, thanks to Mama Virge. But this job required operating a sewing machine; Lula was concerned, but the deacon said they were willing to train her.

So early on a slate-gray Monday she reported to work and was led into the biggest indoor room Lula had ever seen, where two hundred women hunched over big sewing machines and concentrated intently on their work. At first, Lula felt as if she might as well have been driving a car, so imposing and complicated were the machines. But her supervisor was a good teacher, and patient. In a few days, Lula began to get the hang of it; a few days more, and she began to feel comfortable behind the wheel. She found that she enjoyed the work. There was an unexpected comfort to the repetition of it, stitching together piece after piece after piece. She became absorbed in the rhythm. She liked it. She even believed she had a knack for it.

Lula was paid pretty good money—about thirty dollars a week. For the first time in her young life she felt some degree of autonomy and self-sufficiency. She was required to contribute half of what she made to Ilona, to help with her room and board. But the rest was hers to save and spend as she saw fit.

Textile work was difficult. The conditions were less than stellar. The factory was dirty and cold, the air lousy with a fine, poisonous mill dust. The strain of the long hours and the repetitive stress of the machines had crippling effects on the older women who worked there. But Lula was young, barely fourteen; she was strong and supple and had the impervious bravado of youth. She was working and going home with money in her pocketbook, and that made her happy.

Sometimes, on Fridays after work, Lula would get special permission from Aunt Ilona to go to the early picture show with some of the younger women from the mill. She loved the westerns, and the movies about elegant rich people with all their fine clothes and fine manners. One Friday, the girls begged off work early and rode the train into Chicago and saw a young Count Basie perform with his orchestra. Lula was nearly fifteen now and looked older; she did what her friends told her, which was to just walk in that club as if it were no big thing at all. She did, and no one gave her a second look. But underneath her thin guise of confidence was a young country girl in thrall. Chicago pulsated and seemed like a movie all by itself, and the music—so *wonderful*—the music was so full of life and arrow-sharp that it seemed to pierce her heart. She got home shortly before midnight with her head swimming, but with Aunt Ilona none the wiser.

Despite the occasional movie or clandestine trip to Chicago, Lula's social life was very restricted. Auntie liked it that way. There was church, where Lula was a member of the choir. Of course, church was no small force in the lives of its members. Church, in this black neighborhood as well as many others, was the linchpin—not just a place to worship, but a place where the community came together to interact and support each other. In the South, the church had been the one community institution where blacks felt empowered, where they could be *themselves.* In church, blacks could talk freely of their beliefs, their opinions, their views of their white-dominated universe. And faith in God often was the only constant in times of oppression, which made the bond between family and church all the stronger. With so many refugees from the South filling the cities of the industrial Midwest, it was only natural that the church would flourish as the preeminent social force for African Americans.

For Lula, the church provided some additional structure to her life and served as an important emotional link to her childhood in Hurtsboro and the tiny white church at the end of the dirt lane near the old plantation. And she loved singing in the choir; she wasn't considered to have great talent, by any stretch, but her voice was strong and pure, and it gave her great *joy* to sing. I may not be the best singer, Lula would tell Aunt Ilona, but I do know how to make a joyful noise unto the Lord. And praise God for that, Aunt Ilona would reply.

Aunt Ilona was kindly and interested in Lula. So was Deacon Robert, although Lula found him harder to figure. He was a thin man with a broad face and a gleaming smile who wore dark suits and a porkpie hat. Sometimes he would speak from the pulpit, and he was, to Lula, a masterly speaker, spinning ancient Bible tales into lessons for modern living. One of his devices as a deacon was to pepper his messages with the names of congregation members: And so when Saul traveled down the road to Damascus, Brother Phillips, he saw a powerful light, and it was the Lord, and, Sister Johnson, what did the Lord impart unto this sinner? Well, Brother Davis . . .

It was amazing, really, Lula thought, how he could flawlessly deliver his mini-sermons and yet still be searching for the next face, the next name to weave into his words. She asked him, once, why he did it. It's just a little game I play with the congregation, he said. It keeps everybody on their toes.

At home, however, the Deacon seemed different. There was a distance about him. The dinners, when he was there, were quiet affairs. He and Aunt Ilona didn't seem to talk all that much. Lula figured it must be that way when two people have been married for twenty-five years; you've already said everything so many times, you don't really have to say it again.

In fact, the Deacon was gone most of the time. He was an early riser. Lula would hear him in the kitchen, making coffee, long before she ventured from bed. He often did not come home until nearly midnight. He's out doing the Lord's work, Aunt Ilona would say. The Lord's work is never done.

And so Lula's days slipped into a comfortable pattern: work during the week, church on Sundays. It was, in many ways, idyllic, despite the demanding nature of her job. It's better than chopping cotton, Lula would tell herself, although there were frigid winter days in the poorly heated mill when she fondly remembered—too fondly, perhaps—the hot sun on her back as she worked down the rows, with Papa setting the pace.

Lula's first winter in the North finally began to segue into spring. She had turned fifteen, and Little Red no longer was so little. She long ago had begun to attract the attention of the opposite sex, but Auntie was firm: no dating until you're older. These boys are nothing but trouble, she would say darkly. You got plenty of time for all that later. You grow up first.

She had much more to say on the topic of men. The East Chicago area in the mid-1940s was mostly black, with its residents striving mightily toward the middle class. The men left behind by the war and who populated Lula's neighborhood were a mixed bag. Many were just boys, of course, not old enough for the military and either in school or, like Lula, dropouts. Some ran in gangs, of which Aunt Ilona vehemently disapproved. Those boys are going straight down the lost road, she would say, and they don't even care.

But her most pronounced disdain was for the grown men who, for one reason or another, didn't seem to find it necessary to hold down jobs. Street hustlers, Auntie would hiss. Scum of the earth. You see them comin', Red, you just turn around and go the other way. Nothing good will come of it.

How do they live? Lula asked.

Auntie's face gathered into a wrinkle of disgust. They gamble. They steal. They sell that dope. They live off their women. It's a disgrace.

With which Lula wholeheartedly agreed. But there was an air about the hustlers, she had to admit to herself in her secret heart . . . something that the other men didn't have. Oh, they were despicable, all right. But it was sort of like the movies; you always rooted for the cowboy in the white hat, but there was always something thrilling about the *bad* guy, too. It was hard to explain. So she didn't, and certainly not to Auntie.

Lula heard the women at work talk about their husbands and boyfriends. It sounded as if they were all, to a man, worthless and lazy and irresponsible and unfaithful. The work days were filled with the latest accounts of indiscretions or disappointments suffered at the hands of these shiftless creatures. So, Lula asked one day, Why do you stay with them, if they treat you so bad? Why put up with all that?

'Cause if you ain't complainin', you ain't livin', joked one.

I'll tell you why, said Susie, who had four children by three men and to whom Lula felt particularly close. I put up with it because there ain't nothin' like havin' a man in your life. He may not always be a *good* man, but as long as he's tryin', that's all that matters . . . It just feels right to have a man lying next to you. Girl, you'll know what I mean one day. If you don't already. You don't already know what it's like, do you, Red?

Everyone giggled. And Lula flushed with embarrassment, because, no, she did *not* already know what it was like. But something within her wanted to know. I'll know, she told herself, one day. And it will be wonderful. It won't be like they say it is.

She was certain of that.

DESPITE AUNT ILONA'S admonitions and her own convictions about how she would tread a different and higher road, Lula started to step out with young men who told her all the things that young women—*all* women—want to hear. She heard that she was beautiful and smart, which she was. She heard that certain young men couldn't live without the pleasure of her company and her touch, which was debatable. She heard that certain young men had only one way to demonstrate the depth of the love they held in their hearts for her, which was blatantly untrue. But, as it turned out, that demonstration of love, regardless of the authenticity of its underpinnings, was something that was not altogether unwelcome to a young woman coming of age who—despite the fierce affection of an aunt who had taken her in as her own—harbored a gaping emotional wound deep within her, a wound caused by the loss of her mother and all the others she had never even had the chance to love.

So it all began, the whispered longings and stolen kisses and, finally, the inevitable surrenders to the nature of the world. It was wonderful and exciting and confusing and frightening and heartbreaking—all the things that it always is. And, as it often is, it was an imperfect process, and mistakes were made.

THE BEGINNING OF the end with Aunt Ilona and Deacon Robert occurred one fall afternoon of the same year.

She was heading home after a couple of hours with her boyfriend; he had borrowed a car and they had driven along the lake and then spent some time at his place. Then, running late, she missed her bus, and started walking to another stop a few blocks away. She was moving briskly down the street when she saw something that stopped her in her tracks: the Deacon himself, crossing up ahead, heading away from her, in a hurry.

A surge of terror shot through Lula. *He's following me. He knows I'm seeing somebody. Damn it, he knows!*

But wait—where's he going? She watched as he bustled up the avenue and out of sight. *I don't think he saw me. And what's he doing over here? I don't know of any congregation members over here . . .*

Curiosity extinguished her fear. Lula picked up her pace and started tailing him, staying about a block behind. Wherever he was going, he was in a rush. She stayed with him, warily, like a cat tracking a field mouse, all eyes and awareness. A few more blocks and the Deacon suddenly ducked into . . . a bar. A bar? *He don't drink. I know he* don't drink . . . never smelled it on him, ever. Must be someone in trouble. Someone got drunk and called, and the Deacon's goin' to take him home. Okay. That makes sense. Okay.

As she chewed it over, preparing to retrace her steps to the bus stop, she saw the lounge door open again. The Deacon reappeared. She hid behind a parked truck and peered around the side. And right behind the Deacon, stepping out of the bar, a young woman. They glanced around; she slipped her arm into his, and they walked, *very* briskly, around a corner and out of sight.

Caught!

A passing car nearly struck Lula, now fully consumed by the thrill of the hunt, as she raced across the street in hot, all-caution-to-the-wind pursuit. She scrambled to the corner and saw the two of them walking up the stoop of a white frame house about half a block down. The young woman unlocked the front door, and they were in.

Lula nearly swooned from the implications of it all. *There can't be any other explanation . . . can there? Poor Auntie! But maybe I've got it wrong. Maybe he's just comforting her, maybe there's a problem at the house. Maybe I've got it wrong.*

But something told her to get closer, to creep nearer.

With her eyes fixed on the front door, ready to bolt at the slightest sign of movement, Lula walked down the sidewalk to get a better look. The house rose up before her like some mystery castle. It wasn't so big, really, but try watching every surface inch of it while trying to get some kind of glimpse inside . . . she felt like a detective or one of those movie spies.

A tall fence ran between the white house and the neighboring house. No one seemed to be home at the neighbors'. Her heart pounding, Lula slowly walked down the fence line on the neighbors' side. If you peeked through the slats you could see the white house, a little. And then she heard the voices coming through what looked like a kitchen window.

A young woman's voice, hard to hear: Because I like to have a little drink, that's why. Sometimes you're late, and I like to have a little drink.

The Deacon, his voice clear: Well, I don't like goin' in there. It puts me in a bad situation.

Deacon, I hate to tell you . . . *a light little tipsy laugh* . . . I hate to tell you, but you *already* in a bad situation.

Lula peered through a sliver of an opening in the fence. She could see, a little. She could see the young woman standing with a glass in her hand, then taking a drink. She couldn't see the Deacon.

Deacon: You know what I mean. You know I have to be careful. I have obligations to the community. I have the reputation of a church to uphold. I'm not so important, but the church is.

Young woman: You shoulda thought about that before you started sweet-talkin' *me.* But you worry too much anyway—

Then, foghorn-loud: *What you doin'! What you lookin' at!*

Lula wheeled around in shock. The neighbor's front door was wide open, framing an elderly woman who, at that moment, was the very apoplectic picture of moral outrage.

Some kind of peepin' Tom here! Some kind of peepin' Tom! Hey!—

In sheer panic, Lula bolted toward the sidewalk and cut a hard corner in a dead sprint. As she fled, she flung one look over her shoulder and saw, in a split-second snapshot, the young woman's face in the kitchen window, looking right at her; and, behind her, shadowy, maybe-seeing-maybe-not, the Deacon.

IN THE DAYS AFTERWARD, Lula monitored her every interaction with the Deacon like a hawk. But he gave no indication—absolutely none—that she was a suspect in the peeping incident. After a week or so, Lula decided she was in the clear. And what a relief. The last thing she wanted was some conflict with the man who had welcomed her in his home when she had nowhere to go.

But Lula didn't have to internalize her secret knowledge of the Deacon's adventures away from home for very long. It would all come tumbling out into the open soon enough.

It all started one evening at dusk, while Lula and Ilona were preparing dinner in the kitchen. A lady who lived two doors down, a busybody for sure, knocked on the kitchen door. Ilona asked her in, noted the worried look on her face—How are you, Sister? Is everything all right?—and the two of them repaired to the living room. Their voices murmured while Lula strained to hear. She could tell that something was *up*.

In a scant few minutes the conversation was over. The neighbor left via the front door and Ilona returned to the kitchen, looking shell-shocked and stricken.

What's the matter, Auntie? Lula asked.

Nothing, Red, nothing, Ilona replied, her head a million miles away.

Okay, then, Lula said, and went back to tending dinner. Ilona busied herself with setting the table, gamely pretending that things were normal. That lasted for about thirty seconds, until—

That no-good, two-timing son of a bitch!

Lula, stunned by this eruption—she had never heard Ilona so much as say "heck"—turned and looked at her aunt, who stood by the kitchen table, her fists clenched as if she intended to use them.

Auntie, what are you talking—

But Ilona did not hear—she was in another place, now. I've had it with his tomcatting around—

Ilona disappeared down the hallway into the master bedroom. Momentarily she emerged again and walked back into the kitchen. Lula, she said, strangely distant, you stay right here. I'll be back in a few minutes.

Lula's eyes were drawn to Ilona's right hand, which held the six-shot revolver the Deacon kept next to the bed.

Auntie!

You get the table set, Ilona said. And I'll be right back. She headed out the door, the gun drooping from her right hand, making no attempt to hide it.

Piecing the story together later, Lula learned that the neighbor had come calling to pass along a tidy little news item, hot off the local wire: Someone had spotted the Deacon, a scandalous young woman in tow, entering a house behind the neighborhood funeral parlor about three blocks away. (The house belonged to a running buddy of the Deacon.) This particularly noteworthy bit of information leapfrogged backyard fence after backyard fence until it reached Ilona's street; the busybody neighbor, indignant that the Deacon would flaunt his womanizing so close to home and also bound by her busybody nature, determined that this was something that Ilona *needed to know.* Thus the dinnertime call on Ilona and the murmured sitting-room conversation.

Of course, Neighbor Busybody had no way to predict that subsequent developments would take such a glorious turn. Who knew that Ilona—sweet, passive, quiet, genteel Ilona—would react in such a way? Who would have thought that poor Ilona, who had stood by in gallant silence for all those years as the Deacon philandered away . . . for God's sake, he had fathered two children (that Ilona knew of) by other women! . . . who would have thought that this would be the straw that broke the camel's back?

Lula followed as Ilona made her way down the street toward the funeral parlor in the gathering dusk. Every few steps she tried to talk to her aunt—Auntie? Wait a minute! What are you doing?—but Ilona was impervious. She kept marching down the street, eyes straight ahead, her facial expression set in stone. It was as if she were Moses parting the Red Sea; everyone scattered from her path.

Ilona wheeled around a corner and the funeral parlor came into view. From some upstairs window—Lula couldn't tell exactly which one—someone who clearly knew the score yelled, Ilona's got a gun! Everybody *run!*

Ilona made her way behind the funeral parlor to the cottage tucked away there. Lula, with a growing sense of impending disaster, hung back and watched. Ilona mounted the steps, switched the gun from her right hand to her left, and pounded on the door. Open up! she cried. Open this door up before I knock it down! Robert Morris! More pounding, more yelling. Finally the door cracked open, and a bedraggled-looking Deacon stuck his head out. Ilona raised the gun and pointed it right between the Deacon's eyes; he instantly disappeared back inside the house, with Ilona right behind him.

Lula watched incredulously from behind a corner of the funeral home as the sound of screaming and yelling came from within the cottage. Then, abruptly, the muffled explosion of a gunshot—then another—What in the name of heaven was going on in there?

And then the door flung open, and the most naked woman Lula had ever seen bolted from the house as if someone had set her on fire. Screaming in terror, she sprinted down the street, her bare breasts flouncing to beat the band. Lula turned back just in time to see the equally naked Deacon, striving mightily to pull on a pair of pants, stumble from the house and make his own frantic way toward the street; Ilona then appeared in the doorway and started firing again, wildly and indiscriminately, as if she were being attacked by a flock of invisible birds. After four shots the chamber was spent, but she kept pulling the trigger, *click click click,* finally hurling the empty gun in futility in the general direction of the fleeing Deacon. Then she sat down on the steps and began to cry, great wracking sobs, and Lula ran to her and held her until the police arrived.

• • •

SOMEHOW, THE DEACON managed to smooth everything over. The cops, once they learned that no one was hurt, were convinced to let sleeping dogs lie. The Deacon managed to convince Ilona—or perhaps Ilona simply chose to believe—that this slip, this stumble into the sinful flesh, was merely a peccadillo, a onetime incident, something that had never happened before and would never happen again. Ilona knew better, of course—*she had to,* Lula thought. But, shocked by her loss of control, Ilona withdrew into herself. Lula was worried about her, but she soon had her own problem to worry about.

Her period was late—about six weeks late. She told no one but Susie, who just shook her head.

You're probably pregnant, she said, a rueful note in her voice. Some chicken hawk done knocked you up. What's gonna happen now?

I don't think I'm pregnant, said Lula, who had no doubt that she was. She just *knew.*

She found the father, a young man she had been seeing for a while, a young man who had told her all the things she had wanted to hear.

My monthlies have stopped, she said. I think I'm pregnant.

She waited for him to say something. But he just regarded her, his expression unchanged.

What are we gonna do? she asked. I'm scared. What should we do?

We not gonna worry about it right now, he said. What do you know about being pregnant? You been listening to that gaggle of geese you work with, and they got you all worked up. You ain't pregnant.

And for a few weeks Lula drew great strength from what he had said. What *did* she know, after all? Wasn't he right about that? But as the morning sickness began to assert itself and she felt her middle begin to swell ever so slightly, she knew for sure: She was going to be a mother.

After a couple of weeks more, she screwed up the courage to tell Auntie. She *had* to, before Auntie figured it out for herself . . . she was nearly three months in, now, and Lula figured she couldn't disguise her condition much longer. It was just a matter of time.

And so Lula came home from work one afternoon, her heart hammering, and took Auntie by the hand and sat down with her on the sofa in the living room. The tears began to spill out onto her cheeks, before she even started to talk.

Auntie, I—

What's the matter, sugar? Are you hurt? What's happened?

I—I'm going to have a baby.

Auntie was shocked, to be sure. She reeled momentarily, then regained her composure.

And who is it? Who is the father?

Lula steeled herself and confessed all. Auntie sat there, her hand to her mouth, and took it all in, word by word.

Honey, I just can't *believe* it . . .

But Lula could see Auntie wasn't angry. Floored, yes. Disappointed, yes. Worried, yes. But not angry. Lula could see her working through the scenario in her head. She could virtually see Auntie's own mothering instincts taking over. She could see that Auntie was picturing a baby in her house again, life in her house again.

Well, she said, no matter who the daddy is, it's your precious child, and it must be loved and cared for. You're upset, now, you go on and lay down. I'll come up and get you in a while.

And Lula went to her room and slept like the dead.

She awoke to darkness outside and the Deacon's agitated voice from the kitchen. She couldn't make out the words, but she could hear Auntie talking, pleadingly, only to be drowned out by the Deacon's low rumble. A knot of dread replaced the relief she had felt at coming clean with Auntie.

Finally she heard the Deacon walking toward her room. A quick knock and the door swung open. His face, contorted with anger, hovered above her.

49

You've disgraced yourself, this house, and God, he said.

I'm sorry, Deacon—

It's too late for sorry. It's too late for that. Now, you listen—

He stopped talking and walked back to the door and shut it. Then he walked back over to where Lula sat on her bed, kneeled in front of her, and began to spit out his words:

You see, I'm a *leader* in this community. I'm a man of *Got*. (When he was agitated like this, or giving a sermon, *God* came out like *got*.) *Got* has instructed me to provide spiritual guidance to this city . . . I set an example. I have a Christian home. Now, can I go out and instruct the sinners of our world about the value of a Christian home when my own home is despoiled? When my own charge has ignored the teachings of *Got*?

Please, Deacon, don't—

He waved her words away, then stood up and reached deep into his pants pocket and withdrew a fat roll of bills. He peeled a few off the roll, put them in Lula's open palm, and then closed her fingers around them. She quickly counted it: Fifty dollars.

The Deacon kneeled before her again and looked at her intently. When he spoke, his voice was low and cold.

You see, I can't have anyone in my home I can't trust. I think you know what I mean by that, don't you? Don't you, Lula?

So he knows, after all. He knows I saw him that day, through the fence.

His voice dropped even lower.

So you must leave. You mustn't come around here. And if I ever find out that you've told your Auntie anything that would make her *unhappy*—do you know what I mean? If I ever hear that, I promise you I will find you and beat you within an inch of your life, as *Got* is my witness. Do you understand that?

Lula, speechless, nodded.

And you tell whatever hustler you been shacking with that the same goes for him. I better not see his street ass around here. You'll tell him that?

Yes—

All right. Now pack your things and get out. Now. Tonight.

And he stood up, hovering above her again, and walked out the door.

And Lula packed up her things and left. She was gone in less than an hour.

THE FATHER OF her child was nowhere to be found. He was gone. This was no tremendous shock to Lula. Hadn't her father done the same thing to her mother? And then—the cherry on top—her mother had left, too. Well, she didn't intend to leave her children. But she refused to be shocked when a man decided to run out on his responsibility. It was, in her mind, simply the way of things.

She stayed with friends until, with Ilona's help, she found an apartment that was both affordable and suitable. Lula worked as long as she could at the sewing factory, but her pregnancy ultimately forced her to quit. Finally, the day came when she gave birth to her first child, a healthy, handsome baby boy. He was the most beautiful thing Lula had ever seen. She named him Milton.

She couldn't work and take care of the baby, too. Ilona couldn't help with baby-sitting—Deacon forbade it—but she did sneak some money to Lula every month. But it wasn't enough. Something had to give. Ilona kept working behind the scenes; at last, word came that an uncle in Saginaw, Michigan, was willing to take her in until she was back on her feet. They needed some help around the house, so . . .

Soon after Lula packed up Milton and their belongings and boarded the bus for Saginaw. Once again, Lula had been shunted aside, passed along down the line. And she gratefully moved on, toward even colder latitudes.

Four

BLOOD ON THE SNOW

*I*T HAD COME DOWN to this: She wasn't going to lower herself again.

Lula wasn't sure of much, anymore—but she knew that she was *not* going through that anymore, not for Mr. Judkins, not for anybody. Surely she must have lost any notion of who she was, to have *ever* done it, even once. But you do what you have to do, right? When your children are hungry and their father (the man you love) beats you black and blue like some dumb animal, again, and says he'll do it yet *again,* then you do what you have to do.

Because you will do anything for your children. *Anything.*

Then a numbness takes over, a fatigue; the brain is telling the body where to go, what to do, but the heart says, *Leave me out of it.* Because it's too awful to let the knowledge of it seep inside you, because it will poison your very soul. And your own soul, your own private knowledge of who you are, who you still consider yourself to be, despite everything, is all you have left when every other barrier to degradation is under siege, eroding fast.

What had gotten her through it? (Not that it was over yet. She still had to stand her ground, reclaim herself, make her refusal real.) How had she held on to herself, in the middle of . . . *all that*? She had seen the other women who did whatever they had to do to get by. She never talked to them—*I'm not one of them*—but she watched them. She saw the dope they took, to make it all go down like sugar. And she watched the dope become yet another master to be served. Dope was slavery. She was better than that, better than *something.*

She would not forget who she was. And who was she? At those moments when she wondered, she knew this much: She was a twenty-year-old mother of three, standing in the wicked stone cold of this awful town, trying to *survive.* Trying to make enough to hurry back home, maybe with a few pieces of coal for the stove . . . yes, she was all that. But she fervently held on to who she *had* been, who she still believed herself to be, in part . . . an extension of Little Red, that young girl in Alabama surrounded by love, who would walk outside the cabin at night while the singing swelled from inside, and stand among the fireflies that swirled about her like a funnel cloud, as if they would pick her up and take her away . . . gently twisting, twisting . . . and deposit her in the dark, secret, safe place.

She held on to that, because sometimes there was nothing else to hold on to, except God.

And there was Milton, Calvin, and now Stevie.

She had always told herself she did whatever she had to do for *them.* But now she knew she had to stop, for them.

No more. *No.*

And she had said it just like that, strong, direct, in his face: No more. *No.*

Why had the refusal welled up from within her now, today? It had been just like any other Saturday . . . he was up early and gone all day. The sun had come out in the morning for a while, and she had wrapped up the boys in the jackets from the Lions Club and taken them over to the park. Milton and Calvin shrieked and chased and let off steam. Stevie—always happy wherever you put him—pawed around in the sand at Lula's feet. It was cold, but the boys didn't seem to mind. They were used to it. But Lula couldn't stand it; Lula never got used to the cold.

She made a pan of biscuits for supper and put Milton and Calvin to bed. Stevie stayed up longer, as usual. Lula swore that boy had his own clock! Regular time seemed to mean nothing to him, because of his condition.

Stevie had just fallen asleep when Judkins came home. It was nearly midnight, and she could tell right away that he had been drinking (not that she would have had any reason to think otherwise, especially on a Saturday) by the slight list in his walk and by the look in his eye.

He didn't say anything at first. He went straight into the kitchen and started rummaging in a drawer by the sink, digging through it like a dog after a bone.

What're you lookin' for? Lula asked finally.

Cigarettes, Judkins said. I know I left a pack of cigarettes in here. Damn!

You took the last one out of there last night. I saw you.

Judkins slammed the drawer shut, turned, and glowered.

What we got to eat around here?

I got a couple of biscuits . . . but they cold now.

I don't want no goddamn cold biscuits!

Well, there ain't nothin' else in this house. And no money to buy it with, unless you got some.

All right, Judkins muttered. All right. I ain't going to sit here and take this from you. You go on. You go on, woman, and bring back some money. Get off your ass and get out there.

Lula sat in silence. This was how it always started. She looked at Stevie, asleep beside her on the sofa. Lord, the child took forever to go to sleep, and then he could sleep through a hurricane. Well, there was another hurricane brewing, for sure, in this house tonight.

Now go on, he said, unsteadily. I'll stay here with these children. You go on.

And bring me back some cigarettes.

Something in the way he said it—*and bring me back some cigarettes*—that was what tore into her. She had already made up her mind; Pete had helped with that. But after all the pain she had absorbed, after all she had been through, that was what did it. That he would just toss it out there, as if she were just going out to the store, anyway, for her own health or something—that was what did it. It grabbed something inside her and wouldn't let go.

Well, what are you waitin' for? I am not in no mood for this tonight. You go *on.*

I ain't doin' it, Lula said. It came out just like that—slow, quiet, and angry.

What's that? Speak to where I can hear you.

I ain't doin' it.

Judkins walked across the room and pointed a long finger in her face.

I'm tellin' you one more time—

No more. *No.*

He drew back the birdlike arm and backhanded her, straight across the jaw. She pitched over onto the floor. Stevie stirred but kept sleeping.

Lula slowly raised herself up from the floor and stood before him.

I ain't gonna do it no more, she said. You can kill me if you want, but I ain't goin' back out there. I got my children to take care of. It's *your* job to support *your* family!

Judkins flew at her. He grabbed her by the shoulders and flung her across the living room and into the kitchen, where she tumbled headlong into the table with a great crash. She literally saw stars. From the back of the apartment, she could hear Milton and Calvin begin to cry.

Don't you *ever* back talk me! Judkins's chest heaved from the effort.

I'm not doing it, you sorry son of a bitch—

He took another menacing step toward her, then stopped.

I *will* kill you. *Damn* you, woman!

He stopped and seemed to reconsider, then walked closer and pointed his long finger at her again. Lula struggled to her feet against the kitchen wall. She tasted metal, felt the blood trickle from the corner of her mouth. She wiped her mouth and saw a streak of red slathered across the back of her hand. It seemed to give her a wild courage.

I'm taking these children and I'm leaving—

He laughed. Where you gonna go? His face was a sneer. Who will take you in? You and three young 'uns—one of 'em blind as a bat—what a sorry-ass lot! You ain't goin' anywhere.

You go to hell, Lula said.

Judkins, his eyes backlit with rage, struck her across the face again and then raised a fist to do it once more. He didn't see the glint of the knife until it was arcing toward him in a blur and felt it slash across his forearm. He staggered backward, stunned. Before he could regroup, Lula came at him again, the knife busy: swiping, stabbing, hacking, probing . . .

Stumbling, Judkins retreated.

Touch me again, I'll cut you into a thousand pieces! Lula was blood-wild. She advanced again as Judkins looked in disbelief at his arms, the sleeves of his jacket darkening with blood, a howl beginning to issue from his mouth.

And then he ran.

Later, outside, Lula saw blood on the moonlit snow.

I meant to slice his head clean off, Lula would realize much later, when her mind had cleared. *And I would have, I truly believe, had the blood not come a shock-red gusher and had he not started*

screamin' and runnin' like some wounded vampire in one of those hor-
ror movies they play late at night when normal people are fast asleep.

IT WAS SUPPOSED to have been different in Saginaw.

Lula didn't want to leave Indiana. But when Uncle Hone McGee and his wife, Mary, offered to take her in, well, it was an offer she just couldn't refuse. And there was something to be said for raising her child in a smaller town, where life surely was simpler and distractions fewer. And so it would be Saginaw, then, a town of about fifty thousand pressed against Lake Huron some hundred miles northwest of Detroit.

But there would be nothing simple about Lula's life in Saginaw—far from it. For Saginaw, like any other city, held its share of good and evil, both in heaping amounts to be sampled by those eternally attempting to choose between the two.

Hone and Mary were good people, and they gladly welcomed Lula and Milton into their home. Hone, especially, was a live wire, a gregarious man who loved life and was determined to live it to the fullest. Lula quickly learned that Hone's house was a popular gathering place for his neighborhood cronies; that was due not only to Hone's pleasing disposition, but to the fact that Hone allowed crap games and other forms of gambling there—so long as he got a piece of the action. Lula worried at first that it might not be the right environment for baby Milton to be raised in. But, for the most part, the men who frequented the house respected the place and behaved. The games were confined to the back of the house. And despite his affinity for gambling a dollar, Hone certainly was a kind man, impossible not to like. Lula was happy there from the start. So she accepted her good fortune and set to doing her part around the house and taking care of Milton.

Lula was the center of attention virtually from the moment she arrived. She was young and pretty with a wicked sense of humor; she took no grief from any of the men who showed up at Hone's for an evening of rolling the bones. Her gumption amused everyone to no end. When the weather was nice, Lula would sit out on the front stoop with Milton and Aunt Mary and while away the time, visiting with whoever stopped by. It was a casual type of socializing that was the lifeblood of urban neighborhoods in the days before the magnetic lure of television, when people began to withdraw into their living rooms, away from the actual living of lives that was transpiring outside in the real world.

The stoop also was a prime spot to meet and flirt and trade barbs with the men who dropped by with a little spending money in their pockets, eager to try their luck in the backroom. And more than one visitor let it be known that—if Lula was interested—they could step out somewhere. You just say the word, girl.

But it soon became apparent that Lula had eyes for only one man in Saginaw. His name was Calvin Judkins, and everyone knew he was a pure street hustler, living on a small military pension. But did he ever have style! He was an occasional visitor to the backroom, and he always stopped to have a word with Lula and to razz Milton a bit. He had a smile worthy of a movie star, and everyone always talked about how young he looked for his age, which was . . . well, actually, no one seemed to know for sure.

Even when he didn't stop in to gamble, Judkins passed by the house every day, it seemed, as Lula, Milton, and Mary enjoyed their postdinner reverie on the porch. Sometimes he would be alone, sometimes with one or two others tagging along like ducklings. He was tall, lean, sharp-dressed, and, Lula thought, absolutely the best-looking man she had ever seen. Auntie would stare at him with the Look of a Thousand Daggers, while Lula pretended not to notice that he even existed. But she did notice, and she knew that he noticed her, too. He would come walking by with that confident gait of his—Lula had never seen anyone so *confident*—and as he glided past the house he would turn and flash a quick smile and touch the bill of his cap, never breaking that beautiful stride, and casually say, "Evenin'," in a voice like honey. And that would be it. And he would keep on his way, with not quite a swagger but something akin to it, oblivious, it seemed, of the dagger shower emanating from Mary and the studious efforts of Lula to ignore him.

Ain't nothin' but trash, Auntie would say. But fine-*lookin'* trash, Lula would say within her secret heart.

One afternoon, as Lula rode the bus home from some shopping, she saw him turn a corner and duck into the drugstore about six blocks from home. The bus rumbled to a halt, making its last stop before Lula's house. Just like she did every day, Lula got up, made her way down the aisle, said good-bye to the driver, and stepped out onto the sidewalk. Just like she did every day, she turned left and started walking slowly toward home.

But then something happened.

Lula stopped in her tracks. As if in a dream, she stood there for a full minute, then slowly turned around and started walking the other way, toward the drugstore. Much later, she would think about how certain things came to be in her life, and she would think back to the afternoon when she stepped off that bus, stopped, turned around, and started walking the other way . . . *the other way.*

SHE WALKED INTO the drugstore, with the strange sensation that she was watching herself from afar. *This isn't even real,* she thought. It was a large drugstore, with the soda fountain up against the rear wall. She could see him at the counter, where the soda jerk was drawing a Coke into a tall glass. Lula wandered into a middle aisle and strolled slowly toward the rear, as if she were perusing the merchandise. *What are you doing?* Some unseen power pressed her forward.

Now she could hear him bantering with the soda jerk. Something about the sound of his voice stopped her in her tracks. It was . . . mesmerizing. There was a lilt, an agility to it, punctuated by an infectious cackle. *And then I tole ole Mister Jack, heck-heck, I said the next time your ole lady lets you outta the house will be the first time, heck-heck-heck. And he act like he don't know what I'm talkin' about! Heck-heck-heck!*

He threw some coins on the table and got up to leave. A surge of panic rolled through Lula. *Leave. Run. Hide. Don't let him see you here. What are you doing?* But she was frozen stiff. She quickly turned and began to pretend to examine the magazine shelf. She blindly grabbed the first magazine she could reach and started flipping through it, looking but seeing nothing.

She felt him loom behind her.

Well, now, looky here, he said. I think I know you.

Lula was mortified. She was determined not to look at him. *Why did you come in here?* She felt flush, light-headed.

Come on, now, you act like I'm gonna kidnap you or something. I won't bite. I'm just being friendly.

Lula continued to flip the magazine pages. *Don't look. Don't speak. Hone and Mary would kill you.*

What magazine you readin'? he asked, drawing closer. What interests a young lady like you?

For the first time, Lula actually looked at the cover of the magazine in her hands. BODY BUILDING MEN, it screamed. The cover photo was of a muscle-rippled weight lifter, hoisting a barbell above his head. *Oh my God!* Lula dropped the magazine as if it had abruptly caught fire. Her hands flew to her mouth in horror.

Heck-heck-heck. HECK-HECK-HECK.

He threw his head back and let that cackle of his go. Lula couldn't help it; she started to laugh, too.

Well, now, that's a mighty *interestin'* magazine, he said finally, picking it up off the floor and placing it back on the rack. But I think you were just hidin' from me.

Lula mustered up her nerve. She tried hard not to smile, but she could feel one forming at the corners of her mouth. Maybe you give yourself too much credit, she said.

I'm sure *that's* true, he said. *Heck-heck.*

They stood there in momentary silence. Lula felt his eyes looking through her, as if he knew her every thought. *He surely doesn't know my every thought, but he must have a pretty good idea.* She suddenly was keenly aware of his physical presence. He had a good, earthy smell, a *man's* smell.

Well, I've got to run along, he said. Besides, I think I'm makin' you *uncomfortable.* I don't mean to make you uncomfortable.

Maybe you're givin' yourself too much credit again, Lula said. *You're flirting with him! Stop it.*

Probably so, Judkins replied. He smiled broadly. And what a smile it was, at close range. He bowed slightly and touched the bill of his cap. Come back by here sometime, he said, and I'll buy you a soda. Or a magazine. Heck-heck-heck.

And he was gone, striding out of the drugstore as if he owned the world. At that moment, as far as Lula was concerned, he did.

THAT EVENING, the dishes done, Lula, Milton, and Aunt Mary repaired to the front porch. After a while, regular as clockwork, Judkins floated by, that gorgeous peacock stride eating up the sidewalk. It was like every other day. As he sauntered past, he glanced over at Aunt Ilona, touched the bill of his cap, and said, "Evenin'." The daggers flew. And then: "Evenin', Miss Lula. *Nice bein' with you today.*" And kept right on going, as Aunt Mary swung around and gazed at Lula in jaw-hung amazement, as if she had just robbed a bank.

Lula, her face on fire, just stared straight ahead into the distance, into infinity, at something she couldn't quite see.

LULA DROPPED BY the drugstore the next day. Judkins was there, sitting at the counter, bantering with the soda jerk. She sat down—leaving an empty stool between them—and he bought her a Coke. And they began to talk.

The drugstore became their meeting place, for a while. And one thing led to another, in the way that it does. But not right away, because Lula was (rightfully) fearful that Hone and Mary would disapprove, should they learn that Lula was being seen in the company of (in the immortal, hissing words of Aunt Ilona, who was indelibly on record on this subject) *a chicken-hawk street hustler.* Judkins finally convinced Lula to start meeting him farther from home, so they could relax, maybe take a walk together.

And so their courtship began. They would meet in a little diner, dingy and with the obliterating hum of a big window fan straining against the summer heat. Judkins would sip coffee and smoke Luckies, while the words began to tumble from Lula. It was almost bigbrother-little-sister, at first, although Lula knew it wasn't really that way. But he wanted to know about her, what she was like and where she came from, and she spilled it all: Hurtsboro, Papa Henry and Mama Virge, how she learned The Truth. The funerals and the clacking-and-swaying train ride north. And the fireflies—she even told him about the fireflies.

That brought forth the cackle. Heck-heck-heck, I don't know, baby (he just slipped it in—I don't know, *baby*), that sounds *crazy.* Bunch of lightnin' bugs gonna take you away . . . Heck-heck-heck. Lord help.

And what about you, Mister Judkins? (For she called him Mister Judkins for a very long time.)

There ain't much to tell about me, he would say. I grew up around here and had to fend for myself for as long as I can remember. I'm not book-smart, but I know my away around. I'm a *businessman,* just like you see those men out on the street with suits and ties? Except I don't have to do that. I don't have to jump when somebody else says jump. I don't have to wear no damn suit. I'm my *own* man, and . . .

He would go on and on that way. And Lula would interrupt: And so what *is* your business, Mister Judkins?

My business is *my* business. I do what a black man has to do to survive, and I do damn well at it. I ain't gonna go hit no clock for no white man, go jump when he say jump. I do what comes naturally to *me.* A man lays his money on the table and tries to take *my* money, I take *his* money. A man needs somethin' that's hard to find, I help him find it. I know this town better than the *mayor.* Hell, I oughtta *run* for mayor. Heck-heck-heck. Now *that'd* be something. I'd damn near win, too. I *know* people . . .

And on and on, about *that.* Lord, that man could talk (and drink coffee!). It was hypnotizing, the entire Judkins philosophy, as it were. Here was a man determined to trod his own path, make his own way, think his own thoughts. Let others follow the white man and his money around like sheep! Not Calvin Judkins. He'd make his own money, be his own man. Damn the rest of all of it! It was heady, dangerous, exciting talk to a fifteen-year-old girl off the farm with stars exploding in her eyes. And he *was* good-looking, just as good-looking as he could be. He used his piano-keys smile carefully, it seemed; he was well aware of its value, its effect on people. It was sort of like punctuation—he'd be talking along, make a point, and, then, *flash* it. His whole face would reconfigure itself from his street-guy scowl into something that was about a million dollars' worth of public relations. It was his weapon, and he used it well.

Lula lived for The Smile. And when he bestowed it upon her, she felt like a queen.

• • •

AND SO IT wasn't long before the natural course of events began to transpire. The coffee-shop conversations were followed by the long walks, which led to the hand-holding, which led to his gathering her up in his long, birdlike arms, which were strong and knowledgeable, and kissing her . . . which led, inevitably, to Judkins's dark, musty walk-up on an afternoon that was silvery with the late sun and the promise of something sacred. And afterwards she rode the bus the rest of the way home in that singular, delicious daze, her mind full of constantly repeating images, and her heart full of the sensation of how it all *felt*, to be in love, to be a woman.

On a visit back to East Chicago, her friends at the mill noticed the change in her. Lula was quieter when the topic turned to men and their ways. She had disengaged, somehow. No more innocent questions or head-shaking commentary about the "no-goods," as they had taken to calling their men. In a private moment, Susie finally got it out of her: Lula had a boyfriend. They were in love. She didn't know what was going to happen, but they were in love.

So what does Auntie and Uncle think of this, Susie wanted to know.

Well, they don't know.

They don't know? Why not?

They wouldn't like it.

Why not?

Because . . . he's different.

Different how?

Lula began to gush, in spite of herself. Different in a million ways. If you're walking down the street, you'll pick him out of a crowd. He's tall and handsome, and other men just seem *small* around him, you know? And he's smart, and makes his own way in the world. He's a businessman. He doesn't need anybody to tell him what to do . . . and his voice. There's something about his voice . . .

Mmm-mmm, Susie said. So let me ask you something: When you talk about *other men,* what do you mean exactly? How old is this boy?

He ain't no boy, Lula said.

All right then. How old is he?

I'm not sure, Lula said.

Susie, exasperated: Well, how old do you *think* he is?

Best I can figure, Lula said, he's about fifty. But he *looks* a lot younger than that.

Fifty?! Susie nearly fainted dead away. And when she regained her bearings, she had a conniption, right there. Fifty? And you, what, seventeen years old? What exactly is goin' on here? No *wonder* you ain't told nobody about any of this—

I ain't told nobody because it ain't none of their business. Besides, there ain't nothing wrong with it. If I was forty, and he was seventy, wouldn't nobody say nothin'.

He *help* you with that arithmetic?

There's nothin' *wrong* with it.

And then a realization came over Susie.

You already sleeping with that old man? You tell the truth now.

Lula didn't have to say anything. The expression on her face surely said it all. It was an expression of guilt, and acknowledgment, and pride.

Lord help us, Susie said. What you gettin' yourself into, girl? Don't you know they could put that man in jail for doin' that with a girl your age? Did he hurt you? If that chicken-hawk son of a bitch *hurt* you—

It's not like that, Lula said. He didn't hurt me. It's our business. It's between us. It's . . . *wonderful.*

Mmm-mmm. Well, all right then. But you makin' a big mistake, Red. You can't see it, but you are. You goin' down the same road the rest of us did, except you're goin' down the road with a man three times your age, and you already got one young 'un on your hip.

I know what I'm doin'.

Mmm-mmm.

LULA FELT A giddy sense of liberation at having finally shared her secret. But Lula was terrified that Hone and Mary would find out about Judkins, knew that it might jeopardize everything. She had been down this road before; who knew how they might react? And so she insisted on keeping their meetings under wraps, their assignations clandestine. They would meet a couple of times a week—any more, and Auntie would become suspicious and start asking questions—and it remained their private matter. She was determined to keep it quiet. And that was fine with Judkins.

Whatever you say, Red, he would say. But we can't hide out like this forever. It's going to come out, sooner or later.

And, finally, word did get back. Hone confronted Lula with what he had heard from one of the boys: that Lula had been seen out with that hustler Calvin Judkins, the one who was always sweet-talking her when he dropped by the house. He demanded to know: Is that true?

Lula saw there was no use in hiding it any longer.

Yes, sir, she said. We're in love.

Good God, girl! Hone sputtered. That nigger's older than I am!

But Hone and Mary soon realized what untold numbers of people had learned long before them: When a girl's head has been turned, it is virtually impossible to turn it back. And so it was with Lula, who was hopelessly smitten—and nothing was going to dissuade her.

Her faith in Judkins was justified when he later appeared at the house and told Hone and Mary that he intended to take care of Lula and wanted to marry her. This was news to Lula, who was happy to hear it nonetheless.

I can't stop you, Hone said. You're too old for that girl and never worked an honest day in your life outside the service that I know of. But I can't stop her from doing what she wants to do.

A few weeks later, Lula and Milton moved in with Judkins in the walk-up. Not long after that, on a weekend trip, Lula and Judkins appeared before a justice of the peace in Columbus, Ohio, and became man and wife. He was the man of her dreams.

Judkins, unfortunately, was an inconsistent breadwinner at best. He was a street hustler, plain and simple; some days were better than others. Some days he was in on the deal—maybe a good batch of homemade liquor, or a craps game brimming with out-of-town money—and he would be the cock of the walk, cash running through his hands like water. Judkins was the classic case of someone who couldn't abide prosperity for very long—the temptation to big-shot around after a score was simply too great.

Other days the luck of the draw inevitably went against him. Sometimes those days would stretch into weeks, and the money would be tight, and Lula would have to resort to the modest and rapidly dwindling savings she had carefully put away while working at the mill and living with Ilona and the Deacon.

It was during the bad spells that Lula would bring up the issue of regular work with Judkins. But, of course, he told her, she just didn't *understand.* You're askin' me to be somethin' I can't be, he would say. And that would be that.

It wasn't long before their first child together, Calvin, was born. Confronted with this new additional responsibility, Judkins grudgingly agreed to accept a job arranged by a relative at a small furniture factory. Lula was mightily relieved; maybe things would work out in Saginaw, after all. Sometimes she couldn't believe the turns her life had taken; why, they said that Saginaw was right across the water from *Canada.* And to Lula, Canada may just as well have been the

North Pole. (In fact, Judkins frequently would tell his children later that the North Pole was only twelve miles from Saginaw, which they believed for years.)

She loved the man; there was never any question about that. There were times when they seemed happy. She loved his pride, his intelligence, his dignity. But his behavior varied wildly; after a period of relative domesticity, he might suddenly vanish for days. He could be soft and loving, but also abusive and demeaning. He was charismatic, unpredictable, unreliable. And, still, about the best-looking man God ever put on the earth, in Lula's mind. In the ever-springing hope that Judkins would change and accept more responsibility, she stuck with him.

There also was the other small matter of how, exactly, she would survive without him. No, it was better to keep the family together. It was the only family Lula had.

JUDKINS DIDN'T KEEP his job in Saginaw for long. That he would just fall easily into the pattern of the working week and the tiring repetition of the labor was, for anyone who knew him well, probably too much to hope for. The demand for conformity grated on him, and he resented the submissive role he was forced to play. In the end, it was never clear whether he quit or was fired. Either way, a few months and it was over.

In so doing, he quickly exhausted the goodwill of his relatives in Saginaw (and Lula's) who had vouched for him in the first place and loaned him money. On top of all of it was the reality of life in Saginaw at mid-century. East Chicago had been no tropical garden, but Saginaw was an onerously bleak, poor town whose only point of pride, it seemed, was "the world's purest water," according to a city history. In its early days, Saginaw had been a boomtown, propelled by the so-called green gold logging boom of the late nineteenth century. And well into the 1900s, Saginaw was a busy mining center due to the generous mineral deposits in upstate Michigan.

But for the African Americans who filtered north in hopes of participating in the great postwar industrial expansion of the Midwest, there was no discernable recovery from the Great Depression of the 1930s. And Saginaw was, and is, *cold*—the city may not have been twelve miles from the North Pole, as Judkins alleged with mirth in his voice, but the elongated, Canadian-style winters there certainly have an Arctic Circle feel. It was a fundamental cold that, Lula believed, matched the city's soul.

And so with Judkins again unemployed and increasingly isolated, the truly dark days began.

How did it ever start?

They were out of money. They didn't have one red cent. Judkins had left at midday with the aim of finding some day labor. It was bitterly cold, and there was no coal for the stove. Lula had some meal for a little cornbread, but that was it. The children need more than that. The baby needs more than that, she told him.

And so he left and stayed away all afternoon. Shortly after dark, Lula heard the shuffle of footsteps on the stairs outside their tenement door; it was Judkins, she could tell, but it was someone else, too. And then he came in the door with a stranger she had never seen—a short man, a little older. He wore glasses. Lula could tell immediately that they both had been drinking. She could smell it, see it.

Hey baby, Judkins said. This is Mr. Simmons.

How you doin', she said.

Fine, thank you, Mr. Simmons said.

And then he looked up at Judkins, met his gaze, nodded slightly, and walked back out the door.

Who's that? And where did you get any money to drink? I know you been drinkin'.

Mr. Simmons was buyin'.

What are you drinkin' for anyway? I thought you were out lookin' for work.

I was, I was. And I found some.

Well, good. How much did you make? You should have gone to the grocery—

Listen, Lula. Judkins was slurring. He had had more to drink than she had thought.

He came very close and spoke in a near-whisper. His eyes were red-spiked, gone.

I want you to go out and take a ride with that man, he said.

What for? Who is he?

He—he gave me some money. I want you to go and take a ride with him. He's waitin' in his car on the street . . . I want you to go take a ride with him, and be nice to him.

Be *nice* to him . . . what do you mean?

You just do whatever he wants you to do.

Are you *crazy* drunk—

Judkins grabbed her arm and wrenched it, hard. Lula feared it might snap in two. He had her pinned up against the wall now, and his lips spit the words into her ear:

You go out there and do what he says, or I'll beat you like you never been beat. You know I will.

And, in that moment, she *did* know it. She knew beyond a shadow of a doubt.

He shoved her roughly away from the wall. Get your coat, he said. Get out there.

In a daze, she collected her overcoat and shrugged it on. Milton appeared in the kitchen doorway: Where you goin', Mama? I'm hungry—

I'll be back in a little while, she heard herself say. You stay here. Mama'll be back in a bit.

She walked down the tenement stairs to where the sedan idled by the curb. Opened the door. Got in. Simmons, looking half-asleep, regarded her somberly from behind the wheel. And a few blocks away, on a side street with the motor running and the radio loud, Lula did what he wanted her to do. It took about two minutes.

Simmons dropped her off by the curb. She walked back upstairs, shell-shocked. She got a few dollars from Judkins and walked to the market on the corner and bought a chicken for dinner and some coal.

Because, by God, her children were going to have food in their stomachs that night, and they were going to be warm. She would see to it.

LIKE ANYTHING, it became easier with repetition.

If not easier, then more manageable emotionally, for a while. Lula would resist it—she would always resist it, to a point. Sometimes she refused to go "out there," as the phrase developed between them; but she would always be under the heat—or threat—of Judkins's insistence. She was under his sway, and she hated it, resented it, felt revolted by it. But she was convinced that this was the only way, for now, until he got back on his feet, until he figured things out. She finally decided that it was what people in her position *did*, when there was nothing else to do.

A week might go by without going out there. It depended on the money, of course. If there was a little butter and egg money, then there was no need. But inevitably the reserves would dwindle and the argument would begin . . . an argument that Judkins would win. They needed the money. They needed food. They needed coal. You don't think *I've* made sacrifices for this family? he would say. But Lula suspected he said that just to make himself feel better. She couldn't think of any sacrifices on this order that he possibly could have made.

So she would shrug on her coat and go out there, drowning out the protests from every fiber of her being. Sometimes Judkins would bring home Mr. Simmons, or some other gin-pickled version of him, to wait outside. Other times, she was on her own. That was her preference, actually. Walking out into the frigid night and over to the boulevard blocks away, away from her immediate neighborhood, away from judgmental eyes . . . the walking would give her time to steel herself, get her mind right, build up to it. By the time she reached the appointed street—*that* street, every town has one—she would be otherworldly, transported. She understood why the others took dope. It was to get to some other place, any other place than here. Lula didn't have to take dope, *wouldn't* take it. She wasn't about to start throwing away the filthy money she lowered herself to work for. Besides, she could be transported to another place all by herself, on the natural. It was like the fireflies . . . only back then, in Alabama, she wasn't trying to *escape.* It was a matter of wondering what else was out there, a curiosity that flowered from a foundation of love and family. But this—this was like tunneling out of her prison of the moment. Her body, her life, was her prison—so she would leave the body, leave the life, for a while. It would be as if she were watching herself from above; and then, at the last second, she would look *away,* avert her eyes toward the night sky. Because, in the end, she couldn't bear to watch.

She stayed on the periphery of the others. For one thing, you could get hurt. Those people didn't think straight. Lula had seen girls fight each other for a trick. And talk about a *fight!* She had never seen anything like it. A fight to the death, a cockfight, hair flying, fingers clawing at eyes, with the other girls watching and laughing and whooping. They all seemed drunk, high, desperate. Lula understood that. But she wasn't going to get in the middle of that. She would hang back, work the edges, the fringe. She was young, pretty, healthy-looking. Getting work was never a problem. She kept to herself, with a wary eye on the rabble.

Once, early on, a large man, rough trade for sure, came toward her, drifting down the street like a shark. Stuck his face in hers. This is *my* street, he said. And I don't *know* you . . . and so, bitch, why you here?

And Lula stood her ground. I'm here, she said, her voice wavering slightly, because my children are hungry and I want some coal in the stove tonight when I go home . . . so why don't you just tell me where your street ends? And I'll make sure I stay off it.

He was quiet for a moment and then smiled a thin smile. Well, now, you don't have to go and do *that* . . . He appraised her. Lula could see him making the calculations. *Girl this fine can go anywhere. She don't need me, not yet. So . . .*

Tell you what. My name's Oscar. Everybody knows me. I'm easy to find. Like I said, this is my street. I worked hard for it. It's my living, so why don't we make a little agreement. Every once in a while, when you think it's right, when it's goin' good, then why don't you show Oscar a little appreciation? You gonna run your own business, that's fine. But if you're going to be around here, then you need to pay a little rent every once in a while. When you *feel* like it. Okay?

Lula said nothing.

Well, you think about it. Ask around. You might decide there are some . . . *privileges* that go with it. You don't exactly look like you know what you're doin', and not everybody is your friend. *So,* see you *around* . . .

And with that he turned and began his ponderous shark-swim back to the reef.

Not gonna pay rent to some lowlife.

She had him pegged, all right; he was no church deacon. He was the worst among men: an out-and-out pimp. Kept his girls on dope, which kept them in line, Lula supposed. She couldn't respect a man like that. But who was she to judge? She felt as different from him as she would feel different from some alien being. But she was a denizen of this planet, too—as superior as she tried to feel, as distant as she tried to remain, as much as she concentrated on the transport—she was of this world. She was on the street, and despite her knowledge of who she was, Lula knew she was *part of it.*

And so she went about it, in the manner that she saw fit.

She didn't dress like they dressed. Didn't want to, didn't have to. She just dressed like *she* dressed. They could tell if you were available. There was no need for advertising.

And no intercourse, either. Plenty of ways to make money without that. Lula was determined to hang on to at least one feathery shred of self-respect. You just had to make it clear, up front. Just so there were no misunderstandings.

Problem was, misunderstandings seemed to happen anyway, no matter what. Which is why she started carrying the knife—to avoid misunderstandings, like the one that happened on her third night out, when this old man rolled through in a red Ford, pulled over, and started talking.

It all seemed cool. The lines of communication seemed clear. Lula got in the car, and they pulled away. Started talking a bit; sometimes, Lula quickly learned, they wanted to talk, nothing complicated, just chitchat to break the ice. (She also quickly learned that there usually wasn't much talking afterwards, if any.) And so the old man—Lula figured he was past fifty, old in her book—began to talk, ask polite questions, until he parked the car. And then it became clear that he did not intend to abide by their agreement. And, suddenly, it didn't seem as if he was willing to be resisted.

He was wiry, and strong. He balled his fist and struck her, hard, right on the point of the jaw. I'm gonna get what I'm payin' for, he snarled. He hit her again, and again, until she stopped struggling. But when he tried to have his way, she started flailing again.

Finally he gave up, cursing, and shoved her from the car. She picked herself up as he screeched away, and began to sullenly trudge back to the appointed street. Her coat was soiled from the wet, dirty street. Angry tears raced down her swollen face.

Oscar appeared from the shadows as she passed by the rabble. What happened to you? That old man do that to you?

Lula just nodded, and shrugged.

Oscar reached into his pocket and withdrew a wad of bills. He handed her a twenty—a small fortune. Go home, he said. Get cleaned up and take care of yourself. Get yourself something to eat.

So Lula went home and silently cried herself to sleep, the side of her head aching from the beating. The next morning, she searched a trunk of Judkins's things and took one of his knives, a switchblade. And she began to carry it with her, and practiced opening it, over and over and over. She got pretty good at it.

A FEW NIGHTS after the old man beat her up, Lula was back on the street, on the periphery of the rabble. She hadn't been out there long before she saw the red Ford whisper down the street again. As it passed her, the old man gave her a look of disdain and then stared straight ahead. He stopped in front of the others, leaned over, rolled down his passenger side window, and began to talk.

Abruptly, Oscar materialized and walked around to the driver's side and leaned down into the old man's face. Lula could see Oscar's mouth working the words. The old man was shaking his head. At one point, Oscar looked Lula's way; the old man followed his gaze and looked over his shoulder at Lula, and then started shaking his head again.

Suddenly, in a flash, Oscar tore open the car door and pulled the man from behind the wheel out onto the street. They scuffled momentarily behind the car—Lula couldn't see—and then Oscar had control, gripping the old man's tie in one hand and slapping him with the other hand. Then, leading him by the tie into full view of everyone on the street, Oscar began to slam the old man's head against the car. When he crumpled to the ground, Oscar kicked him repeatedly and viciously in the ribs. Then, finally, Oscar dragged the old man back to his feet and shoveled him back into the Ford, where he slumped bleeding in the front seat, semiconscious.

There were whoops from the rabble. Oscar turned and gave Lula a long and meaningful look across the way.

Lula started paying Oscar the rent.

THE WHITE GENTLEMAN started coming around a couple of months after Lula first went out there.

It wasn't unusual to see whites cruise by the rabble. That was something that surprised Lula at first; the street wasn't exactly on their side of town. But cruise by they did, very cautiously, and many stopped and conducted business. Lula figured the lure of what was for sale was a lot stronger than any feeble sense of caution.

He was polite, quiet-voiced, sober. Most of the men who came through usually had been drinking, if not outright drunk, as if they had to get their courage up. But the white gentleman—and he *was* a gentleman, Lula thought—was clear-eyed and reserved. He drove a small pickup, and always wore jeans and work boots. He seemed very out of place the first time he appeared, the truck drifting slowly down the street.

Lula was on the periphery, as usual. The truck didn't stop the first time around; it circled the block and then came back around and stopped in front of her. The white man rolled down the passenger window and leaned over from the driver's side.

How much? he asked.

Depends on what you want, she said.

It's up to you, he replied.

That's a new one, she thought.

77

Twenty, she said.

Okay, then. Get in.

And so he started driving.

He looked small, Lula thought, hunched behind the wheel. Lula figured him for about forty. His hair was cropped short, and he had the air of someone who spent his days outdoors. A nice-looking man, Lula decided. But she was wary, as always, and spooked by the simple fact that he was white. It occurred to her that she had never ridden in the same car with a white person. White people were, to her, as foreign as someone from China. Her world was black, had always been black.

Do you mind if we just drive around for a while? he asked in his quiet voice.

All right. Just don't go too far from here. I get nervous.

Okay, he said. That makes two of us.

Somehow he began a conversation: You from Saginaw? . . . Alabama? I was there once . . . I've got some family in Florida . . . It was like that. Meaningless stuff. They're all alike, Lula thought, white or black; they all got to talk first. That was fine by her. The car was warm, and he seemed safe. Still, bitter experience had already taught her to keep her guard up—way up.

But he kept driving and talking, meandering through the dark city streets and their small-potatoes conversation across their great divide. They talked about Alabama weather, Saginaw weather. Lula wondered when spring would arrive; he told her what to expect. She asked him what he used the truck for; he ran a farm north of the city, he said. The truck comes in handy.

Finally, he pulled the truck over on a quiet street and cut the engine. The bile began to creep up into Lula's throat, as it always did. She could never get past the bile and the churning stomach when the time came. She prayed to God every day that she would *never* get past it.

Look, he said. I thought I wanted to do this, but . . . well, I've never done this before . . . like this. It doesn't seem right. I wish I hadn't come. You—you seem nice. It's not what I expected.

That's okay, Lula said. None of this is what I expected, either.

Keep the money, he said. I'll take you back.

All right, then. Suit yourself. I surely don't mind.

He dropped her off back into the cold on the rabble's fringe. Will you be here tomorrow night? he asked.

If you want me to be, I will, she said.

Lula clutched the twenty in her coat pocket, a good night's work, and watched as he drove away.

HE CAME BACK the next night, and the next, and others after that. Same drill each time: Twenty dollars, a drive, a conversation—about everything.

You married? he asked one evening toward spring.

I'd rather not talk about that.

Children?

Yeah. Three boys. Milton, Calvin, and little Stevie.

Are they good boys?

Well, they're *boys,* you know? But they're good. I'm trying to raise 'em best I can. Stevie's special; he's blind. But you'd never know it, the way he gets around.

I'm sorry to hear that—that he's blind. What happened?

They don't know. He was in an incubator for nearly two months after he was born. They say it could have been that. But they don't know. God is the only one who knows why.

You a religious woman?

I try. But sometimes I think I believe in God more than He believes in me. I don't blame Him for turning His back on me. I guess I turned my back on Him, from the looks of things.

Don't give up. He works in mysterious ways.

It was a month before he told her his name. It was the same night he asked if he could meet her children.

Why on earth would you want to do that?

I'm curious. We've talked so much about them. I wonder what they look like.

Well, they look like me, and their daddy. What else you need to know?

I don't have to actually *meet* them. I'd just like to see them. I'd like to see you with them.

And so a few days later, on a sunny afternoon, Lula took the kids to the park at a prearranged time. Milton and Calvin, as usual, ran and shrieked and let off steam. Stevie played in the sand at her feet. After a while, the pickup pulled up across the way and Pete stepped out. He came no closer, per their agreement, but simply leaned against the truck and watched. Lula stole a glance at him from time to time; he seemed lost in thought.

Finally, it was time to go. Lula scooped up Stevie and called the other boys from the jungle bars. She gathered them all together and, for a moment, looked toward Pete. He gazed straight at them, smiled, and nodded almost imperceptibly at Lula. Lula felt as if she were posing for a family portrait. And what a picture it must have been—a shopworn young mother, defiled beyond her darkest dreams; Milton and Calvin, skinny and virtually dressed in rags; and little Stevie, two years old, perched on her hip, his cloudy, opaque eyes looking at everything and seeing nothing.

I WANT TO show you something tonight, Pete said, the next time they were together. But we'll have to drive a while, okay?

Okay, I guess, Lula said. Where we going?

You'll see.

He pointed the truck north and sped out of town, the shabby, low-slung Saginaw outskirts finally giving way to the pines and hardwoods of the Michigan countryside. Not a word was spoken.

About twenty minutes later, Pete began to slow and turned off the highway onto a narrow country lane that went on for a few minutes more. Finally, he turned again and drove through a large gate that led to a large farmhouse set on a rise. Lula couldn't see much through the darkness, except rolling pastureland and the burning porch lights of the farmhouse as they approached.

Is this your place? Lula asked, breaking the silence.

Pete only nodded. He seemed deeply preoccupied.

They got out of the truck and climbed the steps to the front door. Pete produced a set of keys and let them in. He flipped a switch and the entrance hallway flooded with light.

Lula saw shining hardwood floors and tasseled rugs. A comfortable living room with a brick fireplace. Pictures on the walls of children and dogs, of a younger Pete and a young woman, smiling. The place certainly had a woman's touch.

He showed her around the sprawling house, not saying much. They eventually reached the back porch, where Lula could see a very large barn and a grouping of other outbuildings bathed in floodlights. A nearby open garage, Lula could see, housed two expensive-looking sedans.

I guess I always thought you just *worked* on a farm, Lula said. But this is your place isn't it?

Yes. It's been in my family for a couple of generations. We grow beans and sugar beets. My mom and dad have passed away. It's just me now.

And what about your wife? I saw the pictures.

She's gone. She was . . . unhappy. She had some problems—with drinking. Her parents died and left her some money, and so she left about a year ago. I haven't heard from her. We've got two kids in college; they haven't heard from her, either. She was a very troubled person.

I'm sorry, Lula said.

There was silence for a moment. Let's go back inside, Pete said finally. I'll make some coffee. I want to talk to you about something.

Soon they were ensconced in front of the fireplace. Lula wished he would build a fire but didn't say anything. Pete got to the point right away.

I want you and your children to come live with me, he said.

What? Lula looked at him as if he had suddenly announced he was from Mars.

You heard me, he said. I mean it. Let me explain how . . .

Just then, Lula realized how little she knew about this white man who had basically supported her for the past few months, with forty dollars, sixty dollars, eighty dollars a week. The money had been very nice. *He* had been very nice. It had all been very much like a bizarre dating arrangement for money; he would tell her what night he would be back, she would meet him on the street, they would drive and talk, he would slip her a twenty and drop her off, make arrangements for another night.

He had never so much as kissed her.

And now, in 1953, a Negro woman and her three young 'uns were gonna move in with a white farmer in the Michigan sticks?

I think you've lost your senses, Lula said.

Wait—hear me out on this. I know we can't—we can't be *together*, you know? Not in any public, formal way. And we haven't even discussed how we feel about each other, but I know that I care for you and you care for me. I know that much. I need help around this place. There's a guesthouse out back. You and your boys could live there. We'd find a school for your boys. We'd get some help for Stevie. I need a housekeeper, a caretaker, whatever you want to call it. I'll give you a place to live and pay you on top of it. I know you need help. You can't live like you've been living. I've seen the bruises on your face and your arms. That man is no good for you . . .

Stop it! The sound of Lula's own voice shocked her.

What's wrong—

This is *crazy.* You're talkin' crazy. We can't do this. *I* can't do this.

Why not? Look at it this way: I'm offering you a job. A *good* job. You can get out of that slum—

Lula cut him off. And then what happens when you decide you don't want me around? When you start to worry about what your neighbors are saying about you havin' all these niggers around? When your wife comes back? What happens to us then?

You don't have to worry about that. I'll always—

How can you say that? You seem like a very sad man, Mister Pete. You've had your heart broken—you're mixed up—and I may live in a *slum,* but I'm taking care of my own. I'm trying to keep my family together the best way I know how. And you've been wonderful to me. But I just don't think I can—

I didn't mean to upset you—

Just take me back. Take me back, *please.*

Another wordless ride. Lula's head was aswirl: Was she out of her mind? This man had offered to take care of her, take care of her boys . . . and she was going to stay on the street? She was going to go back to an abusive man who led her to this cold, dark, tawdry corner of the world?

At that moment all the repression and denial of what her life had become seemed to lift away like clearing fog. She had taken a path in life that would have seemed absolutely inconceivable not so long ago—and, yes, she had *taken* that path, chosen it, had allowed herself to become so dependent on Judkins that she no longer felt in control of her own actions, and had succumbed to her own fear of the unknown, her fear of what things might be like without him. And that fear had driven her to become a streetwalker, a prostitute, a *whore.* That word, the word she had buried deep within her some-where, suddenly began to ricochet in her head: *whore.* She was a *whore,* selling herself for money. Oh, she had been strict about her limits, insistent about what she would *not* do; and she had taken some comfort in that, had convinced herself that her sacrifice, her degradation, was not complete. What a joke! *In the name of my own children and my own fear, I have become a whore.*

Where would it end? How long before the older boys figured out what their mother was doing? How many of her neighbors already knew? How long before some drunken, angry customer gravely injured her or beat her to death? How long before she used the knife to kill someone in self-defense? How long before she got sick, like so many in the rabble? How long before she started using dope to dull the heartache, to placate the churning stomach? How long before she ran into trouble with the law? How long before the faint ember of light remaining in her soul went dark?

And now some man, different from her but a good man, comes with some heaven-sent offer of help, and her fear will not let her accept? Was she so paralyzed, so far gone?

She saw it all now. If she could not accept help due to her fear, then she would have to defeat her fear and help herself.

The truck rolled to a stop at the periphery of the rabble. Lula watched through the windshield as the girls milled and flounced and jostled, as a car or two sidled up to the curb, as Oscar glided about the shark shadows.

It's all so *crazy,* she said, as if thinking aloud. She turned and looked at Pete, this odd, quiet, decent man, and leaned over and kissed him, sweetly, for what seemed like a very long time.

Thank you, Mister Pete, she said. And God bless you.

She stepped out of the truck and watched as Pete drove slowly away, like all the times before. Then she turned and started the walk home, for the last time. She didn't intend to come back.

• • •

IT WASN'T QUITE OVER with Pete. A few nights later, a knock came on the door. Judkins answered it; he found three white men standing in the hallway. Judkins was stunned. He figured you could live a thousand years and not see that sight again in this part of Saginaw.

What's this all about? he asked, suspicion dripping from his voice.

I want to see Lula, Pete said.

What for?

I don't want to talk to you, Pete said, quite firmly. I want to talk to Lula.

By then, Lula had appeared at the door. Her hand flew to her mouth when she saw who it was.

Pete brushed past Judkins and stepped into the apartment. Lula, get your children together and come with me, he said. You know you want to. You know it's the right thing to do.

Judkins couldn't believe his eyes and ears: Now wait just a *damn minute* here—

The two burly farmhands stepped closer to Judkins. One placed a hand on Judkins's shoulder. Judkins got the message.

Lula and Pete sat down at the kitchen table.

You shouldn't have come here, she said. I wish you hadn't.

I came because I know you're scared of him. I came to let you know that you don't have to be scared. Just get the kids and the things you need and come with us. Nothing will happen, I promise.

That's not it, Pete. Going with you—it won't work out. We can't be together. I know that's what you want. And this is the father of two of my children. I don't know what I'm going to do, but I know that running away with you to a white man's country isn't going to fix anything.

You don't know what you're saying, Pete said. You're not thinking straight.

Yes, Pete, I am. You need to leave now. Somebody's gonna get hurt.

Pete sat silently for a moment. Okay, Lula, he said. Take care of yourself. If you ever change your mind, or need any help, all you have to do is tell me.

Pete stood and walked back toward the door. He stopped and looked Judkins in the eye.

You ever lay a hand on her again, he said, I will kill you.

Judkins didn't blink. *Get out of my house,* he said, fierce and low.

The door closed behind them. Judkins turned and looked at his wife. Woman, he said, you done gone to the dogs for sure.

I sure have, Lula thought. *I sure have.*

THE NEXT EVENING was when all hell exploded.

Judkins made his demand; Lula refused; the knife, *his* knife, purloined from the trunk, came out and did its work; Judkins fled, baying and bleeding, out into the night and an early spring snow.

When he left, Lula cleaned up the wreckage in the house as if it were just another day. She wiped blood from the floor as if it were merely spilt milk. Then she went and woke up the boys—they had slept through it all, slept through so much—dressed them and gathered their meager clothes together.

She went into the kitchen and reached far beneath the sink and drew out a box of washing powder. She dug into the sweet-smelling powder and withdrew the money—$117, most of it from Pete. She had heard there were jobs in Detroit, good jobs. There was public housing, subsidized by the government. Maybe they could find a place. The shit had surely hit the fan. The money would get Lula and the kids to Detroit and keep them going for a while.

And so Detroit it was. *We'll start over,* Lula thought to herself as the four of them, ragtag, pulling and pushing and cajoling and complaining, made their way downstairs to the snowy, windswept city street. It was another family portrait for the books, for sure.

It will be better in Detroit.

Better for me, better for Milton, better for Calvin.

Better for little Stevie.

Part Two

STEVIE

Five

SOUNDS

In the beginning God created the heaven and the earth.
The earth was without form, and void; and darkness was upon
the face of the deep. And the spirit of God moved upon the face
of the waters.
And God said, Let there be light: and there was light. And God
saw the light, that it was good: and God divided the light from
the darkness.
And God called the light Day, and the darkness he called
Night . . .

—Genesis

DARKNESS EXISTS ONLY to those who know light. Light is
not reality; it is perception. We take the world as we find it.
There are five billion people on the planet, and five billion worlds.

For one who has never known light, there is no darkness. For one
who cannot see, there is no reason to see. Because—

There is touch: Air as it rushes between the fingers of a waving
hand; grass beneath bare feet; warm water upon a face; the face of a
coin against a fingertip; lips pressed against lips.

There is smell: honeysuckle in the spring; a wet dog; grits cooking on the stove; oil on the sidewalk; rain coming.

There is taste: the crunch of bacon; the silky swirl of milk; a crust of bread; bitter medicine; snowflakes exploding on the tongue.

And there is *sound*: Mama talk; brother walk; bird flutter; seesaw screech; radio sing.

LOOK AT YOU! Look at this mess on you!

What mess, Mama—

You got dog manure all over you again! What'd I tell you about that? You got to be careful out there! Now I'm gonna have to clean you up.

I'm sorry, Mama. I was playing. You said I could play.

I know what I said, son.

Milton and Calvin were playing, too. Did they get messed up?

No, baby, they didn't. Gimme those hands so I can wash them off.

That feels good. Ha! That feels good, Mama.

Baby, you got to watch what you're doing out there. I know you can't help it, but you got to be more careful of yourself. You got to figure out a way.

I was just playing, like you said.

Gimme those pants. Lord, what a mess!

I don't want to make a mess, Mama.

Listen to Mama, baby. Are you listening to me?

Yes, Mama.

I know you're a smart boy. You're the smartest boy I've ever seen. But you got to understand that you're different from Milton and Calvin and you just can't do like they do.

I know. I'm blind little brother Stevie.

Who said that? Milton and Calvin say that?

They say that when we out running with somebody new. They say, This is our blind little brother Stevie.

Well, that's right. You're more special than them other kids, like we talked about. You remember that?

Yes, ma'am. We'll be out running and they'll be somebody new and they'll say, What's wrong with his eyes? And Milton and Calvin will say, That's our blind little brother Stevie. He can't see. And they'll say, He can't see nuthin'? and Milton and Calvin will say, That's right. He's blind as a bat.

Here, now put these on and sit down. We're gonna talk about this. You're nearly five years old. You're old enough to understand this now.

Okay.

See, sugar, you being blind means you're special and different, like I said. But sometimes I think you believe it's just different in the way that some people are tall and some people are short. There's lots of tall people and lots of short people. But there's not many blind people like you, not at all. You got to understand that, son. You got to realize that. Do you really understand what it means to be able to see?

It means your eyes work. That's what Milton says.

Okay, but do you understand what that means? Do you know what your eyes do for you?

I . . . don't know.

We all live in this big world, Stevie. How can I explain it? And your eyes show you everything that is happening, where everything is. If Milton or Calvin are playing outside in the yard, then all I have to do is look out the window and my eyes will see them. I can tell that they are out there. But you can't do that, because your eyes don't work.

I know when Milton and Calvin are in the yard.

I *know* you do, honey. Your ears tell you. But your ears don't tell you everything. They don't tell you if something's in your way; they don't tell you if there's dog mess where you sit down and play.

How come my eyes don't work, Mama?

I don't know, child. Only God knows that. We don't always know what He has planned. But I do know that God has looked after you and that you are a special child of His. I *do* believe that . . . you are a special child, but you have to take *special* care of yourself. Mama can't always be with you.

Yes, ma'am.

You have to beware of where you are. You have to pay attention to what's around you at all times. You promise Mama?

Yes, ma'am.

Okay, then.

Can I go back outside now, Mama? Mama? Are you crying?

It's all right, son.

Why are you crying, Mama?

It's all right. It's just a trial, that's all. I know God has His reasons, but I *do* wish you could see. I worry about you. And that makes me sad.

Don't worry, Mama. I'll be careful.

Okay, darling. Come here and give your Mama a big hug. And then you go out and play.

THE LABOR STARTED two months too soon. Lula had experienced no trouble giving birth to her first two boys, and both were healthy and strapping. Everything had gone like clockwork. But this one—this one was different and difficult, almost from the beginning.

It was a fact that she had worried about this baby. Winter in Saginaw was neither the best time nor place to carry a child. It was brutally cold, and sickness abounded. Respiratory contagions blazed around the city's poor neighborhoods like wildfire. Pregnancy was no less than a risky physical condition. Birth defects were a common part of life.

So when the contractions started much too early, Lula feared the worst. *Something's wrong. He wouldn't be trying to come out so soon unless something was wrong.* Even then, she figured it was a boy. Even then, she figured that he was going to have a different and difficult road in this life.

Don't worry, Judkins had told her. Everything will be all right. That child just can't wait to get started, that's all. Just raring to go, that's all. Everything will be all right.

Stevland Judkins was born on May 13, 1950, a Saturday, the day before Mother's Day, a day framed by a bleak gray sky and a chilly wind off Lake Huron, although summer was only weeks away. He weighed barely four pounds. The tiny baby was greeted by a slap on the rear; a song issued from his lips. At least it sounded like a song to his spent, near-delirious mother, who watched through the layered gauze of her pain and effort as her new baby boy was taken from her to be placed in an incubator.

Will he be okay? she asked the doctor. Seven months can't live, can they?

The doctor was encouraging: He looks good so far. We're going to put him in an incubator in the special baby unit. It's standard operating procedure. He'll need to stay there for several days, more than likely, until we can be sure he's breathing well enough on his own. We have to give his lungs a chance to develop fully.

All right, then. But he seems okay? Is everything normal?

Yes, everything seems fine. But there is always a danger when a child is born prematurely. We have to be very careful.

Yes, of course. Thank you, doctor.

After a while, a nurse helped Lula into a wheelchair. Judkins and the boys escorted her down to the special baby unit. They gazed through a big window as a nurse tended to little Stevie in the big, clunky-looking incubator. To Lula, he looked like the smallest and most vulnerable creature in the world.

As they watched, another nurse brought another infant, big as nothing, to the incubator and placed the child next to Stevie. Lula noticed another young couple nearby, watching the process with great concern. Like Lula, the young woman wore a hospital gown and an anxious look on her face. The young man next to her held her tightly against him.

Lula rolled over to where they stood, crumpled against the glass window.

My baby is the one on the left, she said. Is the other one yours?

Yes, the young woman said. That's our little girl. Nine weeks too soon . . . they don't know if she will make it. We named her Eden—and we call her Edie. We named her Eden because she's our whole world, a new beautiful world starting from the beginning. What's your baby's name?

Stevland. I think it's a big, strong name. I hope it will give him strength.

The young woman dabbed at tears. I pray that it will, she said. But I'm afraid—I'm afraid that our little Edie won't make it. The doctor said the chances aren't good. We lost our first baby, too—

That's okay now, Lula said. You try not to worry about that. We will pray and God's will be done.

That's right, that's right. Praise God in the highest and His will be done.

Judkins and the nurse rolled Lula back to her room, where she prayed and fell into a deep sleep. She dreamed that she was awake and walking down the hospital corridor to the special baby unit and the big window. She looked through the window at the incubator, where only little Edie lay. Then there was the doctor at her side, talking with his words silent, shaking his head. She jolted awake, heart hammering.

LULA WAS RELEASED from the hospital a few days later. Stevie stayed behind in the incubator. He was struggling, the doctor said, and could not leave until he was stronger. But he's a little fighter, the doctor told her. He's got guts. I still think he's going to be okay.

Lula held on to that scrap of optimism as if it were gold.

As she regained her own strength, Lula spent most of her time at the hospital, as if her very presence would provide a shield against anything happening to Stevie. She hovered about the glass window of the special baby unit like a ghost, willing her child to breathe more deeply, to improve, to live. Edie's mother was there, too, maintaining her own vigil. The two of them talked and prayed and talked and prayed some more. They watched their babies for any sign of change, good or ill. They constantly buttonholed the doctors and nurses who examined and cared for their children, buffeting them with questions. The doctors and the nurses understood, and were patient. Some of the nurses prayed with them.

Another week went by, then two.

Midway through the third week, Lula came back to the unit from lunch and looked through the big window at the incubator, where only little Stevie lay.

She looked around wildly. No one in sight. She walked hurriedly down the corridor toward the nurses' station; farther down the hall, she could see Edie's mother and a doctor in a deep conversation. Lula could see the back of her head and the doctor's face. His lips were moving, the words silent. He was slowly shaking his head, back and forth, back and forth.

ON THE FORTIETH DAY, the doctor called Lula into his office and shut the door.

I have news about your son, he said.

What's wrong? Lula demanded, terrified. Is he okay?

Nothing has happened. He's doing fine. We hope to let him go home in perhaps another week or so.

Lula was confused. So then what's the matter? I know something is wrong.

The doctor drummed his pencil on his desk. We've noticed that Stevland doesn't react to light or movement. It is a very subtle thing in a child, and you don't always notice it right away. But we're very concerned, and we're going to run some tests.

I'm not sure I understand.

We fear that your boy can't see. We're afraid your boy is blind. Well—we know he is blind. But we don't know why, and we don't know if we can do anything about it.

But—how could it happen? Lula choked the words out.

It could be any number of things. We believe he was able to see when he was born. Our initial routine tests seemed to indicate that. It could be from too much oxygen in the incubator, but without that oxygen he never would have survived. But there is no way to know for sure, at this moment, what happened.

Lula sat stone still, in shock.

I wanted to tell you, because it is something you will have to prepare for, the doctor said.

Lula began to cry. I can't believe it, she said. Why would God do such a thing? Born too soon and now this—I must have done something wrong—I must have not have taken good enough care of him, good enough care of myself—

You can't look at it that way. We don't know why it happened. It probably had nothing to do with you. I've seen you in here every day. I know you love this child. Don't blame yourself.

I still can't believe it.

Don't give up. There may be something we can do—just give us some time.

But, as it turned out, there was nothing they could do. For Lula, it was the beginning of a long journey that would take Stevie before what seemed like dozens of public welfare doctors, quacks, and faith healers, all in a fruitless attempt to restore his sight—if, indeed, he ever did see. It was to be a long and heartbreaking process, with hopes rising countless times only to be smothered by reality: Stevie was blind, and there was nothing anyone could do.

Lula was only at the very outset of that journey as she bundled up her baby nearly two weeks later and prepared to take him home for the first time. Stevie had spent fifty-two days in the incubator. She chose to look at things this way: It was a blessing that he was even alive. When she felt despondent about his sightlessness, she thought of little Edie—and then she felt like the luckiest mother on earth.

She said good-bye to the doctors and nurses and the rest of the staff. I'll tell you, one nurse said, I didn't think that boy would make it. He's a special little man. He is a fighter! And he is so *sweet*. There really is something about that one . . .

Of that Lula was convinced. As she attempted to come to grips with the fact of Stevie's blindness, she became convinced that God had spared him for some reason. She knew that sightless people were among the most disadvantaged of God's children, but she also knew that the blind held a unique spiritual place.

I will love and protect this child until my last breath, Lula told herself. *This child is a gift.*

Six

DRUMMER BOY

I'm goin' to Detroit, get myself a good job,
Tried to stay around here with the starvation mob,
I'm goin' to get me a job up there in Mr. Ford's place,
Stop these eatless days from starin' me in the face.

—"Detroit Bound Blues," by Blind Blake

Please, Mister Foreman, slow down your assembly line,
No, I don't mind workin', but I do mind dyin'.

—"Detroit, I Do Mind Dying," by Joe L. Carter

I F YOU SET out to design the perfect urban laboratory for enlight-
ened young black people to absorb both the bitter realities of life as
well as its infinite possibilities, then you couldn't do much better than
Detroit, Michigan, in the 1950s.

For Detroit had it all: large doses of both oppression and opportunity. Oppression came in the form of racism and intolerable conditions for the legions of blacks who had migrated to the city ever since

the mid-nineteenth century, when Detroit served as the last stop on the Underground Railroad (just across the Detroit River was Windsor, Canada). Opportunity came in the form of relatively decent factory jobs for huge numbers of black citizens—decent, at least, compared to the backbreaking field-labor jobs from which many had fled in the South.

Like Chicago, Cleveland, and other industrialized cities of the Midwest, Detroit for generations had been a magnet for African-American families who sought relief from the spartan, cruel, dead-end conditions of the Hurtsboros of the world. Like the fictional Joads in Steinbeck's *The Grapes of Wrath,* who mirrored the exodus to California of countless real-life Dust Bowl refugees in the 1930s, black Southerners like Lula Hardaway heard the stories about the Promised Land to the north—and, once there, found much to be grateful for. But they also discovered that the riverbanks didn't exactly flow with milk and honey.

Yet despite the hardships that most blacks encountered as they settled in Detroit, it was a place where they found a very tangible emphasis on identity and self-worth. Perhaps black families were crushed together in slipshod tenement housing; perhaps they fought a constant battle for fair treatment in the workplace; perhaps they still suffered, in one form or another, the racist slings and arrows simultaneously suffered by their brothers and sisters back home in the South. But there was a very real strength in numbers in Detroit. Its burgeoning black community, at once sprawling and tight-knit, gave itself the legs to stand on its own cultural values and the heart to pursue its own destiny as a people. To many blacks in Detroit, who had seen firsthand the abject brutality of the South, that alone was worth the price of admission.

While Detroit is widely known as the locus of the American automobile industry, its role in the cultural history of American blacks is equally notable. By mid-century, the city had begun to produce such cultural, economic, and political institutions as the Broadside Press, one of the first black-owned publishing houses in the country; WCBH, the first radio station in America to be built, owned, and operated by African Americans; the Concept East Theater, the first black theater company in the urban north; the Booker T. Washington Trade Association, one of the largest chapters of the National Negro Business League; the Dodge Revolutionary Union Movement, which became the League of Revolutionary Black Workers; and the Freedom Now Party, the first all-black political party in the country. In the early 1970s, the Congressional Black Caucus was formed by Detroit congressmen Charles Diggs Jr. and John Conyers. Detroit also gave birth to the Nation of Islam and the Shrine of the Black Madonna, a denomination that celebrated black culture and promoted black Christian nationalism.

From its inception, Detroit was a "tough, militant, take-no-shit town," as writer Charles Shaar Murray put it. As exemplified by its role in the Underground Railroad, Detroit was a center of abolitionist activity in the early 1800s. Throughout its early boom days, Detroit boasted a very real and politically active black middle class, a strata that included citizens like Benjamin Pelham, the publisher of the *Detroit Plain Dealer*, who became known as the "Czar of Wayne County."

By the early 1900s, however, the standing of blacks in Detroit had eroded. The fledgling auto industry was rapidly expanding, and large numbers of blacks were lured into the city to fill the most distasteful jobs for less money than other workers. During the 1920s, Michigan registered the highest percentage gain in black population in the country. The city's housing infrastructure was unprepared for the onslaught, and most of the new arrivals lived in horrid circumstances.

Many whites, competing for the same jobs, saw the incoming surge as a threat to their own economic welfare. By the mid-1920s, there were an estimated 875,000 Ku Klux Klan members in Michigan, the most of any state.

In 1925, a notorious racist incident ended in an important legal civil rights decision and helped cement Detroit's role as a critical battleground in the struggle for black equality. A black doctor named Ossian Sweet purchased and moved into a house in a white neighborhood on Detroit's east side. In less than twenty-four hours, a belligerent crowd of whites gathered and began to shatter windows with stones. A police contingent on hand made no attempt to thwart the mob. As things worsened, shots were fired from within the house into the crowd, killing one man and wounding another. Sweet and his companions were all arrested and charged with murder.

Enter Clarence Darrow, the most famous defense attorney of his day, who won acquittals for all the defendants. He later wrote: "The verdict meant simply that the doctrine that a man's house is his castle applied to the black man as well as the white man." The case and its verdict were a national sensation and helped spread the notion that Detroit was a place where blacks, despite fearsome obstacles, were gaining equal treatment under the law.

But the opportunity/oppression dichotomy continued. Despite the Sweet acquittals, Detroit also remained a place where racism and down-spiraling economic conditions maintained a vicious edge. In the 1930s, the Great Depression smothered the job boom in Detroit and led to even more egregious living conditions for blacks.

Oppression: Housing conditions were onerous for everyone, but it was worst for blacks—and the white business structure sought to keep it that way. Opportunity: Suddenly, blacks were being hired for positions in the workforce that in the past had been denied them. Oppression: Even though the United Auto Workers Union encouraged equal opportunity for all workers, whites objected to having blacks on their assembly lines. This antipathy was exacerbated by various racist organizations. Sound trucks patrolled the streets by the factories and broadcast racial epithets that found sympathetic ears inside the factory walls. A typical refrain: "I'd rather see Hitler and Hirohito win than work next to a nigger."

Soon Detroit exploded into civil war. On June 20, 1943, a riot erupted among one hundred thousand picnickers at Belle Island on the Detroit River.

Soon rumors circulated in the black ghetto that a mob of whites had thrown a black mother and child off a bridge. Violence began to spread and soon the black ghetto was in flames, stores were looted, and white motorists coming through the area were stoned.

Detroit soon was the scene of a pitched race war. Blacks and whites alike were attacked, beaten, and killed, although blacks received the worst of it by far. When order finally was restored, thirty-four people had been killed—twenty-five blacks and nine whites. More than two million dollars in property damage was reported. Many families were left homeless, mostly in black neighborhoods.

The scars from this tragic series of events in Detroit never really healed, certainly not by the time little Stevie Judkins began to come of age in the late 1950s and early 1960s. Conditions and attitudes continued to deteriorate, leading to another uprising in the black community in the summer of 1967. But out of the ashes of oppression came opportunity, in the form of a determination by blacks in Detroit and elsewhere to make their own destiny. Soon, black leaders like Dr. Martin Luther King Jr. and Malcolm X began to be heard.

DETROIT SEEMED ALMOST balmy after the cruel winter rigors of Saginaw. It was frightfully cold in Detroit, too, to be sure. But Lula noticed that the wind didn't blow quite as wickedly off the water in Detroit, compared to Saginaw; the nights didn't seem quite as unforgiving and frigid. Maybe there wasn't much difference—maybe it was all in her head. Maybe she was just determined that Detroit would be better, come hell or high water. If so, she thought, so be it. She would take it.

Her escape from Saginaw had not been as clean as she had hoped. After she had cut Judkins—what a mess that had been!—she gathered up the children and distributed them among various friends and relatives, for she had word that the police were going to arrest her. Judkins had pressed charges, and there was going to be trouble. She was going to have to lay low for a while.

After a few days, Judkins cooled down and dropped the charges. That bullet had been dodged, but there was another problem: In the first panicky days after the fight, she had succumbed to temptation and had passed some forged checks that a friend had given her. The police had identified her as the culprit; again the word came through the grapevine that a warrant was out for her arrest.

So it was past time to leave town. But she needed help. Despite the money in her pocket, she knew that starting over in a new town would be tough. She knew no one in Detroit to speak of, no one that could take her in.

She decided to make a deal with the Devil.

Lula arranged a meeting with Judkins. He was all apologies and contrition. I've treated you wrong, baby. I've been a bad husband. Give me another chance, I'll make it all up to you, swear I will.

She agreed, under one condition: that they move to Detroit. Judkins readily agreed. He knew people there, they could probably get a place in the Brewster Projects. I'll take care of it, baby. We'll be all right from now on, you just wait and see.

Lula had no intentions of making everything right with Judkins. He had used her; it was her turn now. She would use *him.* Judkins's connections would help with the move to Detroit, and as soon as she could get enough money together she would be gone. *I'll leave him flat as a pancake,* she vowed to herself.

Lula and Judkins drove to Detroit and, just as Judkins had predicted, were able to arrange to rent an apartment in the new, federally subsidized Brewster Projects on Hastings Street. Because of Stevie's blindness, in fact, they were able to secure one of the more desirable apartments, number 2701, on a ground floor. With living quarters secured, they quietly slipped back into Saginaw, collected the children, and headed back to Detroit.

Judkins, true to form, didn't knock himself out looking for work; as always, he was content to collect his small pension and let the chips fall where they may. Lula found work right away at a fish market in downtown Detroit. It was hard, cold work, and the bell rang early: She had to be on the job by 4:30 A.M. But her work day ended by lunchtime, which meant she was back home relatively early in the day. Soon, her half sister, Nellie, came from Alabama to live with them and was able to help with the children.

It was merely the living of life in the ghetto, everyone pitching in and struggling to get by—the most ordinary thing in the world. But amid the daily, numbing struggle for survival, as Lula began to put her life and her family back together again, she began to realize that, in spite of everything, her children seemed to be thriving. It was a glorious thing, to see them grow and adapt and persevere, because God knew that the children had been through hellish times, right alongside their mother. She figured those times weren't over yet. But there was something else . . . it was about Stevie. Lula had come to realize that her Stevie was different from other children, different beyond the simple reality of his blindness. The little boy born too soon, the wisp of an infant that nearly died and then was visited with a handicap that broke his mother's heart, was a real pistol. Everybody talked about it: That boy was . . . *something*.

THE COIN CLATTERED on the table, finally wobbling to a stop.

  What's that, Stevie?

  Dime.

Another coin, another wobble.

Quarter.

Another.

Quarter again.

Whoops and laughs all around. Lord, I ain't *ever* seen nothing like that! That child doesn't miss a trick!

How do you do that, Stevie?

They sound different. It's easy.

Maybe to *you*. You got some kind of ears, Steve.

Can I go outside now, Mama?

Okay. Give your Aunt Ilona a kiss, and go on. And be careful!

Yes, ma'am.

Run outside. Hear Milton and Calvin down the street. Walk to the sidewalk and then run to their babbling voices.

Hey, Stevie! We gonna play army. You wanna play?

Yeah. I'll play!

Okay, we're gonna be the Americans—Lamar talking, one of the older boys. He said, Milton and Calvin and Stevie will be the Germans. We'll go camp over here and you come find us, okay? Give us a little while and then you come on patrol. See if you can find us. Everybody take some gravel, and whoever gets hit with gravel is dead. Okay?

Okay.

The Americans rustle off down the alley, murmuring strategy.

Okay, Milton said. Here's how we'll do it: We'll go around the block and come in the other way. Then we'll send Steve up ahead. We'll be watching you. When you hear 'em, you point to where they are. And then we'll circle around and ambush 'em. Okay, Stevie?

All right. Let's go.

The long way around the block. Stevie knew it by heart. The grind of car brakes at the intersection at the corner; the sound of Mr.

Roland's radio, always on, halfway down; right before the alley, the lurch-and-screech of the big swing set. From the sound of the lurch-and-screech, Big Regina was in the swing (except nobody called her Big Regina to her face—unless you wanted her to beat the crap out of you).

Hi, Stevie.

Hi, Regina.

Hi, Milton. Hi, Calvin.

Hi, Regina.

Okay, Milton said. Stevie, you go ahead. We'll watch.

Stevie was *so* good at this. Creep cat-silent. Listen for signs of the would-be GIs amid the cacophony of noise that was his every waking moment. His radar blanketed the alley. Creep, listen, creep, listen . . .

There—a giggle. And there—a *shhhh.* Lamar shushing Davey. They were off to the right, two postage-stamp tenement yards over.

And over there, to the left—a rustle, just beyond the fence. That would be the other three members of Lamar's platoon—he sensed them there.

He knew that Milton and Calvin were watching. He held up a hand with two fingers and pointed to the right, toward Lamar and Davey. Then pointed three fingers to the left, at the others.

They knew what to do. Stevie could hear Milton and Calvin begin to make their way behind the tenement row to the right. They would surprise the three soldiers behind the fence from the rear. Meanwhile, cat-silent, Stevie would try to get in position to deal with Lamar and Davey.

Creeping, creeping . . . he was *so* good at this.

Stevie knew exactly where they were. They were expecting some-one to come down the side alley, right past where they perched low on top of a shed, one of a network of small, mostly uniform outbuild-ings that clung closely together and dotted the backyards of the small houses and larger tenements that comprised the block. From that vantage point, Lamar and Davey were waiting to pounce up and fling gravel at any unsuspecting German soldiers on patrol.

A commotion from across the alley: Milton and Calvin had successfully ambushed the guys behind the fence. Stevie decided to seize the moment and flush out Lamar and Davey. He pulled himself above the fence line with one arm; Ha! he yelled, and with his free hand he hurled a spray of gravel in their direction. Ow! cried Davey. Davey's dead! Davey's dead! Stevie shouted. He could hear Milton and Calvin racing toward the new battleground.

He heard Lamar exclaim: Shit!

Stevie followed the sound, and then he heard Lamar make his escape, jumping from one shed to the next. He's on the sheds! Stevie shouted. He's getting away!

Milton and Calvin scrambled past him in fierce pursuit. He heard them scale the first shed and then run and jump to the next—running footsteps, grunts, and then *thump!* Footsteps and grunts and *thump!* Steps grunts *thump!*

Stevie fumed for a split second. The game was getting away! He wasn't allowed on the sheds—no one was, really—but he knew where they were, knew the spacing between them. Why should his brothers have all the fun? *I'm going after Lamar, too.*

He climbed the fence and pulled atop the first shed. He felt the unfettered sun blast his skin, sensed his new elevation.

He heard Davey, who had lagged behind in the alley. Davey was, after all, dead now.

Hey, Stevie, Davey said. What're you doin' up there? You better watch it.

Stevie ignored him. He could hear the steps grunts *thumps* of the others grow fainter. Quickly, he judged the location of the edge of the shed. And then he took off running—

Davey, alarmed: Hey, Steve, you better *not*—

And Stevie was airborne.

Thump! Onto the flat roof. Made it!

He had the spacing down now.

Run-run-run-juuuuuuuuuuuump-*thump!*

Wahoo!

Run-run-run-juuuuuuuuuuuump-*thump!*

Yow!

Run-run-run-juuuuuuuuuuuump-*thump!*

He was catching up! He heard Milton and Calvin laugh: Attaboy, Steve! Keep on comin'!

Run-run-run-juuuuuuuuuuuump-*thump!*

Run-run-run-juuuuuuuuuuuump-*thump!*

Suddenly: *Stevie Judkins!*

He stopped dead in his tracks. It was the neighbor lady, Mrs. Buchanan.

Stevie! You gonna kill yourself! You better get down from there right this second! Why, you must be out of your mind! You *get* down from there!

But the frenzy of the chase had Stevie in its grip. He meant to catch up with the others, or die trying.

She yelled again: *Stevie Judkins!*

Stevie yelled back: *Aw, shut up!* And shocked himself in the process. But he had to keep going—

Run-run-run-juuuuuuuuuuuump-*thump!*

Milton and Calvin: Come on, Steve!

Run-run-run-juuuuuuuuuuuump-*thump!*

Run-run-run-juuuuuuuuuuuump-*oof.*

The next roof wasn't flat—it was slanted. *What?!* It was like running into a drunken wall. Stevie's knees and shins hit first, and the wind burst out of him. Dizzy, shocked, his balance lost, he rolled down the slope of the roof. He felt the edge, and clawed desperately for it. Tried to catch hold—*aaaaaaah!*

He seemed to float for a lifetime. Then he met the ground with a jolt and crumpled into it. His hip took the brunt of the blow. He was stunned.

A presence loomed over him. A hand grabbed his arm and pulled him to his feet.

Mama!

Lord have mercy! Boy, are you all right? Where did you hit?

Right here—he rubbed his hip—but it's okay.

All right then, she said. And then Stevie realized, too late—*she was mad.*

Boy, what *are* you doin' up there like a fool?

We were chasing Lamar—

You think you're Superman or something? You tryin' to kill yourself?

No ma'am, I—

And you talkin' to Mrs. Buchanan like that? You think I didn't hear that?

But—

Pull those pants down, boy—

No, Mama—

Yes, Mama. You know what I got in my hand right now?

I'm sorry, Mama—

Oh, you're sorry *now.* You'll be real sorry here in a minute!

Stevie felt the awful sting on his legs. The ironing cord! The ironing cord was for special whippings . . . Ow. *Ow!*

Stevie starting running home with Lula right behind—driving him home like an errant mule.

MILTON AND CALVIN got ironing-cord whippings, too, when they got home, along with a lecture for the ages about looking after their little brother. Stevie, snuffling back tears, dutifully plodded over and

apologized to Mrs. Buchanan. The house was quiet that night, as the boys reflected on their transgressions and their still-stinging legs.

Stevie went to bed early. He didn't mind the whipping so much. He knew he had been bad. Just before sleep, he felt the sensation again—not of the whipping, now forgotten. It was the sensation of soaring above rooftops, of leaping and defying the pull of the earth . . .

WAITING ON MAMA to get home from work.

Milton said, Let's play with the cards I got for Christmas.

Okay, Calvin said.

I want to play! Stevie said.

You can't, Milton said. You can't see the cards.

Please? I want to play cards with you.

But how can you play? You can't see which cards you have. We'll have to tell you every card you have. It won't be any fun that way.

Aw—

Stevie sat down on the floor and began to cry. Milton shuffled the cards listlessly.

Calvin said to Milton, It's not fair. How come he can't see?

Mama said nobody knows. Maybe because he was born too early.

It's not fair. Do you think he can see anything at all?

I don't know. Ask him.

Stevie, quit crying now. Listen . . . listen. Can't you see anything at all with your eyes?

Like what? Stevie snuffled.

Like . . . anything. Can you ever see anything move? Any shapes or anything?

Nope. Sometimes I think I see something, but Mama says it's just my 'magination.

Maybe you're not trying hard enough. Sometimes when I'm trying to see something far away, I have to look real hard to see it.

But I can't see nothing.

Leave him alone, Milton said. He said he can't see anything.

I wish I could play cards, Stevie said. I wish I could see. And Mama wouldn't be sad no more.

Mama's sad? Milton asked.

Yeah. I can tell, sometimes.

Like when?

Like when she'll hug me sometimes and tells me everything will be okay—I can tell she's sad and worried about how I can't see. And then sometimes at night I can hear her pray for Jesus to take care of all of us and for Jesus to allow me to see.

I never heard that, Calvin said.

She says it real low. She don't think anybody can hear. But I can.

I wish you could see, too, Milton said.

I wish I could play cards, Stevie said.

Wait a minute, Calvin said. I've got an idea. Maybe Stevie can't see because there's not enough light for him.

What do you mean? Milton said. It's the middle of the day.

I know, but maybe Stevie just needs more light than we do.

How we gonna do that?

Well, maybe he could see enough to play cards if we built a fire or something. Remember how they built that big bonfire on the Fourth of July in the park? Even though it was nighttime and dark, when they built the fire you could see. So maybe we could build a fire for Stevie, and he could see enough to play cards with us.

Yeah! Stevie said. I want to play cards!

Maybe we'll play cards in the kitchen and use the garbage for a fire, Milton said. They just burn it anyway outside.

Calvin and Stevie chorused: Okay!

They set up shop on the kitchen floor. Milton pulled the garbage can into the center of the room and inspected the contents.

There's not enough in here, he announced. Calvin, go outside and

bring some of those old newspapers down the hall in here. That'll work good.

Calvin quickly returned with an armload of newsprint, dumping it into the garbage can.

Milton reached up and snared the big box of matches from the stove.

Okay, he said. Y'all start playing cards, and I'll light this. Stevie, you tell us when you can see, okay?

Okay!

Milton struck a match and held it to the top sheaf of newspaper. It caught quickly and began to smolder.

Here we go! Milton said.

I'm dealing! Calvin said.

And I'm gonna play cards! Stevie said.

Flames began to shoot up from the metal can. Black smoke began to billow.

How about it, Stevie? See anything yet?

Not yet!

Flames crackled. Black smoke began to fill the apartment.

Boy, it really *smells*, Calvin said.

I can't see yet! Stevie said.

Suddenly the front door crashed open to reveal a panicked Lula, burdened with two bags of groceries. Her gaping eyes took in the scene: *WHAT IN THE NAME OF SWEET HOLY JESUS—*

MILTON AND CALVIN got an ironing-cord whipping that night, after Lula threw water on the flaming trash and then cleaned up the black sooty mess and aired out the place. It was a miracle they hadn't set the whole tenement on fire. But it wasn't much of a whipping; her heart wasn't much in it by the time she heard what the boys were up to.

She told Milton and Calvin: I'm not whipping you because you tried to help your little brother. I'm whipping you because you played with matches. Y'all understand that?

Yes, ma'am.

All right. Now pull down those pants.

That night, Stevie could hear his mother pray to Jesus, thanking Him for not burning their house down, and to please let her little boy have the power of sight. Then he heard her cry herself to sleep, ever so quietly.

FIRST IT WAS PERCUSSION: Baby Stevie, wooden spoon in hand, banging on a table. All kids do it; Stevie never stopped.

Then it was rudimentary, homemade percussion pieces: cans, pots, and pans battered with spoons or sticks. The little toy cardboard drums popular with small children in those days had no chance under Stevie's assault. Every Christmas, Stevie would get another toy drum set; by New Year's Eve, it would be in shreds. He drummed with the radio; he drummed by himself; he drummed night and day.

Sometimes Lula heard drumming in her sleep only to wake to silence, realizing the noise of the day was reverberating in her head. Lord, that boy and that drumming. But whatever makes him happy.

Then came the Fourth of July picnic at Belle Island. Stevie was five; it had been an even dozen years since the bloody riots began there. Somebody had hired a band. Stevie had heard plenty of live music in church, which he loved; but that was with only a piano and organ playing along. This was a real band, with guitar and bass and, yes, *drums*.

Stevie, as always, was the center of attention. Look at him dance to that music! He's right with it! Law', that little boy has *got* it. People laughed and clapped and rubbed his head like a prized puppy. That boy has a *spark*—

The band was smitten with the little blind kid who danced to the beat. During a break, the band's singer walked over to talk.

Hey, little man. What's your name?

Steve.

You like that music, huh?

I sure do.

Well, you a mighty good dancer. What kind of music you like, anyway?

I like church music. And I like what I hear on the radio, too.

Oh, yeah? Like what?

I like the *Sundown* show on WCHB.

Everybody does! What songs you like on there?

My favorite song is "Pledging My Love," by Johnny Ace.

We play that one. What else you like?

I like B. B. King, and Little Walter, and Bill Doggett, and Jimmy Reed, and Bobby Bland, and Jackie Wilson, and the Coasters, and Chuck Willis, and LaVern Baker, and—

Hold on, kid! Heh-heh—you're gonna name every act there is!

You know what else?

What's that, son?

I can play the drums.

Is that right?

Yes, sir, I sure can. Play 'em all the time.

Well, that's great. Hey, tell you what—come here with me for a minute.

The singer led Stevie over to the bandstand, where the drummer was settling in behind his kit for the next set.

Guess what? the singer said. This young man says he's a drummer, too. Maybe we ought to give him a little *tryout*, heh-heh.

The drummer smiled. Sure—boost him up here. C'mere son, sit in my lap. You ever played a real set of drums before?

No, sir! Stevie said.

All right, then. Here's the sticks.

He placed the drumsticks in Stevie's hands. They felt heavy and polished and magnificent compared to the small, coarse sticks that came with his toy sets.

Little different from the stuff you been using, huh? the drummer said, cackling.

Yeah. They feel good.

Stevie banged around a bit. The drummer showed him where the pieces were, the snare, the cymbals, everything.

Here, the drummer said, hold the sticks like *this*—

He did. And he banged around some more.

Hey kid! the drummer said, laughing. You ain't half bad. You got some real punch! Hey, Eddie, look here at this little guy . . .

The rest of the band mounted the bandstand. The singer said, Let's do a little bit of "Pledging My Love." Okay, on three—

The band broke into the bluesy shuffle. Stevie whacked away, somewhere in the neighborhood of the basic beat. The drummer said, That's right, that's right! Now don't forget about that cymbal up there!

The band mercifully kept the song to one verse. At the last refrain, Stevie gave the cymbal one big last *gong*.

The singer boomed out over the PA: Let's hear it for Stevie, the little drummer boy!

And then Stevie heard it: the clapping and the cheers! It shocked him: He had been so intent on the drumming that he had blocked out everything else. He didn't even know anyone had been watching . . . but it sounded like a multitude laughing and cheering and yelling his name: That's it, *Stevie!* Way to go, *Stevie!*

The drummer lifted him from his lap to the ground next to the bandstand. There was Mama and Milton and Calvin and a herd of others, some he didn't know. All hugging him and laughing . . .

Here you go, son, said a strange man's voice. He took Stevie's hand and placed some coins in his palm. The voice laughed: That was good playing, son. You keep practicin'—you'll be good for real.

Stevie felt the coins against his skin. *Three quarters!*

Look, Mama!

I see that. You thank the man.

Thank you!

Three quarters . . . it was a staggering fortune. But worthless compared to the feeling of playing those drums while *everyone watched*, and making them clap, and laugh, and cheer; the sudden sharing of joy at the center of the universe.

IT WAS THE OLDEST TRICK in the world. But it was working.

It was the old hole-in-the-mattress trick. Lula would bring her pay home from the fish market. She would reach down into the mattress on Nellie's bed and extract the roll of bills, bound together with a rubber band, and add another dollar or two—some weeks maybe five—and hide it again.

No one else knew it was there, except for Nellie, who slept on it every night.

She didn't trust banks. And she certainly didn't trust Judkins.

The mattress money was *her* money, *her* future. It was a way to get the boys out of this tenement, to get them out of this place. And, God willing, she would do it. And she was *doing* it. The bankroll in the mattress was proof of that.

BUT TIMES STILL were hard, the winters still cold enough to slice your heart in two.

It happened more than once:

The weak sun, overwhelmed by frigid air and the low-hanging gray-bleak sky pregnant with snow, would drop from the sky, ushering in the night and the cold wind off the lake that seemed to invade the marrow of every bone in the city. And the cold scaled the tenements like an invisible, omnipresent burglar, alternately seeping and bludgeoning its way through the flimsy brick and mortar that represented a futile, even laughable, barrier against the elements. Even with coal in the stove, the cold nights were hardly bearable; with no coal at all, the winter nights didn't even seem survivable.

And so those nights would come, no coal and just enough money to put food on the table until the next payday finally arrived. And the dark would descend and you would think: *Maybe it won't be so cold tonight. Just bundle up and keep warm and put the boys under the covers, and it won't be so cold.*

But the cold infects all. And when you talk you can see your words, shrouded in steam, words condensing in midair.

Don't think about it. Pretend, instead, the air is like a wondrous warm liquid and the crickets begin to rumble and the lightning bugs are darting and fluttering, their tiny yellow lamps flickering as if there is nothing amazing or spectacular about it at all. And there isn't, not when you're a little girl and you believe the world is a place where things are good and constant and make sense.

But the here and now is relentless. Here comes Milton, padding from the boys' room, rubbing sleep from his eyes.

Mama, it's so cold.

I know, baby. Go back to bed and try to go to sleep.

I can't, Mama. Too cold.

And then the resolve goes out of you as you look at your child wrapped in a blanket, shivering as if he were standing barefoot in snow, his words forming frigid little clouds in the air. And you hear another of your children in bed, hacking with the croup. And the little one, stirring under a blanket on your lap, glomming onto his mother for every last watt of body heat she can provide.

You think about the bankroll, hard-won, hidden away in the mattress like a pearl. And you say to yourself: *I could take some of that money and buy enough coal to last until payday. The money is right there. Just peel a few dollars off the roll and go down to the dry dock and give it to the night clerk. Bring home the coal and your children will be warm.*

But then: *No. You promised yourself. That money is the future. That money is escape. That money is for something of worth in this life that no one can take away. That money is self-reliance and pride.*

And then you know that you will do what you have to do.

Mama—

Hush now, Milton. Go get Calvin up and you boys dress up warm. We're gonna go out and get something. Stevie, wake up, baby.

Even though it is nearly midnight, you bundle up your children, and you grab two gunnysacks from the pantry. And the four of you venture out into the cold black night, the wind buffeting and loud and ice-wet.

You make your way through the slicing wind and past sleeping tenements and shuttered stores, past business being conducted in the pitch-black alleyways that you know all too much about.

There is always that. But never again.

You come up on the railroad yard, where a lone pale light shines from within the clerk shed. You know the clerk is inside and will stay there unless he is summoned or becomes suspicious that someone lurks outside. Beyond the shed is the loading dock, where the piles of coal lay.

You look down at Milton and Calvin and put a finger to your lips. They nod; they know. She squeezes Stevie's hand. He knows, too.

This is not the first time.

And so like refugees crossing a dangerous border hand-in-hand in the dead of night, you slide through the opening in the fence and you steal across the big yard, peppered with heavy machinery and stacks of lumber and brick and rock and Lord knows what all. Milton trips on something and sprawls with an audible *oof* to the ground; every-one freezes. You look across the way at the shed. No movement, no sign of life. Milton picks himself up. You keep moving.

You reach the dry dock. You fill up your sacks. Calvin holds onto Stevie, whispering inaudibly to him: Be quiet, Stevie, be quiet.

But Stevie knows to be quiet.

The gunnysacks bulge.

You steal back across the big yard like panthers. The barely con-tained panic that has pulsated inside you begins to fade. The awesome cold, momentarily forgotten, reasserts itself. No words are spoken, not yet. The four of you slide through the fence, cross the street and quicken your pace down the sidewalk. You already can feel the warmth of the stove filling up the apartment, returning the feeling to your hands and feet, obliterating the word-fog.

And then you are back at home, the deed done, everyone con-vulsing in shivers from the cold. You pour some of the shiny black craggy gold into the stove and light it . . . and it is as if the place can't get warm fast enough. The four of you huddle around, grasping each other, four of you huddled against the cold world.

And you think: *I have sold my honor under the watchful eyes of the Lord. And now I have stolen another man's goods and have taught my children to steal, showed them how to steal by my own example. I have included them in my crime. I have corrupted myself, and now I seek to corrupt my children.*

And you pray: Dear God, forgive me for my weakness. God, grant me the strength to provide for my children. Forgive them for their sins, which have come at the behest of their own mother. Grant us a peaceful life. In Jesus' name we pray, amen.

You open your eyes and see your children arrayed around you. You feel the warmth of the stove begin to radiate throughout the room. You see these boys, who only moments before suffered and shivered, become drowsy from the pure luxury of the heat.

You think of the bankroll, hidden away in the mattress like a pearl, intact.

And you know that you will do whatever it takes.

And you know that, tonight at least, your children will be warm.

And you say to yourself: *Let no one but God judge.*

Seven

SAINT, SINNER

The Negro with a trumpet at his lips, whose jacket
has a fine, one-button row, does not know upon
what riff the music slipped its hypodermic needle
to his soul. But softly, as a tune comes from his
throat, trouble mellows to a golden note. And
suddenly the smoky air grows sweet and dreams
come back to tumble down the street.

—Langston Hughes, "The Trumpet Player"

STEVIE ATTENDED THE Fitzgerald School for the Blind and
dutifully learned Braille and expressed nominal interest in all
the usual subjects. But his passion for music overwhelmed everything.
Music made him light up; music gave him the buoyant quality that
made him so irresistible to others. He clearly had talent, and despite
his blindness—or, more accurately perhaps, because of it—people
indulged him.

By the time Stevie was of school age, his musical inclinations were
well known in the neighborhood. One Christmas, the Lions Club held

a party for blind kids and gave Stevie his first proper drum kit. He was thrilled, and was so eager to flail away that he began playing the drums upside down, with the sticks clattering against the metal snares stretched across the drum skins. (When his benefactors tried to get Stevie to turn the drums over to the correct side, the boy protested.)

Other people directed musical charity in little Stevie's direction as well. A next-door neighbor owned a piano; Stevie, still a half-pint, often would noodle around on it and sound out songs, casually developing a substantial repertoire. When Stevie was seven the neighbor moved away but left the piano behind for the budding prodigy. He could barely reach the pedals.

But it was the harmonica that ultimately would become his favorite instrument as a child. When Stevie was very small, his mother often took him for haircuts to a family friend who was a barber. The barber had a key ring with a small harmonica—a charm, actually—that Stevie always clamored to play. Finally the barber, amused, gave the harmonica to Stevie—his first. Adaptable as always to any musical instrument, Stevie played the harmonica constantly and learned to play on his own, quickly becoming very proficient.

When Stevie was about eight, he received a Hohner chromatic harmonica as a gift from an uncle. The chromatic was a much more sophisticated instrument than the toy harmonicas to which he was accustomed, and Stevie became even more intrigued with the instrument. By mimicking and expanding upon the music he heard on the radio, Stevie was an outstanding harmonica player by the time he was nine, bordering on outright virtuosity. He became the leader of the harmonica band at school and kept finding new chords, new tunes, new ways to squeeze feeling and complexity from this most rudimentary of instruments.

Stevie picked up music the way most people pick up a cold. There was no formal training. Had there been money for music lessons or scholarships or some other opportunity to enter the culture of music teachers and recitals and the like, it is by no means clear such an environment would have abetted Stevie's evolution as an artist; it may have had the opposite effect. As it turned out, the musical structure he needed was right at his fingertips, in great abundance in Detroit in the late 1950s. There was the gospel choir at church; there were the rhythm and blues emanating from the radio and the street. Stevie Judkins absorbed it all like a greedy sponge, and then wrung from himself his own sound, unfettered, entirely on the natural.

From the very start, he had the chops—that much was apparent to anyone who cared to pay attention. In the beginning, some thought it was the work of God, that He sent a special angel to earth to spread joy. But other people figured it was the other way around, that maybe the Devil had something to do with it. But it always seemed like God and the Devil were both mixed up in everything anyway, so everybody was right.

SAINT, SINNER. Sinner, saint.

It was like this:

Saint:

The choir room. Sister helps with the robe, as always. The robe always feels nice. Had to have a small robe made special. There now, Sister says, you look nice. All ready to make a joyful noise unto the Lord.

Sinner:

Sundown on the radio. They're playing the blues. Jimmy Reed. Bobby "Blue" Bland. They sound good. They sound nasty. They sound real, like they come from somewhere. Some songs sound made up, as if somebody said, Here, sing this. The blues singers sound like they're coming straight from their dark soul. Their girlfriends have been mean to them and they're letting it all out because they can't stand it no more. Or they know they been bad and the guilt is too much.

Saint:

March out into the church. Pass some brothers and sisters along the way. There's little Stevie, mister junior deacon! How you doing, Brother Steve? You gonna let the Lord hear it this morning? Praise God!

Sinner:

The harmonica sounds good with the blues. You can make it go *low,* like this, all the way down here, when you're sad and feel bad. You can make it go *high,* all the way up here, when you're happy and you feel like dancing. And you can make it go everywhere in between. *Sundown* comes on, take the harmonica and play the harmonica and saxophone parts. It's not hard. Listen where they go, and then go there, too. And then go wher*ever.*

Saint:

One of the big deacons talking to the congregation: We *welcome* you to the Whitestone Baptist Church. We do the Lord's work here. Everybody is equal under the eyes of the Lord. *Rich* and poor. *Black* and white. *Young* and old. The *strong* and the infirm. God works His miracles in this place. We work *our* miracles in this place, and then we go forth and do the Lord's bidding. For Jesus said, Ye are the light of the world. A city that is set on a hill cannot be hid. Neither do men light a candle and put it under a bushel, but on a candlestick; and it giveth light unto all that are in the house. Let your light so shine before men, that they may see your good works, and glorify your Father which is in heaven. Amen, brothers and sisters . . .

Feel it: A song stirs In There.

Sinner:

Here's one I like, turn that *up* . . . I can do this one *good* . . . *When things go wrong/Go wrong with you/It hurts me too* . . . That's a low-down song. Hey, all right, here comes John Glover. I hear you coming, John Glover. You bring your guitar?

Yeah, right here. Who's that playing? Sounds like old McKinley Morganfield.

Naw, man, it's Tampa Red. *You love another man/But I love you . . .*

Say, Steve, they was asking out there if Stevie and John was gonna play today.

Sure, you wanna?

Sure.

Let's go over on Twenty-sixth Street. We'll catch the first shift comin' home. Hey listen: Marvin Gaye! Here we go: *Mister Sandman . . .*

Saint:

The deacon's getting worked up. Ye are the light of the world!

He shoulda been a preacher himself.

Let your light so shine!

Feel the song stir In There. Feel the spirit *well up.* Hear the choir start to rustle. Hear the Sister at the piano hit a chord, let the piano say *amen,* let that chord hang in the air. That chord says, *get ready.* Because if that deacon keeps going like that, he's gonna *start* something . . .

Sinner:

Harmonica in a pants pocket. Uncle's bongos on one hip. Tin cup. John Glover got his guitar. Trek over to Twenty-sixth Street. Shake some money outta those folks. Take that harmonica outta that pocket so some money can go *in* that pocket. They always like to see Stevie and John.

Hey, Stevie and John! Y'all gonna play? Where at?

Hey, Stevie and John! Y'all gonna do that new one by Smokey?

Hey, Stevie and John! Y'all do good today!

Set up here, right on the corner. Get 'em coming *and* going.

All right. Feels good. We ready . . .

Saint:

Deacon on *fire.* Feel the song stir. Stand *up.* You know it's what they want you to do. Deacon says, *Shine* the light in the mornin'! *Shine* the light in the evenin'! *Shine* it when it feels *good, shine* it when it feels *bad! Shine* a light—

Here goes—can't stand it any longer—got to *tell* it—besides, ain't this what they came for? Start *clapping* hands—hear the rest of the choir pick up the beat: *Clap*—yeah-yeah—*clap*—yeah-yeah—*clap*—yeah-yeah. Now it ripples through the congregation—*clap*—yeah-yeah—*clap*—yeah-yeah—

And now, songbird-pure, ringing through the *clap*-yeah-yeahs to the heavens—

This little light of mine
I'm gonna let it shine . . .
Sinner:
Here we go now—
John Glover starts on guitar, a nice and slow blues strum . . . and then just jump in.
Sugar mama, sugar mama
Please come back to me.
Sugar mama, sugar mama
Bring my granulated sugar
And ease my misery . . .
Feel the people begin to stop and gather around—
Saint:
Everybody clapping now, the whole church in sway—
Oh Jesus, this little light of mine
I'm gonna let it shine.
Get *with* the Lord. Hear the deacon chime in on the downbeat—
When I cross over Jordan, Lord.
Tell it young brother!
I'm gonna let it shine.
Amen amen!
When I cross over Jordan, Lord.
I'm gonna let it shine
And now the choir and everybody joins in—
Let it shine,

Let it shine,
Let it shine.

Don't let it go yet—stand in your seat—keep clapping and moving and swinging—hear the response from the deacon and the congregation—everything gets *louder*—Sister throwing all of God's glory down on that piano—

Sinner:

I'm so wild about my sugar,
I don't know what to do.
It's that granulated sugar
Mama, ain't nobody got but you.

John Glover hits the last chord. Lots of clapping and laughing—some change hits the tin cup—start up again fast, don't let 'em go—hit that chord, John—

When a girl gets to be eighteen years old,
She begin to think she grown.
You can't never catch that kind of little girl at home.
You have to go see her early in the mornin'
Baby, 'bout the break of day.

Quick harmonica blast—*wa-wa-wa-waaa-waaa*—John Glover punches the chords—

Now you ought to see me hug my pillow
Where my baby used to lay.

Hoots from the crowd—He's tellin' it from the mountaintop! How old is that kid? Eight? Nine? Lawd, lawd . . .

Saint:

The big deacon is on the verge of speaking in tongues. Feel his strong arms embrace and *lift*, and suddenly the full-tilt tumult that the church has become seems far below. Deacon is dancing to the *clap*-yeah-yeah, *clap*-yeah-yeah, the congregation is in a chantingsinging uproar, the noise and song and fervor a rising tide, the deacon parading up the aisle with the lamb of God atop his shoulder—and every set of eyes riveted on the little blind boy with the herky-jerky head, clapping and you just have to clap *with* him, singing and you just have to sing *with* him, the little junior deacon with a smile bestowed by Jesus himself, setting the place *aflame.*

Sinner:

Blow straight into "Rollin' and Tumblin'"—the song moves like a locomotive. John Glover is laying the guitar down just right. Harmonica *driving.* People clapping, feet shuffling on the sidewalk, people jostling around. Who's playin' that—why, they just little *kids*—and that one's *blind*—

Keep *driving* it. Don't let 'em go. Make 'em want to reach in that pocket. Make 'em want to hear another one. Try not to let 'em see that this is so much fun that the money makes no difference. Kick the harmonica into another *gear*—let's tear it *down*—

More hoots and hollers and chortles—them little fellas better be careful, they gonna blow themselves *up*—and the crowd is four-deep now, craning for a look and pushing and laughing and shaking their heads, wondering just what *in the hell* is going on here on Twenty-sixth Street, where every set of eyes is riveted on the little blind boy with the herky-jerky head who plays the harmonica like Gabriel's horn and sings like he done already seen every corner of this mean old world, all with a grin bestowed by the Devil himself, setting the place *aflame.*

SOMETIMES WORLDS COLLIDE. Stevie and John took to playing on porch stoops in the neighborhood—the closest thing around to a stage. More than once, Lula would start looking for Stevie around dinnertime and find him blocks away, set up with John Glover on a stoop and playing his heart out on the harmonica or the bongos, singing some blues song off the radio. And people would always stop to watch and maybe throw some money into the tin cup. Every so often, a passerby would be so impressed he would try to give Stevie a dollar bill or two—but Stevie didn't want it. Stevie wanted quarters. Stevie wanted to hear the money *jingle*. If it didn't jingle, it wasn't money.

One afternoon, a woman who was a member of the Whitestone Baptist Church happened by. She was particularly pious, actually a member of the local Sanctified Holiness church as well as being on the roll at Whitestone. Stevie and John were deep into a rendition of the Miracles' "Bad Girl." The sister was agog.

Oh, Stevie, I'm so ashamed of you for playing that worldly music out here, the sister said when the song was over. I'm so ashamed of you.

The sister then went on her way, shaking her head, but that wasn't the end of it. A few days later, one of the big deacons came calling right before dinner. He explained to Lula that the leaders of the church were very concerned to learn that little Stevie was playing devil music in the streets. In fact, he said, Whitestone was officially stripping Stevie of his membership in the church.

Well, Lula said, that means I won't be showing up anymore, either.

The deacon tipped his hat as if to say, So be it, and took his leave.

Well, Mama, Stevie said, I guess I just became a sinner.

IN 1955, Berry Gordy Jr. woke up one morning and found himself working on the assembly line at the Ford Motor Company. It was *not* what he had in mind for his life.

His family was more fortunate than most in Detroit. Berry Gordy Sr. had built a successful business as a plastering contractor. Berry Jr. was fourteen when the 1943 riots swept through the city, sparing the family business but decimating the black community.

The unrest made a vivid impression on the young Berry. There were lessons to be learned. Lesson number one: You must be the master of your own fate. If you depended on others to fashion your life path for you, then you were powerless.

So, to his father's great disappointment, Gordy Jr. would not go into the family business. A pugilistic sort anyway, he had another career path in mind: He would become a professional boxer.

Detroit was a tough town, and to succeed there as a boxer you had to be a tough customer. Berry fought as a featherweight; he was more creative than brutal and wasn't half-bad. But his boxing career ended when he was drafted in 1951 and sent to Korea. He was discharged in 1953 and then opened a record store in Detroit, the 3D Record Mart, which trafficked mostly in jazz.

But the business failed, and Gordy—by then married with three children and bills to pay—found himself punching a clock in a factory. He was troubled and unhappy. In 1957, his wife, Thelma, sued him for divorce. Gordy knew he needed to change his life, to take things in another direction. He decided to give songwriting a try.

Gordy had always loved music and frequently dabbled with songwriting in his spare time. He was very much a part of the scene at the Flame Show Bar, a center of Detroit's black nightlife, where his sisters sold cigarettes. He felt like he knew a good song when he heard one; now he meant to see if he could write good songs himself.

The going was slow until he discovered that an old friend, Jackie Wilson, had become a singer and was looking for songs to record. With some help from his sister Gwendolyn, Gordy put together some songs and offered them to Wilson. One song was "Reet Petite," which became a modest hit. Wilson wanted more songs; Gordy wrote "Lonely Teardrops," which became one of the biggest hits of 1955.

With a little folding money in his pocket and with an always-roving entrepreneurial eye, Gordy decided to go into producing and publishing music. With a shopworn recording machine, Gordy used his house as the setting for a studio. Anyone with a song and a little money could get recorded there. Gordy occasionally would accompany the performers, playing some of the instrumentals on the records, and he and his second wife, Raynoma Liles, would sing backing vocals.

After "Lonely Teardrops," Gordy was a known name in the music industry. He quickly capitalized on his new status with a hit for Marv Johnson, "You've Got What It Takes." But Gordy was disillusioned. He made promising, high-quality records, yet he still had no choice but to shop them around to the major record companies, and that consumed time and money. Whether any record company would agree with his judgment of a particular record was a roll of the dice; even if they did concur and decided to buy it, there was no guarantee that they would back it properly. A great record might simply languish due to the whims of some distracted record company hack.

It also began to dawn on Gordy that there was a deep well of black musical talent in Detroit going undiscovered. He knew this from his matriculation within the university of Detroit's nightclubs, churches, and talent shows; there were performers out there with amazing talent going nowhere. Slowly, Gordy began to construct the idea of forming his own record company.

A fundamental building block presented itself in the form of Smokey Robinson, the marvelous singer with the white-chocolate voice and front man for the Miracles. Gordy's relationship with Robinson had flowered while producing two Miracles hits written by Robinson, "Got a Job" and "Bad Girl." Robinson was a great source of encouragement to Gordy, convincing him to finally take the plunge and kick-start his own operation. Gordy borrowed $800 from his father and Tamla Records was born, with Gordy as president and Robinson as vice president. After some debate, the principals decided on a corporate name: Motown, as in the Motor City of Detroit.

The embryonic enterprise began operating in a rundown clump of houses on West Grand Avenue. It was a Gordy family operation through and through. His brother and sisters were placed in charge of various departments within the company. "Pops" Gordy was the maintenance man. When sister Gwendolyn married Harvey Fuqua, owner of the Chicago-based Tri-Phi and Harvey record labels, Gordy arranged a merger that brought Fuqua to Motown along with a cadre of musicians that included Marvin Gaye and Junior Walker and the All-Stars.

Motown's first hit record came virtually before the dust settled. Gordy, broke from start-up expenses, wrote a song for Barrett Strong called "Money (That's What I Want)," which cracked the Top 40 and later would be covered by the Beatles. It was a startling breakthrough, given that the song was hashed out around the piano and produced on the slenderest of budget shoestrings. "Money" was cut strictly by the seat of Gordy's pants.

Then came "Shop Around," by the Miracles. The song hit like wildfire, and instantly established Robinson, Gordy, and Motown as local legends. That sudden street cred was plainly evident in the growing numbers of wannabes who competed for Motown's attention, would-be recording artists of all ages convinced that they were destined to be the next Smokey or Jackie. Gordy finally dedicated an afternoon a week to listen to aspiring stars that surged through his office like trout swimming upstream.

One hopeful who ultimately made his way across Gordy's field of vision was about chest-high. At age ten, he already had been plying his trade in the street for years. And he couldn't see his hand in front of his face.

Eight

SIGNATURES

L ULA WRESTLED THE mattress from atop the box springs, reached up into the hiding place within and conducted a balance inquiry. The FOR SALE sign had bloomed in front of the house over on Breckenridge Avenue like a spring flower, and she had thought of nothing else since.

The bus was lurching and heaving home from work and she had spied the sign from her perch the way a crow spies a glinting treasure on the ground below. Lula got off at the very next stop—attracting a mild look of curiosity from the driver, who knew good and well where she usually disembarked—and doubled back to take a look.

It looked *good*. It wasn't going to win any garden club awards, mind you, and it was the picture of modesty—a small brick house with a small front porch and what passed for a picture window. But it had a nice feel, even from the street. It looked unoccupied, so Lula cautiously clambered up on the porch and peered through the window. From what she could see, it was clean and in good shape. She saw enough to know that she wanted to see more.

She memorized the real estate agent's phone number on the sign and walked briskly to the pay phone at the corner market. It was a nice little street, she thought, a nice little neighborhood. Nothing fancy—nothing fancy *at all*. But Lula didn't need fancy. Lula wanted a house, away from the din and paper-thin walls and dead-end feel of the projects. She wanted a home.

She got lucky on the phone and caught the agent at her desk. Yes, the new listing at 3347 Breckenridge. The owner wants $8,000. We can probably get you in it for ten percent down, if everything checks out. Are you interested? I can come out and show you the place right now if you like . . .

And so within thirty minutes Lula was inside the house and in the trance that occurs when people imagine their lives unfolding in a new world. A nice big kitchen. A good stove. A furnace in the hallway. Four bedrooms. A small backyard. A sound roof. The wallpaper was worn, and the hardwood floors needed a good cleaning, but Lula didn't see much else wrong with the place. Milton *here*, Calvin *there* . . . I could put Stevie and those infernal drums *way* back here, and he could bang away to his heart's content . . .

What do you think? the agent asked, sizing her up. Should we write up an offer?

Lula thanked the lady and said she would be in touch. With a stern note in her voice, the lady advised her to act quickly if she was seriously interested. This is a nice little place, she said; it won't last long. And we'll have an ad in the paper this weekend.

Lula thanked her again and caught the next bus, her heart in her throat. She *wanted* it. It was time. It was *her* time.

She bustled into the tenement and tore into the mattress. It had been a while since she had counted the roll of bills, even as she had religiously continued to add to it every payday. It was a mass of ones and fives and tens, with some twenties grudgingly interspersed. It took a few minutes to get it all together. Then she sat cross-legged on the floor and counted it, down to the last dollar. Twice. It took about ten minutes.

Nine hundred and two dollars.

She had worked like a damned fool for that money. She felt as if she were holding her very body tissue in her hands. She felt certain she would never have so much money together again in her life. She wanted to make it *count*. This way, she figured, the money would always be there. A house would be tangible evidence of her hard work and hard times. And it would be *hers*, acquired by her own lights and by the sweat of her own brow, owing to the bank but to no man.

The agent had explained the way it would work. She would need about $800 for a down payment. The payments would run about $100 a month. That sum represented a significant portion of what she brought home each month from the fish market. It would be tough, but it seemed doable.

The bank would never lend $7,000-plus to a single black mother of three; Lula knew that much. The agent knew as much, too, and assured Lula that if she could get the down payment together that she would work as a middleman to arrange the mortgage. If necessary, she said, they would work something out directly with the homeowner.

Lula made her decision. She called the agent and made arrangements to meet at her office the next afternoon. She made her way home the next day and took the cash and stuffed it in a Mason jar, which she in turn stuffed into her purse. Thus armed, she took the bus to the real estate office, walked in, and placed the jar delicately on the agent's desk, her hand trembling slightly.

The agent watched her and then hefted the jar and smiled. You worked hard for this money, didn't you?

I surely did, she said in a quiet voice. I worked hard for a lot of things.

All right then, she said. Let's get started.

So many papers . . . and a lot of talk that Lula didn't understand. But the agent was honest and kind—and wanted the sale. Soon everything was complete. She gave Lula a receipt for the money and said she would drop by in a day or two to let her know where things stood.

Two afternoons later, a knock sounded on Lula's door. She found the agent in the tenement hallway, dangling a set of keys in her hand. Here you are, she said, it's all been arranged. We can go over the details later, but you can move in anytime. You just need to sign this agreement.

She produced an envelope that contained a densely worded legal document. She spread the document in front of Lula and handed her a pen. She felt a momentary wave of uncertainty—the words swam around on the page, undecipherable—but regained her balance and confidently signed on the bottom line.

She placed the keys in Lula's palm. She looked at them, almost uncomprehendingly, and then bear-hugged the agent as if she were a long-lost sister.

Thank you for your help, she said, her vision blurring.

My pleasure, the agent said. Congratulations and good luck.

And so Lula grabbed her coat and set out into the neighborhood and found her boys and, ignoring their protests, loaded them on a bus for Breckenridge Avenue.

Where we going, Mama? Stevie asked, clutching her hand.

You'll find out soon enough, baby.

They got off the bus, and Lula led the boys like ducklings down the street to the small white frame house.

Whose house is this? Milton wanted to know.

Well, Lula said, from now on, it's *our* house.

The children were speechless. Shocked silence engulfed them for what seemed like hours.

Is it a *nice* house? Stevie finally asked.

It sure is, Calvin said.

Well . . . let's have a look, Lula said.

And so Lula fished the keys from her purse and fumbled with the unfamiliar lock, finally solving it. The door swung open, and Milton and Calvin tumbled excitedly inside, with Stevie groping along behind. Then the three of them ripped room to room, taking it all in, exploring and babbling and arguing.

Lula stood in the living room and gazed out the small picture window, taking it all in, looking onto the street, and listening to the empty-house echo of the kids and their buffalo-herd rumble as they raced about the place.

I have a home, she thought to herself. *My family has a home.*

She thought fleetingly of Papa Henry and Mama Virge, and of the old home place bulging with song after supper, and wondered what they might think of this house, this city, this life.

And then Lula was back in the present. She began to think about where to put her meager collection of furniture in her new home, this monument to her survival on Breckenridge Avenue in Detroit, Michigan.

They went back to the projects and, with the help of some friends, moved out that very afternoon before Judkins returned. Stevie's piano had to be left behind, but they got most everything else. When Judkins got home that evening, he found a curiously empty apartment and not so much as a note.

Flat as a pancake.

DETROIT IN 1960 was a big city and a small town, especially where its black residents were concerned. It was a sprawling, densely populated place, but the sense of community was strong. Blacks continued to flood into the city from the Deep South and elsewhere in search of opportunity and to be with family that already had made the leap. (According to census figures, the black population in Detroit more than doubled from 1950 to 1970, from about 300,000 to more than 660,000. The rise in the percentage of blacks in relation to the overall Detroit population rose accordingly during the same period, from 16.2 percent to 44.5 percent.) Despite the ever-escalating numbers, it seemed that everyone in the black community knew everyone else, or knew someone who knew the someone in question, knew *of* the person in question, was related to or knew someone related to the person in question.

And so it was that one of Stevie's best childhood friends was Gerald White, who was a brother of Ronnie White, who was one of the Miracles—as in Smokey Robinson and the Miracles. At that juncture, Motown was only getting its wobbly colt-legs anchored under itself. Robinson and the Miracles had made a few records, and Gordy had enjoyed some success as a songwriter, but Hitsville U.S.A. still was very much a fledgling enterprise. And yet the Miracles and Motown already were virtual household names among Detroiters, particularly black Detroiters, who paid even scant attention to the local music scene or listened to WCHB.

Convinced, like virtually everyone who heard Stevie perform, that his friend was a special talent, Gerald White relentlessly badgered his brother to investigate Stevie on behalf of Motown. Ronnie White, like everyone else associated with Gordy, was under constant siege from family, friends, and strangers, all of whom were convinced that they or someone they knew was a hit maker in waiting. More often than not, Ronnie made his excuses and put these people off. And why not? It was usually a waste of time, and, besides, he was an entertainer, not a talent scout.

But Gerald was persistent, as was Ruth Glover, the mother of Stevie's musical partner John Glover. Ruth Glover buttonholed Ronnie one day and gave her own testimony regarding Stevie's abilities.

Finally, Ronnie—more from exasperation than expectation—agreed to drop by the White home and check Stevie out.

On the appointed day Ronnie arrived with Pete Moore, another member of the Miracles, in tow. Stevie already was there, kibitzing around. Everyone repaired to the living room and talked for a while, getting comfortable. Finally, Ronnie said, Okay, Stevie, we heard you were a good singer. Is that right?

Yes, sir. I can sing real good. I can sing badder than Smokey.

White and Moore fell all over themselves, laughing. Badder than Smokey, huh? Kid, you got some attitude, I'll say that much. All right then, Mister Badder-than-Smokey. Let's hear something.

And then Stevie began to sing "Lonely Boy," a song he had written himself.

The smug smiles evaporated from the two Miracles' faces. The voice emanating from the little blind kid was strong, gorgeous, note-perfect, *expressive.* Maybe this kid had something after all . . .

Midway through "Lonely Boy," Stevie pulled his chromatic from his pocket and pealed off a solo that seemed to flutter around in the heavens. Holy shit, the kid could *play.*

Stevie finished the song, stuck his harmonica back in his pocket, and fidgeted.

Finally Ronnie spoke: Is this some kind of joke? Kid, who taught you to sing and play like that?

Stevie shrugged. Nobody, he said. I just started playing and singing along with the radio. That's all. And I used to sing in church, too.

Used to?

Well, it's kind of a long story.

Never mind. What are you doing tomorrow afternoon?

I don't know. Why?

You're coming with me down to Motown.

• • •

LULA HAD NOT even been aware of the audition for Ronnie White.

Stevie had banged out of the house that afternoon, yelling something over his shoulder about going to visit Gerald White. That boy was always charging out into the neighborhood like some kind of rhinoceros, she thought; from a distance, you'd never suspect he was blind, probably, as long as he was in his element, his familiar surroundings. Get closer, however, and his affliction would become apparent: the opaque eyes, the way his head rocked back and forth. Everyone had tried to get Stevie to concentrate on stopping that odd mannerism, but he said he couldn't—he didn't even realize he was doing it. The doctor called it a "blindism." Lula just figured it was the rhythm in his head.

Lula finally had arrived at a measure of peace with her son's blindness. It still broke her heart every day. She still sent fervent prayers that something miraculous would happen, that some sort of cure would be found, that something behind Stevie's eyes would suddenly dial into place—*click*—and he would just as suddenly be able to see the glory of the world around him.

But it was different now. When Stevie was smaller, she would find herself mired in deep, shadowy periods of gloom as she fretted about his blindness and struggled with the unanswerable question of why God would deny the ability to see to her son, the picture of strapping health in every other regard.

She blamed herself. Surely, she figured, God recognized the capacity within her to do the sinful things she ultimately did back then to survive. Stevie's blindness was, somehow, retribution for the earthly crimes she had committed. She had stolen. She had sold herself. She had nearly killed her husband in a knife-wielding rage. And while she had done none of these things until after Stevie was born, until after his condition was apparent, she deduced that God had known of the terrible things of which she was capable, knew of the weaknesses in spirit to which she would succumb.

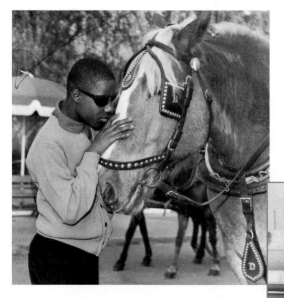

Stevie and Lula at Disneyland. Stevie's blindness never kept him from pursing the same childhood joys as sighted kids.

Stevie poses with a four-legged acquaintance during a trip to Disneyland in 1964.

Stevie at sixteen.

Stevie and Lula, riding high in 1975.

Lula acknowledges the cheers at the 1973 Grammy Awards.

Lula and Stevie meet President Nixon in the Rose Garden at a ceremony for disabled youth. Stevie later became closely associated with Democratic Party causes and candidates, including Bill Clinton and Al Gore.

July 14, 1903 - November 28, 1976

In Loving

Memory

of

Calvin Judkins

OUTER DRIVE UNITED PRESBYTERIAN CHURCH
4849 West Outer Drive
Detroit, Michigan

Rev. Henry Walsh, *Pastor*
Rev. Charles Nicks, Jr., *Officiating*

Saturday, December 4, 1976 - 1:00 p.m.

The cover of the program for the funeral of Stevie's father, Calvin Judkins.

Lula's Aunt Ilona, a significant maternal figure in her life.

Stevie and John Travolta, circa *Saturday Night Fever*.

Lula relaxes shortly after the move from Detroit to her
new home in Los Angeles.

Lula and Motown founder Berry Gordy Jr., circa 1975.

Lula and Stevie at a family gathering in 1979.

Lula, circa 1995.

Stevie and former UN Ambassador Andrew Young, two of the formidable forces behind the drive for a Martin Luther King Jr. national holiday.

Lula with Ewart Abner, a former
Motown executive who served as
Stevie's personal manager.

Who says the good life doesn't
have its perks? Lula meets
Tom Jones in Las Vegas.

Lula in her kitchen at Christmas time, circa 1990.

And yet, and yet . . . Lula was convinced that God had never placed a happier child on the face of the Earth. Almost from the very beginning, he had been an absolute ray of celestial light, with a glow that seemed to bathe everyone who came into contact with him. He was absolutely undaunted by his inability to see. He relished his life, his family, friends, his music. Lula had realized long ago that it was useless to pity Stevie for the fact that he lived in a world of darkness; Stevie did not know what darkness *was*. He did not know light; so how could he know darkness? To him, it was perfectly normal and natural. So he bumped into furniture in strange houses, tumbled down steps, learned to read with his fingers, willingly groped his way through the world. As far as Stevie was concerned, didn't everyone? There were times when Lula was convinced the boy saw much more than anyone who was saddled with the curse of sight. He could tell you who was coming down the street. He knew who was in a room before he entered it. He could surmise someone's emotional state without the benefit of seeing the pain or the joy written across his or her face. He was wholly attuned to the world that surrounded him.

That power of perception was the key to one of the watershed emotional moments in Lula's life, the moment when she finally was able to stop torturing herself about her son's plight. Stevie couldn't have been six years old at the time; Lula had been in one of her dark, bottomless funks, despairing over the boy's lot in life. Night terrors flooded her sleep with images of Stevie stumbling his way through a cruel world of hardship and, worse, the overwhelming *insignificance* that seemed to her to be the undeserved fate of so many disabled people, shoved aside to the margins of the world.

He had come to her in the night, as she had awakened from a dream and realized that she had been crying in her sleep. He could always tell when she was depressed and often took it upon himself to cheer her up, clowning around, making up silly songs. But on this night he seemed to know that his mother needed comfort beyond a juvenile joke. She felt his hand upon her face, and she sat up in bed and held him fast to her, wishing she could envelop him forever and deny his good heart even a pinprick of pain.

What's wrong, Mama . . . what's wrong?

There's nothing wrong, baby. Sometimes Mama just gets sad.

Yes, there *is* something wrong. Please tell me.

No, it's all right.

Tell me what's wrong. Are you sick?

No, baby. I'm just—it's just that I get upset and worried sometimes about you.

About me? How come, Mama?

Because of your condition, son. I worry because I can't always be there to watch after you. I worry that you won't be happy, because you'll always wish that you could see. And there's nothing Mama can do about it.

And, then, Stevie said it:

Don't be sad, Mama. I'm not sad.

And at that moment Lula realized that it was true: He *wasn't* sad. He wasn't burdened with the weight of his affliction. He didn't feel sorry for himself or seek pity from others. He accepted his state of being and the world in which he existed as he found them. Part of that, of course, was due to the simple truth that he was a child, innocent and still unexposed to the callousness of unfeeling people and the treachery of the knockabout world. But anyone who knew Stevie, anyone who was even around him for thirty seconds, knew that he was nothing if not gloriously, effusively, phenomenally *happy*—full of a spiritual glow, a boat floating effortlessly on the rising and falling tide, always at full sail. He was unfazed by his blindness. Perhaps that was out of some blissful ignorance, but Lula didn't think so; she believed Stevie had a larger grasp than that, even at six years old. So at that moment she resolved to let it be. Yes, she would worry. Yes, she would continue to pray for a cure. Yes, she would watch over him the way every mother watches over every son.

But she also would stand back and *let him be happy.* Because it was clearly what he wanted to be. Why should she take that away from him because of her own fears?

There was another consideration, one that Lula kept entirely to herself.

She had long known that there was a fervent school of thought, particularly among black folk, that the blind possessed special powers. She had heard it referred to as "second sight"—an innate, shamanlike ability to connect to spirits and visions and worlds that "normal" people couldn't even fathom. Stevie's uncanny talent for music and his phenomenal perceptiveness about people and their thoughts and emotions often left Lula wondering if her son had the gift of second sight. But she didn't dare discuss her suspicions; people regarded her son differently enough without introducing some witch-doctor business into the mix. Yet she was convinced that, one day, it would likely be revealed that Stevie was different, special, gifted, "powerful"—and the thought gave her great discomfort. Her fear was that, somehow, he would be taken away from her, that he would be put at risk out in the world away from her protecting arms.

When Stevie exploded into the house the afternoon he wowed Ronnie White, Lula knew that the day she had feared had finally arrived. Stevie was walking on air—Ronnie White is gonna take me down to Motown! I told him I could sing badder than Smokey!—but her chest was filling up with fear, the way a running faucet fills a kitchen sink. *They're coming to take a piece of my precious boy.*

AND SO IT wasn't exactly on angel wings that Lula accompanied Stevie, Milton, and Ronnie White down to the rundown-looking house on West Grand Boulevard, the one with the HITSVILLE, U.S.A.

sign draped in front. But what happened that afternoon was a sight to behold.

The first stop was the office of Brian Holland, talent scout and songwriter extraordinaire, the anchor of the Holland-Dozier-Holland songwriting team that ultimately would become one of the most prolific and successful in popular music. White already had prepped Holland about Stevie, and Holland had agreed to give the kid a quick hearing to determine if White's instincts were correct. Holland's office was brimming with people and noise—the entire house was teeming and chaotic, always, as if in the middle of an air raid—so the group moved outside onto the front porch for an audition. It wasn't much quieter out there, with the sound of traffic emanating from West Grand; but, Holland said, it will have to do.

Holland talked to Stevie for a minute or two to break the ice, asking about singers he liked and how he became immersed in music. A quizzical—even dubious—expression crossed Holland's face when Stevie ticked off the list of instruments he played: harmonica, piano, organ, drums. Finally, Holland asked Stevie to sing and play something on his harmonica.

Stevie launched into a Miracles song, punctuating the lyrics with harmonica riffs. Holland couldn't believe what he was seeing and hearing—the kid seemed to light up the afternoon sky. Not much more than a minute had gone by when Holland cut Stevie off.

All right, he said. Let's go see B.G.

THREE TEENAGE GIRLS named Florence Ballard, Mary Wilson, and Diane (later Diana) Ross—recently signed to a Motown contract as a singing trio called the Supremes but who had yet to cut a record—sat in the downstairs living room that served as Motown's lobby and watched the unusual proceedings.

First, in came Ronnie White with a gangly little kid, apparently blind, accompanied by a woman who looked to be the kid's mom and a teenager who probably was the blind kid's older brother. The girls watched as White ushered the group into Brian Holland's office, and then as they reemerged and headed back outside. Next, with increasing interest, they tracked Holland as he led the entire entourage up the stairs to Berry Gordy's office. About ten minutes later, the group came rumbling back down the stairs with Gordy leading the way, headed for one of the makeshift studios. Curious, the girls fell in behind.

Gordy had heard Stevie sing and play the harmonica in his office. He kept a poker face, but he thought the kid was fabulous. Intrigued by Stevie's claim that he could play almost any instrument, Gordy decided to take the boy into the basement recording studio. Stevie found the piano and played a couple of gospel tunes with a flourish.

Gordy grinned. What about the drums, Stevie?

Stevie made his way over to the big drum kit, grabbed the sticks, and practically detonated the room. His playing was strong, sure, natural, animated, and sophisticated.

Okay, then, Gordy said. What else can you play, Stevie?

Stevie went around the studio. He spent a little time with each of the instruments he had played around with at school—a trumpet, a saxophone, percussion instruments, even a xylophone—and went around the block a few times with each piece. Gordy and the others watched with growing amazement.

This kid, Gordy whispered to the girls, Holland, and White, is truly some kind of young musical genius. They could only nod in agreement.

Even Lula and Milton, who certainly needed no convincing of Stevie's ability, were taken aback by his exhibition of talent that day. They knew he could sing; they knew he could play the harmonica; they knew he could play the piano; God knows they knew he could play those damned drums. But horns? Percussion? That was a surprise. But more than that, the shock was in seeing Stevie perform through the eyes of others. It was . . . *a revelation.* They had seen the kid grow up from an incubator baby the size of a water bug and gradually pick up this instrument and that and carry a tune. They had seen him take over the choir and raise the roof within the friendly (for a while) environs of the Whitestone Baptist Church. They knew he was a precocious little operator who could take his harmonica and charm money out of strangers' pockets over on Horton Street. They knew he was extraordinarily gifted. Of *course* he was—everyone in the neighborhood knew *that.* It was just an accepted fact. And yet, still, they weren't quite prepared for what they saw that day—to suddenly see Stevie in full flower, playing every instrument in the house, hypnotizing these important-seeming men in suits. It was like watching a tree grow in the front yard for years and years, seeing it every day of your life, and then coming across an old photograph of the house with the tree as a sapling. Only then does it hit you, full force, how much the tree actually has grown. Lula and Milton had been too close to Stevie to see it all come together until that afternoon at Motown, when they saw Berry Gordy's eyes widen with discovery and then narrow with calculation.

GORDY WASN'T TERRIBLY sure about the best course of action regarding the prodigy who had literally landed at his doorstep on West Grand Boulevard, practically wrapped in swaddling clothes. The kid had talent, sure—a hell of a lot of it. But what to do with it? It was difficult enough recording and promoting adult artists, much less some ten-year-old pipsqueak who, by the way, was stone blind, too. Blind or not, minors were a problem. He had resisted signing the Supremes for that very reason; there were liability issues, child labor law issues, tensions with parents, all of it. But with the girls, he had finally relented, realizing there was something very special—and very marketable—at work there. He intended to bring them along slowly. Nonetheless, working with kids meant that you had to walk around on eggshells. Now, here was this half-pint Ray Charles.

I don't know what we'll do with him, he told Mickey Stevenson, Motown's street-smart A&R man, but we'll think of *something.*

But first things first: Stevie had to be signed. And to sign Stevie, Gordy would be required not only to get Stevie's signature, but Lula's approval on the dotted line as well. And the entire affair would have to be monitored by state labor authorities. Despite all the hassle, Gordy decided it was worth it. He could start shaping Stevie's career right away. The boy was a gem in the rough, but with some excavation and polish, who couldn't say the kid might make it? If nothing else, he could provide instrumental backing for other artists. Besides, how hard could it be to sign him? That should be the easy part, right?

Right . . .

WHEN IT CAME to signing Stevie, Lula was about as cooperative as a rodeo bull attempting to gore the clowns. Everything about the process unnerved her. Stevie, of course, could not have cared less about the details of the contract. He was, after all, only ten years old. His head was swimming with the heady notion of actually *making records*—records that, as Gordy told him, might just wind up on the radio, maybe even on *Sundown.* Gordy told the boy it would all depend on how hard he worked and how much faith and trust he put into Berry Gordy and Motown Records.

He told Stevie: We want you to be a part of the Motown family.

Stevie replied: When can I start?

The boy already was hanging out at Motown in the afternoons after school with the likes of Smokey Robinson and Marvin Gaye, listening in on recording sessions and monkeying around with what seemed to him to be a treasure trove of musical instruments. If Stevie had had any money of his own, he likely would have paid Gordy for that very privilege alone, rather than the other way around.

But Lula was a much tougher customer—for a while. Like many people deprived of education, she was highly suspicious of anything that involved paperwork, signatures, and the like. Her distrust of banks had led her to keep her life savings squirreled away in a mattress for years; a fire or theft could have meant disaster. The same principle applied to the "negotiations"—one-sided though they were—between Lula and Motown. It all seemed like gibberish to her. She had been lucky when she purchased her home; her agent had been an honest woman. She knew that the agent easily could have taken advantage of her. But she had sensed that she was worthy of her trust, and her intuition had proved correct. But this was a different situation entirely. This was a situation where money—who knew, maybe even lots of money—would be coming to Stevie and his family if things worked out. She could tell the Motown people were anxious for her to sign the contract, but her inner alarm was clanging like church bells on Sunday morning.

Lula, of course, was haphazardly educated at best and was poorly equipped to provide Stevie with the guidance he needed when Motown came calling. The contract specified, among myriad other things, that Stevie's earnings would be placed in a trust until he became legally responsible at the age of twenty-one; Gordy would control the money until then. It also stipulated that Motown would control Stevie's music publishing and management.

Gordy saw his position in contract negotiations with his artists as eminently defensible. He already was well aware of the vagaries and unpredictability of the music business. Nothing was guaranteed. The odds of developing an artist into a successful recording star were slim, no matter who the artist was or how talented he or she may have been. Producing a hit record took guile, hard work, and a mountain of luck.

And, most of all, it took time and money. Countless hours would have to be spent working with the artist, finding the right style, the right voice, the right material. Money would be spent on recording sessions and promotion and clothes for live appearances around the city (another part of artist development). Gordy also hired a cook and fed his Motown crew every day from the kitchen at the house on West Grand; shouldn't that count for something? Not to mention all the other overhead and salaries for which he was responsible at Motown.

In short, Gordy was putting himself and his own money on the line when he agreed to sign artists to his label. And while he strongly believed in the talent and potential of the already-burgeoning roster of artists he had signed—Smokey Robinson and the Miracles, Mary Wells, the Temptations, Marvin Gaye, the Four Tops, the Supremes, Junior Walker and the All-Stars, some of whom had already put records on the charts—Gordy knew that finding a hit was like finding a needle in a haystack. The likelihood was that Gordy would spend substantial amounts of money on behalf of an artist before he would ever see a penny in return, if ever. He figured it this way: He was sowing the seed money and molding these people into stars. Shouldn't he reap the lion's share of the rewards?

His logic seemed to compound in his favor when it came to Stevie. Here was a ten-year-old blind kid who was a heavenly talent but, still, as raw as anyone could imagine. Everyone agreed the kid had *something,* but what was it? How do you go about trapping this lightning in a jar? Do you make him into some sort of Ray Charles knockoff? Something else entirely? Can a kid so young get away with singing love songs? What's gonna work? Did the kid really have what it takes—the work ethic, the smarts, the swagger, the *soul*—to pull it all off? Could he perform onstage and connect with people? Could his personality translate over to a vinyl record? Could he handle being separated from his family? Well, could he?

The bottom line is that no one knew for sure. But Gordy was willing to bet his time and money to find out. And, by God, he would arrange the terms to shelter his risk.

And so in his upstairs office in the rambling old house on West Grand, Gordy and Mickey Stevenson spread the contract before Lula and began to coax her to sign, while Stevie lolled distractedly on the furniture and then escaped to roam the halls. *We believe that Stevie has a chance to be a successful musician. He's a very talented young man. He's enthusiastic. He's willing to learn. We think we can work with him and develop him into something special. But it's going to take a while. It's going to take a lot of work and a lot of money. But as long as we all go into this together as a family . . .*

Lula fixed Gordy and Stevenson with a baleful, decidedly un-familial glare. She wasn't buying any such crap. She might damned well sign, but it wasn't going to be because she believed that Berry Gordy had anyone's interests above his own. She radiated Aunt Mary–sized daggers while she listened to the pitch and the explanation of the contract, delivered in a tone usually directed at second graders. She knew they were patronizing her, but the cold facts were that all the contract talk may as well have been in German. It all fluttered over her head like a flock of birds heading due south for the winter.

We'll treat Stevie as if he was our own child. We're a family around here. Ask Smokey. Ask Diane and the girls. You saw Pops Gordy cleaning up the place . . . we all stick together. And you'll be family, too . . .

What about money?

Well, when we make money, Stevie makes money. The way it goes is, three percent—

I heard all that. What I want to know is, if Stevie makes a record, then how do you handle the money? You can't give it to him. He's just a boy. He don't even care about money that much. You give him a quarter and he thinks he's got a million dollars in his pocket.

And how we handle that is, see, is with a trust. All of Stevie's proceeds, if there ever are any, will go into a trust—

A trust? What's that?

It's a special bank account. And Stevie will get any money from that trust that he has coming when he turns twenty-one. That's all right here on page nine—

At twenty-one? He doesn't get any money until he's twenty-one?

Well, we'll pay his expenses, of course, but because he is a minor—

And who's in charge of this trust?

We are.

Why can't his mother be in charge of this trust?

We're—uncomfortable with that.

And so that's it? He works for you, and nobody but you gets anything for it for eleven years? I know that can't be right.

But that way, the money is protected—

It doesn't sound right.

This is a wonderful opportunity for Stevie. Now, you don't want to deprive him of that opportunity, do you?

Don't put it like that. I'm just trying to look out for my boy.

And yourself. Isn't that right?

What's that supposed to mean?

Why don't you just tell us what it is you have in mind?

I'm leaving. This doesn't sound right, and that boy is just fine doing what he's doing now and living like he's living now. Stevie! Stevie, get in here—

Now hold on a minute—

What is it, Mama?

Put your jacket on, son. We're going home.

But we just *got* here. I was gonna—

I said put your jacket on. We're going home.

Wait. There's no need—

155

Good-bye. Come along, Steve.
Lula? Lula!—Aw, hell.

LULA RESOLVED THAT they would not sign with Motown. She had meant what she said; they didn't need this complication in their lives. The family finally was in a settled place. They had escaped the despair and cruelty of their lives in Saginaw and of the early days in Detroit. Times still were hard—times were *always* hard, it seemed—but hadn't they fought their way out of the darkness? She had worked hard and saved her money and bought a home. She had a steady job. The boys were doing well enough in school, Stevie included. He was smart and popular with anyone he came into contact with; he could learn a trade and, his teachers said, probably become self-sufficient by the time he was an adult. He would need some help to get there, but they all said Stevie could do just about anything he set his mind to.

But Stevie was devastated by the turn of events. He couldn't quite understand what had gone wrong with his mother and Gordy at Motown. And, in truth, Lula had a difficult time trying to explain it to him. Her concerns about how the money was being handled were lost on the boy. He could not have cared less about money, as she suspected. His head was full of dreams of being a part of the doings at Motown, a place that for him was like waking up to Christmas every day. At Motown, music was the order of business around the clock. People there talked music, listened to music, *lived* music. And the music that Berry Gordy was developing at Motown was music that Stevie loved, music with the soul of the old blues singers that he worshiped and mimicked but with the driving, irresistible beat of rock and roll. It was new, exciting, *infectious*. And he wanted to show them that he was as good as the rest of them, that he could make records, too, that he really could sing badder than Smokey.

At first, Stevie sulked and pouted. He was genuinely distressed, a condition that was highly unusual for him and did not go unnoticed by those around him. Compounding the situation was that word of Stevie's triumphant audition at Motown had ricocheted around the neighborhood like cannon fire; everyone, it seemed, knew about the audition and knew that Motown had offered Stevie a contract. Stevie could go nowhere without someone stopping him and congratulating him and wanting to hear all about it, which only added to Stevie's funk. Mama doesn't want me to do it, he would explain, which unfailingly prompted an array of flabbergasted responses. What!—Why, I never—How come she—Woman must have lost her mind! You tell her I said—

It was the first real conflict to come between Stevie and his mother. Not that he had been the model of the well-behaved child; far from it. She had punished him for plenty of transgressions, of which leaping across rooftops was only a minor chapter. She had washed his mouth out with soap on several occasions, once when Stevie decided to mimic within her earshot a raw routine he had heard on a Redd Foxx record. And even at his tender age and condition, he already had found that he could insinuate himself with the opposite sex. More than once, Lula had caught her boy smooching around with one neighborhood girl or another who obviously had fallen prey to Stevie's persuasive persistence. It didn't hurt that he was able to serenade his young love interests with his harmonica.

But all that was natural, boys-will-be-boys, growing-up stuff. While she had made frequent use of the ironing cord, she secretly thrilled to the knowledge that he was confident enough, brave enough, *normal* enough, to attack the world in the way that he did. And never had either of them felt the other had betrayed them in any way. They had always been close, in perfect sync emotionally. That, no doubt, was the result of Stevie's absolute dependence on her as a baby and, then, as a youngster. All children rely on their mother for sustenance and guidance as they totter about and explore their vivid new world with all its light and color and visual splendor. For Stevie, though, his mother was for a very long time his primary vessel for navigating his world that had no light, color, or visual splendor.

Now, for the first time, Stevie felt let down by his mother. It was incomprehensible to him that she would not allow him to make music, which to him was the most natural thing in the world. Even at age ten, he felt that music was what he was, *who* he was. Music was the thing he was meant to be. He had no idea of becoming famous or amassing a fortune; he could barely conceive of making a record. He just knew this: After carrying the torch of his musical absorption and prowess for all of his young life among people who perhaps cared for music but did not *live* for it, as he did, he had suddenly found a refuge teeming with like-minded people to whom he was powerfully drawn.

After a few days, Stevie's sulking segued into outright campaigning for Lula to change her mind. He was a formidable salesman. He begged and pleaded, keeping up a relentless assault. Even though he didn't really understand it, he instinctively knew his mother could be stubborn—even mule-headed—about certain things, particularly when she felt she was out of her depth. So he set about letting there be no mistake about how much this opportunity meant to him.

And, predictably, Lula began to weaken. There was the onslaught from Stevie, with his incessant beseeching that, more than once, bordered on nagging and wheedling. There was peer pressure from her neighbors and coworkers, whose smiling, excited faces uniformly melted into disbelieving frowns as she explained and defended her concerns with less and less conviction.

But more than all that was her awareness that money really wasn't the obstacle she made it out to be. In the moments when she was brutally honest with herself, she knew that it was something else all together that was fueling her recalcitrance: fear. *They're coming to take a piece of my precious boy.* That was it. Her boy, her special blessing, was no longer hers and hers alone. He had been found out. He had been discovered. It wasn't fair! She had given him birth; watched over him like a haggard, bandaged, war-zone sentry as he spent fifty-two days in that incubator; nursed him and fed him and loved him; buffered him from an abusive father; sold herself into slavery to keep his belly full and the ghost chill from his bones; dragged him to every doctor, quack and faith healer in three states; stuffed money into the deep labyrinth of her mattress for years to provide a roof over his head; and watched over him the way a lioness watches over her favorite cub, which is to say with a great, swelling, instinctual, inexplicable love in her heart and murder in her eye. And now these strangers, these highwaymen, these pimps in business clothes, were going to take him from her? Not without a duel to the death, they weren't.

More to the point: What would happen to him? Who would look out for him? Who would have that mother's radar, that finely tuned, oscilloscopic sense that always knew when he was in need, always detected danger? Berry Gordy? Please.

But also: In her heart she knew that this was a boy who had been watching out for himself for years. He would always need her, the way a boy always needs his mother, even as a man. But he had known love, had known a loving, protective mother and brothers, and he carried that with him wherever he went. He was armed to the teeth with love. How else did he have the courage to step into this new and foreign world? What else gave him the mettle at ten years old to even contemplate stepping off the precipice into the dark void to see if anything would break his fall? And when Lula thought about it, she realized that this was nothing new. Stevie had been vaulting from the precipice into the dark void his whole life. That was what his life *was*. It always had been, always would be.

IN THE END, it was the drumming that closed the deal.

After a couple of days of begging and pleading and wheedling and nagging, Stevie took to his room and his drums. And he began to drum, and drum, and drum, and drum and drum and drum drum drum drum drum drummmmmmmmmmmmm. He drummed from early morning until late evening, a wall-quivering, brain-numbing, ear-deadening, resolve-battering, aural and psychological assault, a sonic declaration of anger and want and frustration and will. Lula—despite a softening due to her around-the-clock internal debate over the issue—held firm and ignored it. And, anyway, she had never *ever* ordered him to stop playing any musical instrument, other than to send him to bed. But after the first fifteen minutes or so of the Drumming from Hell, she understood what he was up to . . . and decided to let it go. Besides, how long could he keep it up?

One day stretched into two. He stopped for fitful sleep and wordless meals; otherwise, drumming—unrelenting, ferocious, savage, vicious, frenetic, unmerciful, frothing, rabid, turbo-charged, take-no-prisoners, cauldron-boiling-over, water-on-a-gasoline-fire drumming, drumming that threatened to swallow the house and the neighborhood and then, inevitably, city, state, and planet. Neighbors begged Lula for relief, only to flee in retreat upon witnessing, writ large on her vaguely irrational face, the true and terrifying nature of the clash of wills in progress.

Two days stretched into three. Lula rode home from work on the bus, got off at the stop, and walked down Breckenridge toward home; she heard . . . nothing? A fragile peace had come over the land. Birds sang grateful choruses in the trees. A faint swell of victory rose in her chest. Her heel clicked imperceptibly on the front porch *and the drumming began anew,* the world shuddering, neighbors' windows shuttering, traumatized birds fluttering.

Finally, that evening—as the very house itself seemed as if it might slide off its foundation in broken surrender—Lula walked down the hallway toward the sound and shoved open the bedroom door.

ALL RIGHT! she yelled into the great maw of the storm.

The drumming stopped.

And she looked with resignation and awe at the boy, who raised his head from his toil to reveal his ashen face, opaque eyes swollen from fatigue and tears. Blood-streaked drumsticks clattered to the floor. He stood up unsteadily and made his way across the room and embraced his mother and buried his head in her breast.

Thank you, Mama, he said. And then he let it go, great gasping sobs crashing out of him in waves, the last time Lula would ever see him cry.

GORDY AGREED to give Stevie a small allowance of a few dollars a week, and Lula a stipend of about $200 a month to help with her family's needs. It seemed like an inconceivable windfall. Stevie persuaded a bemused Gordy to pay his allowance in quarters. Lula signed her name as neatly as she could on the last page of the impenetrable contract, trying her best not to appear nervous. Stevie quickly etched an X. (His surname also was legally changed to Morris, an old family name, as a preemptive strike against any attempt by Judkins to cut in on their sudden good fortune.) A photographer brought in for the occasion bathed the boy in flash. And everyone clapped and hugged each other, while Lula pretended that all this wouldn't change anything, not a single thing.

Nine

LITTLE STEVIE WONDER

At the [Ford] plant cars started out as just a frame, pulled
along on conveyor belts until they emerged at the end of the
line—brand spanking new cars. . . . I wanted the same concept for my company, only with artists and songs and
records. I wanted a place where a kid off the street could
walk in one door an unknown and come out the other a
recording artist—a star.

—Berry Gordy Jr.

Have you heard Stevie Wonder's in town?

—From "Don't You Know," by Little Stevie Wonder,
recorded in 1962

B Y 1961, MOTOWN already had produced Barrett Strong's
"Money (That's What I Want)" and put out its first million-
seller with "Shop Around." But despite this validating success, the
studio still was very much in its infancy. There was tremendous financial pressure on Gordy and the musical and business brain trust he
had assembled to turn out moneymakers—and turn them out quickly.

Turn them out they did. With early songs like "Please Mr. Postman" by the Marvelettes, "Do You Love Me" by the Contours, and "You've Really Got a Hold on Me," by the Miracles, Motown produced a succession of hits that poured the foundation for the "hit factory" juggernaut that came to fruition in the mid- to late 1960s. The impact was immediate, so much so that the Beatles recorded "Please Mr. Postman" and "You've Really Got a Hold on Me" on their second album.

Motown during this period often has been likened to an automobile assembly line, not unlike the Detroit factory where Berry once made his living, trotting out hits the way Ford trotted out Thunderbirds, and there is some truth to the analogy. There was an undeniable sameness in the sound of many of Motown's seminal hits, attributable to the booming acoustic resonance of the cobbled-together studios on West Grand. After a while the songs themselves also began to follow a familiar pattern. Certainly by the middle part of the decade, as the in-house songwriting team of Brian Holland, Lamont Dozier, and Eddie Holland began to issue forth a string of blockbuster hits for the Four Tops and, especially, the Supremes, Gordy knew that he had hit upon a winning formula: a scrupulously measured witches' brew of gifted singers, irresistible hooks, and a relentless, dancing-in-the-street backbeat powered by the combustion-chamber rhythm section of bass player James Jamerson and drummer Benny Benjamin. Gordy, a notorious control freak before the term ever was coined, also exercised an iron grip on every aspect of every artist's career at Motown. He held (and used) veto power on everything from song title to shoe color to what the Motown kitchen was serving for dinner. Berry Gordy believed within the tiniest atom of his soul that he knew what made records sell; he made sure—*damn* sure—his vision was implemented down to the last scrawny detail.

Did Gordy know what he was doing? In 1966, a remarkable 75 percent of the company's releases made the music charts. By 1970,

Motown had racked up twenty-two number 1 hits on *Billboard*'s pop chart and forty-eight number 1's on the R&B chart. It was the most lucrative black-owned business in the country. Motown had developed what was arguably the signature sound in American popular music; its artists were familiar names in households of every ethnic stripe, and Gordy was justifiably recognized as perhaps the most accomplished music mogul of his time. Motown had become, in short, a stanchion of popular culture. White artists like Elvis Presley had exposed white listeners to rock and roll infused with African-American influences; Gordy's Motown was bringing the music of the street—albeit with a distinct commercial sheen—directly from the source. In today's world of militant, profane, in-your-face rap music, it is difficult to fathom Motown music as cutting-edge. But in the 1960s it was undeniably authentic, and introduced whites to a black aesthetic that continues to dominate popular culture today.

Yet this phenomenal success still was years away as young Stevie began to settle in at the bustling house on West Grand. For all the assembly-line metaphors that have been applied to Motown, Gordy actually followed a relatively conservative production philosophy that emphasized quality control and extremely cautious decision making about which records would be released. Gordy's goal was to produce a limited number of extraordinarily polished and fully realized singles that had the best possible chance, in his view, of becoming hits. That approach was a far cry from how a giant, established record company of the day—such as, for example, RCA—might flood the market with product, figuring that the law of averages dictated that something would strike a chord with the listening public. Gordy's logic was that a new and struggling record company needed credibility with radio stations and retail outlets, and credibility came by exhibiting the ability to add an exciting new layer to the hit-and-miss process of making successful records.

The in-house competition was brutal. Gordy, according to

Motown legend, even repeatedly rebuffed the early lyrical efforts of Smokey Robinson. If Gordy had a song with potential, every singer or group in the house might audition for the right to record it. Gordy was a nightmarish perfectionist, driving his performers and songwriters and producers to do it again and again, to make it sharper, tighter, brighter, better. Gordy was a slave to the eternal conundrum that tortures anyone in the business of assessing art. He may have had trouble explaining what made a hit record, but he knew one when he heard it.

(One of Gordy's favorite anecdotes involves "Shop Around" by the Miracles. After sweating over the production of the single for what seemed like centuries, Gordy finally released it. Shortly thereafter, Gordy was driving in his car late at night when he heard the song on the radio for the first time. It hit him: the song was too *slow*. He sped to Motown, got on the phone, and jangled Robinson from bed, instructing the Miracles to return to the studio immediately. At about 3 A.M., a surly congregation of bleary Miracles and musicians congregated in the basement studio and, with Berry at the dials, recorded a livelier, up-tempo cut of the song. It was a smash.)

So what to do about Stevie? For several reasons, Gordy decided that he would be well advised to take it slow with the kid, to take pains to develop his talent in the right way. For one thing, Gordy at first wasn't completely sold on Stevie's singing ability. He had a nice, pretty voice and was a very confident singer—there was no lack of confidence in this boy—but the fact remained that Stevie's voice still was maturing and a little thin. Nonetheless, there was a unique quality to it that held promise. What Gordy liked most and wanted to build upon was Stevie's contagious exuberance for music, his amazing facility with the harmonica, and an already-discernible knack for making any song his own.

Thus Stevie became a Motown "project." He worked with a variety of producers and began to record a few songs almost immediately, some of which he had written himself. The first song he recorded was a Latin-flavored song he wrote called "Mother Thank You," originally called "You Made a Vow." The song ultimately was renamed "Thank You (For Loving Me All the Way)" and released years later as a B side. But most of Stevie's early labors in the studio wound up in the trash bin. It was all part of the process of developing a sound for the young performer. Increasingly, Stevie began to work with gifted producer and songwriter Clarence Paul, who became the boy's mentor at Motown. Paul, affable but highly opinionated in matters of music and life, began to fill in the gaps of Stevie's musical education and served as nothing less than a father figure for his young charge.

Paul, whose real surname was Pauling, had grown up in North Carolina in a very religious and musical family. His mother and sister were singers, as was his brother, Lowell, with whom Paul formed a gospel duet called the Royal Sons. (Paul soon left the group, which ultimately would become the non-gospel 5 Royales, which had several R&B hits, including "Baby Don't Do It" and "Help Me Somebody.") Paul went on to sing with gospel groups such as the Coleman Brothers and Wings Over Jordan before serving in the Army during the Korean War. When he was discharged he began to record non-spiritual songs for labels such as Federal and Roulette. By the early 1960s he found himself in Detroit and landed at Motown, where Gordy made good use of Paul's ample composing, arranging, and producing skills.

Initially, Paul and Stevie experimented with recording a variety of standards, hoping to hit on something that could be released as a single—singles being virtually the exclusive focus of Motown at the time. None was exceptional, although Stevie was becoming more comfortable in the studio. In casting about for the best method to capture Stevie's talent, Gordy and Paul conjured up what was, at the time, a revolutionary idea for Motown, given its emphasis on three-minute pop 45s. The concept: Stevie would record an album's worth of instrumentals—no vocals—intended to advertise his considerable abilities with a variety of instruments. The album would be called *The Jazz Soul of Little Stevie.*

To some degree, the decision to make an instrumental LP reflected Gordy's continuing ambivalence toward Stevie's singing. The kid could sing, but no one had figured out, just yet, how to showcase his vocals. An instrumental album would buy some time while he continued to evolve. Meanwhile, Gordy and his brain trust would continue to muse over his future. The contradictory title of the album itself (Jazz? Soul?) was a clue as to the internal debate at Motown as how to bundle Stevie's disparate abilities. So Paul began writing most of the material for the album and worked out the arrangements for a big band that would accompany Stevie. Now eleven, Stevie was somewhat overwhelmed by the big production, but he gamely stood his ground in the eye of the storm. What came out of those sessions was a series of recordings that were a wild departure from the music being produced at that juncture by Motown. The big band provided a lush backdrop for the entire album, while Stevie wandered around, a little aimlessly, from track to track, noodling on his harmonica, bongos, piano, organ, and drums. A studio version of "Fingertips" was recorded, a song that, later recorded again live, would figure prominently in Stevie's eventual breakthrough. On *The Jazz Soul of Little Stevie,* however, the song was workmanlike and unspectacular. Indeed, on this version of "Fingertips," Stevie plays the bongos rather than the harmonica, an error that would be corrected—and then some—on the subsequent live version.

Despite the oppressive big-band arrangements on *Jazz Soul,* Stevie's talent managed to peek through. His harmonica playing on songs such as "Square" and "Session Number 112" was startling in that, even as a preteen, he clearly already had developed the virtuosity for which he later would become famous.

When the *Jazz Soul* sessions were complete, Gordy and Paul listened carefully and confirmed what they already had suspected:

There was no apparent single to be found, and as a consequence it was pointless to even consider releasing the album. Stevie's debut as a recording artist would have to wait. Whatever the proper vehicle for the kid was, Gordy decided, *The Jazz Soul of Little Stevie* wasn't it. Motown would just have to consider the album an investment in Stevie's future, and leave it at that.

Gordy and Paul then reverted to Plan B: Ray Charles.

Charles, the immensely talented soul singer, pianist, bandleader, and songwriter, also blind, was one of Stevie's idols and a monumental influence on his music. Even though Charles was not even a Motown artist, Gordy and Paul put together an audacious scheme to attach Stevie to Charles's coattails. They envisioned an album on which Stevie covered a number of Ray Charles songs, mixed in with original songs. For good measure, the thinking went, they would provide Stevie with some Charles-style sunglasses and see what happened. The big difference with this effort, of course, would be that Stevie actually would be allowed to sing.

What happened was, well, nothing. As with *Jazz Soul*, Gordy was dissatisfied with the results of the album that came to be known as *Tribute to Uncle Ray*. Again, he heard no single; again, the big-band sound that Paul carried over from *Jazz Soul* didn't seem to hit the nail on the head.

Still, Gordy and everyone else at Motown were more convinced than ever that Stevie was something special. Even though *Jazz Soul* and *Uncle Ray* were deemed failures, evidence abounded from those two sessions that it was just a matter of time before something clicked. Even on *Uncle Ray*, as he once again struggled against the onerous big-band backing and with material that often was ill-suited for his reedy, still-developing voice, Stevie had his moments. His version of Charles's "Hallelujah I Love Her So" was impressive, but the album's highlights may have been his renditions of the traditional folk song "Frankie and Johnny" and Charles's "Come Back Baby." In both songs, his voice finally was released from the tyranny of the lower registers and roamed free and pure.

There was yet another element working in Stevie's favor. Gordy had begun to slowly work Stevie into the lineup of live shows around Detroit featuring Motown acts. This was done carefully for several reasons, not the least of which was that Gordy lived in constant fear of somehow running afoul of the labor authorities when it came to Stevie. The boy was barred from performing in clubs; only public venues like city-owned auditoriums were appropriate. He also could not perform beyond a certain hour. In addition to those concerns, there was the obvious consideration of breaking the boy in slowly before live audiences, particularly black Detroit audiences, who could be merciless and unstinting in their condemnation of a performer who failed to impress.

Gordy soon realized he needn't have worried about Stevie. Audiences *loved* the kid. And it wasn't just because people felt sympathy because of his age and his disability, although certainly Stevie was given some latitude in those departments. No, Gordy surmised, the simple truth was that the little rascal was *good*. He was a natural on the stage, with an ability to connect immediately with the folks in the seats. Gordy decided that the kid didn't have a nervous bone in his body. Stevie loved going out there and showing them what he could do; that was something you couldn't teach a performer. And damn it all if the kid didn't always get the loudest applause. There had to be a way, Gordy mused, to channel all that charisma—for that is what it was, *charisma*—onto vinyl.

It began to dawn ever so gently on Gordy and Paul that what Stevie needed was *less* structure, not more. But that was a radical notion within a tightly harnessed operation such as Motown where spontaneity, in Gordy's view, was about as welcome as the tax collector. To Berry Gordy, there was nothing accidental or serendipitous about making a hit record. It was 1 percent talent, by his calculations, and 99 percent hard work. But he also realized after watching Stevie perform for a while that you could send the little knucklehead out there with the oldest, tiredest, most raggedy-ass song in the book and he *still* would have people up on their feet, clapping and laughing and slapping each other on the back. Gordy would stand in the wings like a sentinel and watch the kid work, trying to puzzle it out.

FINALLY, ON AUGUST 16, 1962, Motown released Stevie's first single, a tune called "I Call It Pretty Music (But the Old People Call It the Blues)," written by Clarence Paul. It was an unremarkable song, and it sank like a stone in water, prompting barely a rustle in the music world.

But there was one notable aspect to "I Call It Pretty Music." On the record label, the artist was identified as "Little Stevie Wonder." Gordy always was referring to the boy as a "wonder," and finally it struck him that the appellation would make a fine stage name. This, after toying with Stevland Morris, Little Stevland Morris, Little Stevland, Steve Morris, Little Stevie Morris, or just Little Stevie. Then, finally, it became Little Stevie Wonder, certainly one of the more inspired monikers in the annals of popular music.

The reception, or the lack thereof, to the first single was a crushing disappointment to Stevie and everyone else at Motown. But Gordy took solace in the fact that now, at least, Stevie was *out there.* At the very tender age of twelve, he was a bona fide recording artist. And, for Stevie's part, he had no doubt that there would be more records; all you had to do was ask him. Mr. Gordy—for Stevie, and all of the other young artists as well, always called him Mr. Gordy—Mr. Gordy had told him time and again that if he worked hard enough, he would be a success.

And Stevie believed him, more than anything in the world.

Ten

SHOWTIME

Can I play?

—Stevie Wonder, "Boogie On Reggae Woman"

S TEVIE STOOD IN the wings at the Regal Theater in Chicago
and listened to the audience out there, nickering.

The Marvelettes had just finished their set, and Stevie was sched-
uled to go on before Mary Wells took the stage. It was a big night, one
of the first excursions from the friendly confines of Detroit by the so-
called Motown Revue, a package show Gordy occasionally put
together. Everyone was anxious to make a splash, particularly in
Chicago, a city with a rich musical heritage by virtue of its blues
roots, its status as headquarters for recording labels such as Chess
Records, and it being the hometown of such musical greats as Jerry
Butler, Curtis Mayfield, and the Impressions. But there was another
reason why Stevie in particular was focused on taking his performance up a notch: His set was to be recorded for what Gordy hoped
would turn into a live album, one that would vividly demonstrate the
excitement his youngest artist generated.

Gordy's idea had pivotal implications for Stevie. Since the release of "I Call It Pretty Music," Gordy had put out two more singles by Little Stevie Wonder: "Waterboy" with the B side "La La La La La" in October 1962, and then, two months later, "Contract on Love" with "Sunset" on the flip side. The release of "Waterboy" barely budged an eyebrow out in the record-buying world; "Contract on Love" was only slightly more successful. But "Contract," in Gordy's view, was significant in that the record moved ever closer to capturing the essential Stevie, the one that caused so much infectious excitement whenever he played before people, be it one listener or a thousand. Stevie *rocked* on "Contract," a record that starts with rhythmic hand-claps and features a snarling and wickedly confident vocal perform-ance by Stevie with backup vocals by the Temptations. *We're getting there*, Gordy thought.

And Stevie had continued to blow the roof off any venue he played live. Since he was legally barred from playing nightclubs due to labor restrictions and contract stipulations, Stevie's opportunities to play before audiences revolved around the Motown Revue tours. Despite appearing on the same bill with supremely talented and expe-rienced performers like Wells, the Miracles, and Marvin Gaye, Stevie more often than not would steal the show.

This was a source of both amusement and consternation to Gordy and Paul. Like every other aspect of Motown, the revues were painstakingly planned out down to the last bow of the last encore, and ran on a schedule befitting a railroad. The artists were to take the stage, race through their sets, and then get off as quickly as possible so that the next act could launch into its set before the proceedings lost momentum.

Stevie, to put it mildly, didn't always follow the program. More than any other Motown artist, he fed off the emotion of the audience; he couldn't see their reaction, so he wanted to *hear* it, to *feel* it. So, despite Clarence Paul's best efforts to keep Stevie on his marks, the boy invariably would depart from his set and start probing the crowd with revival-style, call-and-response exchanges, working himself and the audience into a frenzy. His backing musicians loved the challenge of keeping pace; Stevie would exhort them to play *one* more song, *one* more chorus, *just a little bit louder,* and, of course, the audience would roar in agreement. And he would just keep riding his whip hand, pushing the band and the audience to a fevered plane, finally taking his sunglasses off and *flinging* them into the crowd, ripping his bow tie from his collar and *hurling* it out there . . .

As a result, Gordy's carefully calibrated clockwork would crumble to dust. More than once, Gordy, annoyed, would find Paul, cuff him on the shoulder, and growl, "Get him *offa* there!" And Paul dutifully would hustle onto the stage and bodily carry Stevie away from the microphone toward the wings, the way someone might fetch a calf that had wandered too far from the cattle drive, with the boy still locomotoring away on the harmonica and gesturing for the band to keep playing, all of which only brought another roar from the lathered-up audience and left them happy, cheering, and spent. God help whoever had to follow *that.*

That excitement was what Gordy hoped to capture on tape at the Regal that night in Chicago. Stevie's stage-hogging shenanigans aside, the kid undeniably was a kinetic performer who had developed a fairly polished repertoire. So they would roll the tape, take it back to Detroit, and see what developed.

Meanwhile, as he waited for his cue, Stevie's competitive juices churned. Certainly your average twelve-year-old kid would have had every reason imaginable to be at least a little nervous at such a moment; not Stevie. Part of it was that he was simply unconscious of many of the machinations that surrounded his germinating career. That they were recording his performance on this night hardly affected his approach at all. It was all about the music, the audience. He loved to perform. He knew that he had the ability to *excite* people.

Musically, he wasn't yet on a par with his idols Smokey and Marvin, and he knew it. But he would *get* there, he just *knew* it, and in the meantime he would give no quarter when it came to setting fire to the people who heard him play. Making a record tonight? Okay, *just stay outta my way.*

And so Motown Revue master of ceremonies Bill Murray intoned into the microphone: *Right about now, ladies and gentlemen, we'd like to continue with our show by introducing to you a young man that is only twelve years old, and he is considered as being a genius of our time. Ladies and gentlemen, let's you and I make him feel happy with a nice ovation as we meet and greet Little—Stevie—WON-da! How 'bout it, huh?*

Stevie took the stage and enthusiastically attacked a set of songs from *The Jazz Soul of Little Stevie* and *Tribute to Uncle Ray.* He battered the bongos on "Soul Bongos" and got the audience working on "Don't You Know" (*Have you heard Stevie Wonder's in town?*). But Stevie saved the best for last. His finale was "Fingertips," and it was a performance that would make him a star.

Congas and handclaps kick off the song. Then Stevie throws a *yeah-yeah* at the audience, which picks up the beat and begins to stir. Almost conversationally, Stevie tells the crowd that the song is "Fingertips," and pleads for them to clap along—they do—and then the youngster, already gyrating and wobbling like a top, begins to unleash:

*Stomp your feet
Jump up and down and do anything that you WANNA do!*

A squeal from the crowd, the drums avalanche in, and Stevie starts goosing the harmonica, playing a wandering little intro for a few bars; then, just as he whinnies the harmonica way up high, the horns and the rest of the band blast into the song, and instantly every-thing is working full-tilt, Stevie see-sawing back and forth on the harp, repeatedly building up to a crescendo and then backing down again into a galloping solo. It's a frighteningly well-oiled machine, with Stevie gliding along on the harp as the band rolls merrily behind him. The intensity builds, and suddenly Stevie interjects a *yeah* that brings another squeal from the crowd—but Stevie and the band keep cooking. Things are *steaming* now, Stevie playing inexhaustibly, alter-nately with just the drums and then the full band again, kicking the song into yet a higher gear . . . it is now fully three minutes and thirty seconds into the song and abruptly everything careens to a halt—

A call-and-response, more *yeahs*. The audience is frothing. Then, wickedly, Stevie bites off a last *yeah,* as if he doesn't have *time* for it, because he knows he's supposed to wrap it up now, but he's off and blistering on the harmonica again, *pulverizing* it, only to once again stop on a dime—

And the noise swells up from the crowd again and everything kicks in anew, Stevie's harp, drums, horns, everything bleating and taunting—then the band downshifts to a stop again, clearly cuing Ste-vie to WRAP UP—but the kid is having none of it, keeps going, juic-ing the harp, the hall clapping and rocking, he won't quit—so the band charges back into the theme, sewing it up for surely the last time and putting on the brakes—

But—

Stevie is still operating at warp speed, threatening the audience with yet another chorus, and then from the blue he mockingly peels off a "Mary Had A Little Lamb" riff, eliciting guffaws from the crowd. Seeing its opening, the band rushes in with a big finale, no doubt feeling fortunate to have locked down "Fingertips" at no less than five and a half minutes. The crowd cheers lustily as Paul leads Stevie away and the band launches into a jaunty, home-free exit theme.

Emcee Bill Murray reappears and bellows, *Take a bow, Stevie!*

A mistake (or a blessing)—because Stevie breaks from Paul's grip and commandeers the mike yet again, like a Marine retaking some embattled hill, and starts playing the harp again, sizzling—and the crowd *loves* it—

Mayhem ensues. The band is clearly befuddled. What to do? Let him keep going by himself? Jump back in? *We gotta jump back in.* Gordy's cardinal rule for live performances was, in the event of disaster, *keep playing no matter what.* Mary Wells's bass player is already on stage for the next set, plugged in, and caught in the crosshairs—*What key? What key?* he asks, audibly—and finally the band gains a toehold and gallantly reenters the fray, the crowd responds with one voice, and the entire place is on *fire.*

Stevie, in a near-manic state, exhorts the band to "swing it" once more—and they oblige, piling on yet again, more inspired than ever, molten lava–hot; who cares anymore, hell, let's just *play,* son—

And Murray wrestles the mike away from the little troublemaker, Paul regains his grip on the boy—*How 'bout it, huh? Let's hear it, everybody, for Little Stevie Wonder!*—and Stevie at last acquiesces and is led away, a megawatt aren't-I-naughty grin shooting off sparks, the crowd aswirl, and the whole glorious, weaving, cartwheeling seven-minute circus of a song finally clanks and clatters and collapses in a heap, may it rest in peace and live forever.

BERRY GORDY WAS, above all, a formula man. He knew what made hit singles: sweet, taut, punchy songs so lovingly produced that they glistened, songs that told a story that people could relate to. But while Gordy could be unrelenting about what he wanted in a record, no one ever accused him of looking a gift horse in the mouth. Sometimes unfiltered talent was its own best testament, and Gordy took pride in his ability to pluck a pearl from a clamshell. Wasn't that how he discovered Mary Wells? Hadn't she tugged on his sleeve on the packed floor of the

20 Grand in Detroit, accosting him as he was making his way from directing a set by Marv Johnson to direct a set by the Miracles on the other side of the club? Didn't he tell her he didn't really have time to listen to the song she had written, but if she wanted, she could sing it right then as she followed him through the shrieking crowd? And didn't he stop dead in his tracks when he heard her sing, despite the din?

You know you took my heart
And you broke it apart
Why did love, baby, ever have to start?
You know you took my love, threw it away
You're gonna want my love someday.
Well, bye, bye, baby . . .

That was how he discovered Mary Wells . . . Yes, he liked things his way. But sometimes things just happened free-form, on the natural, and there was nothing you could do but stand aside.

And so it was to Gordy's immense credit that he saw the silver lining in the hodgepodge dog's breakfast that was Stevie's performance of "Fingertips" recorded at the Regal. It was wild and reckless and powerful and unrepentantly undisciplined, with Stevie playing masterfully and with total abandon, the audience responding in kind. You could hear that *something was going on.* Again, Gordy marveled at the boy's precocious skill and enthusiasm. At last, he felt that he had captured what made the kid such an affecting entertainer. And yet this was no single, as Gordy saw it. It was seven minutes long, too long for one side of a 45; it would have to be cut. There were no lyrics per se—just Stevie's fevered harp and his exhortations of the crowd. And there was the rickety finale, with everything going hilariously wrong. What would people make of all that? It would have to be cut.

But Gordy kept rolling the tape, again and again. The backing band was in fine form, and Gordy could only laugh every time he heard the ramshackle confusion at the end when Stevie may as well have set off a string of firecrackers in the midst of the stage. If you listened carefully enough, you could actually hear Mary Wells's bass player curse as he fumbled around, calling for help from the other band members. It was one terrific, crazy, idiosyncratic recording.

Finally, Gordy made a decision that went against every by-the-numbers instinct that he possessed. The live version of "Fingertips" would be released as a single, warts and all of it, with the song spilling over both sides of the record. Side one—"Fingertips—Pt 1" on the record label—essentially was the body of the song, while "Fingertips—Pt 2" on the flip side contained the encore that wouldn't die. With this move, Gordy not only suppressed his beliefs in the omniscience of the mixing board, but released a live recording at a time when such performances simply weren't marketed as singles.

Stevie was thrilled with the decision. He loved the cut, loved the way it sounded, loved the way the very molecules on the record seemed to vibrate with the joy of performer connecting with audience. He felt *excitement* when he heard it. To actually be able to hear for himself, away from the stage, the way in which people responded to him only heightened his confidence and his resolve. His budding commercial instincts told him that the live "Fingertips" was a knockout, and he told Gordy as much.

The record was released on May 21, 1963, a few weeks after Stevie celebrated his thirteenth birthday. Ten days later, Motown put out a live album—*Little Stevie Wonder: The 12 Year Old Genius*—culled from Stevie's set at the Regal, which contained the uninterrupted version of "Fingertips."

What happened next was one of those developments that makes record industry executives contemplate other careers, or at least consider taking an ax to the marketing budget, because who, really, can anticipate the desires of the record-buying public? "Fingertips—Pt 2," the B side with its effervescent anarchy and utter lack of structure, became a sensation. It introduced to the world a fresh and audacious new talent, this little black blind kid from the ghetto fronting a crack band and driving a packed house wild, swinging from the heels and kicking *ass*. It was great R&B, but it also was fabulous rock and roll. That summer, people listening to "Fingertips—Pt 2" on their radios felt what the audience in the Regal Theater felt that night: wonderful.

"Fingertips—Pt 2" went to number 1 on the pop charts, the first live recording in history to hit the top spot. In a matter of weeks, Little Stevie Wonder went from being a Motown "project" to one of the hottest acts in America.

BUT STEVIE STILL was just a kid, as his behavior around the Motown studios suggested. He was a relentless prankster, especially in his first year or so there, filling the downtime that inevitably is a part of the recording process by romping around and generally being the preteen that he was.

He was an uncanny mimic. The same facile quality of voice that Stevie used so nimbly in the studio also was a lethal weapon when he turned its force on imitating someone. He quickly developed a stinging impression of Gordy that he was always happy to unveil as long as his audience didn't include Gordy himself.

One afternoon at Motown, Stevie was entertaining a small circle on the front lawn with his best, overdrawn Berry Gordy:

If you make a mistake, I don't care, go with it! As far as I'm concerned, there are no mistakes. If the mike falls on the stage, you fall with it, and you sing right there on the ground like it was *planned* like that . . .

Everyone but Stevie in the group could see Gordy walking up from behind. Stevie was on a roll:

And another thing: That song you wrote is *gabbage*—

At which point Gordy intoned: And so is your impression of me, Stevie.

Everyone had a big laugh, Stevie included. Not that it dissuaded him from further mimicry. Stevie was fascinated with the network of phones in place at Motown, which provided him with a prime venue for mischief. He memorized all the intercom numbers and buzzed various offices at random, frequently imitating Gordy himself. He was particularly successful in fooling the business staff, convincing them on at least three different occasions that he was Gordy, instructing them to order a special tape machine for "that great young artist, Stevie Wonder." Stevie, who later in his career would become a technological wizard and would make groundbreaking use of the Clavinet and the Moog synthesizer, was fascinated by gadgets and studio equipment and coveted the tape machines the way another kid might ache for a new bike. Gordy finally gave Stevie a tape machine for Christmas, and he was ecstatic.

On another occasion, not long after Stevie had signed with Motown, he and a young friend were snooping around in a storage room and stumbled across some two-track tapes. One was a master of "Shop Around," not yet released. Stevie and his buddy promptly stole the tape, accidentally tearing it up in the process. Not long afterward, the tape was missed and a search was launched; Stevie was asked several times if he knew anything about it. He kept mum, terrified that he would lose his contract. The experience made an impression. He made a point to leave well enough alone from then on.

But Stevie continued to be the master of the put-on at Motown, often using his blindness as a prop. Knowing when he was being watched, he would pretend to stumble and fall, only to laugh when the concerned onlooker rushed over to help. He would ask someone to describe what a certain person was wearing, and then would proceed to lavish praise on that person about her dress or his suit, as if he could suddenly see. Dionne Warwick may have been the most successful brunt of this particular routine. Backstage one evening, the Shirelles saw Warwick in a bright red dress that the group didn't especially care for, and decided to recruit Stevie, always a willing accomplice, to their cause.

Stevie always knew Warwick by her perfume (Shalimar). When she approached the boy that evening, he recoiled as if struck by lightning. It's that awful red dress, he told her. Warwick, shaken, took the dress off and never wore it again, although it cost her a hefty $3.98. Only years later did the Shirelles confess their conspiracy to Warwick.

Stevie also developed a huge schoolboy crush on the older Diana Ross, then still called Diane. It was the voice; he loved to hear her sing, and he loved to hear her talk. Love-stricken, he would listen to the Supremes' "Time Changes Things" over and over, simmering in heartache.

MOTOWN WAS A fantasy world for Stevie. He loved everything about it: the toy-shop array of musical instruments upon which he was free to experiment to his heart's desire; the constant emphasis on performing, both in the studio and onstage; the relationships he formed with the artists and other personnel at Motown, who embraced him and treated him as both a prodigy and a kid brother. He felt very much at home in the growing complex on West Grand Boulevard, and had it been up to him he would have spent every waking hour there.

But it wasn't up to him. There was the matter of his education, which became a significant issue for Stevie and Motown, particularly after the success of "Fingertips." Suddenly, Stevie was in much demand, and Gordy wanted to put the kid out on the road whenever possible with the Motown Revue, fast becoming one of the most popular touring shows in the music business. All of which was fine with Stevie; what kid wouldn't choose the mystery and excitement of touring the country as a professional musician over the relative drudgery of school?

The situation presented a mini-crisis for Lula, who wrestled with the same conflict that had haunted her from the beginning of Stevie's flirtation with Motown. On one hand, she wanted nothing but happiness and success for her gifted son. During that summer of 1963, as "Fingertips—Pt 2" scaled the charts and, it seemed, poured forth from every radio on the planet—she could walk down her street toward the bus stop past her neighbors' houses, the windows flung open, and "Fingertips" would come on WCBH or WNRL (they played it almost constantly), and the entire block would fill with the sound of Stevie at the Regal, Little Stevie Wonder in neighborhood surround sound. It was thrilling, and suddenly she found that she was a bit of a local celebrity, too. Her life went on more or less as it had before—she had always been Stevie's mama, anyway, the way the kid got around and always lit up the sky—though certainly the extra stipend from Motown helped with the household budget, made her life considerably easier. They had a refrigerator now, an incomprehensible luxury just a year earlier. She also was in a new relationship with a gentleman she cared for very much. Most of all, she saw how much it all meant to Stevie. The kid was in the clouds. She had never seen him happier. It seemed clear that he was meant to be a musician, just like everybody always thought, even though the sheer scope of his success that came so quickly—C'mon, a *number 1* record at thirteen? Number 1 in the *country*?—was mind-boggling. It seemed like it all had happened so fast.

And yet, Stevie still was just a boy, and she worried about him throwing himself so completely into Motown. What if it didn't work out? She figured that if things went south, if there weren't more hits, Gordy could just as easily drop him like a sack of rotten potatoes. How would Stevie react to that? Would he always be tortured by his brush with the world of professional music? Lula was the first to admit she didn't know much, but she knew enough to realize that there were no guarantees in show business. She had heard the stories of all the washed-up has-beens, broke and forgotten.

There also was the matter of her fear that Motown would take her son away from her, that she would somehow lose him. She certainly was beginning to see that happen, even now. When school was in session, Stevie would spend every afternoon at the studio. That wasn't just what Stevie wanted—that was what Gordy demanded. They constantly worked with the boy, adding polish, trying out new songs, searching for something that sounded like a hit. Stevie ate it up like ice cream, but Lula worried that he was becoming detached from his home life. In the summer, Stevie would be gone for weeks at a time with the Revue. Lula accompanied him on some of these trips, but she had her other children to raise, too. It wasn't that she worried for Stevie's needs when he was away; the Motown entourage was chaperoned to the hilt (Gordy, who insisted on exemplary behavior, saw to that), and the other artists and Motown people on tour watched over the boy like hawks. And the rock and roll road in those days was a far cry from the debauchery and excess that came to be its calling card in later years. In any event, Gordy wouldn't have stood for it, and she knew it. Her concern was rooted in the simple separation anxiety that one would expect any mother to have, especially involving a child blind from birth who, despite his very acute independent streak, had always depended on her mightily.

And then there was the matter of school. It would become more difficult for Stevie to attend his classes regularly as opportunities for out-of-town performances arose, and as he hit the charts and became well known in Detroit, there were stirrings at the board of education regarding his schooling.

Part of it was Judkins, who, in Lula's view, was upset that he was not allowed to share fully in his son's success (translation: money). So Judkins—certainly in part from genuine concern, certainly in part from spite—made a complaint to the board that Stevie was neglecting his schooling, which Lula says resulted in the board giving her a stern warning as the 1962–63 school year came to a close: If there was no education, there was to be no performing. It was within the board's legal authority to keep Stevie in school, and officials told Lula in no uncertain terms that they were perfectly willing to exercise that authority. The message was clear: Unless some acceptable arrangement could be worked out, Stevie's career would be put on hold.

Stevie was devastated by the development. He had attended the school board meeting, and when the decision was announced, he began to cry. He then went into the bathroom and fervently prayed that God would find a way to allow him to continue at Motown.

Complicating things was that Stevie was, indeed, having trouble at the Fitzgerald School for the Blind. The demands of his career made it more difficult for him to keep up with all of his studies; that was indisputable. And because he was an absolute anomaly—that is to say, a blind ghetto youngster who also was a professional musician— Stevie received conflicting responses from his peers. Even before "Fingertips," when he would occasionally get some radio play in Detroit with "Contract on Love," Stevie would be virtually mobbed by starstruck schoolmates; others taunted him and wanted to fight. Some of the kids called him "Stevie Wonders," which he found hurtful. One bully, one of the big kids, picked a fight with Stevie—and promptly was shoved down a flight of stairs for his trouble. Eventually, however, Stevie's relations with his classmates modulated as they realized he wasn't conceited about his seedling career and wasn't willing to be pushed around.

Yet Stevie's most daunting obstacle at school came, oddly enough, from his teachers. Very conservative and suspicious of the "street music" with which he had aligned himself, many of his instructors aggressively lobbied him to stop dabbling with Motown and apply all his attention to his education.

One teacher was particularly blunt:

You should just forget about that old music, she told Stevie one day. You need to face facts. You've got three strikes against you—

you're poor, you're black, and you're blind. You will *never make it* against those odds. You need to put that music aside and buckle down to your studies. Because if you are an uneducated black and blind man, the only thing you'll be able to do with your life is make rugs and potholders!

All this was enormously painful to Stevie. The boy knew enough to realize that the teacher didn't understand what he was about, didn't understand how important his music was to him—but that didn't make her scare tactics any easier to digest. The conflict with his teachers only served to make him feel even more alienated from school, and to gravitate more than ever to the friendly confines of Motown.

As timing would have it, Stevie's troubles with the school board came at the close of the academic year, which meant that Lula and Motown had until the fall to come up with a solution. After some brainstorming, Lula placed an ad in the newspaper soliciting suggestions from educators about ways to resolve the situation. A woman who taught at another blind school in the area responded and put Lula in touch with the headmaster at the Michigan School for the Blind. An arrangement was worked out by which Stevie would be required to spend at least two weeks each month at the school, and then would be tutored two hours a day on the road by a private teacher named Ted Hull, recruited after a nationwide search by Motown. With the help of some intensive lobbying by Gordy, the school board signed off on the plan. Stevie would essentially be home-schooled.

Stevie was free to pursue his career, and—now that he had been largely spared from the time-consuming, comparatively boring daily routine of traditional school—he pursued that career with a vengeance. But changes were on the way, along with an unexpected creative dry spell that would jeopardize Stevie's future in the business. Little Stevie Wonder wasn't long for this world; the question was, who would Stevie Wonder be?

Eleven

UPTIGHT

Mama, they're not playing my record on the radio anymore.
—Stevie to Lula, 1965

*B*ERRY GORDY HAD a knack for finding ways to control a great many things—Motown's recording sessions, his artists, his artists' contracts—but there was at least one aspect of the career of Little Stevie Wonder that he was powerless to manipulate: the onset of puberty.

That Stevie's voice would change was inevitable, of course, and Gordy and everyone else at Motown had resigned themselves to this particular fact of life with the requisite amount of dread. Who knew how the change would go? The youngster's pipes might mature into a richer, more powerful version of the singing voice that served him so well as a fledgling star, or it might break off into some inferior facsimile that could grind his career to a halt. All anyone could do was wait and see.

After the success of "Fingertips—Pt 2," and the album *The 12*

Year Old Genius (which also hit number 1 on the pop charts), the next single by Stevie was "Workout Stevie, Workout," with the B side "Monkey Talk." "Workout Stevie, Workout" featured a fine vocal performance by Stevie and some trademark harp play. It was a great-sounding record, and hopes were high. The single was released in September 1963 and peaked at number 33 on the pop charts, a far cry from the top but, in Gordy's view, hardly a disaster. Gordy, always looking at the big picture, also found solace in the realization that, at long last, the spark so evident when Stevie was onstage finally had been replicated in the Motown studios.

"Workout Stevie, Workout" would be the last Stevie Wonder record released before his voice started to crackle and delve. By the time Stevie appeared in the studio in late 1963 to record his fourth album, a collection of ballads to be entitled *With a Song in My Heart*, Clarence Paul found that the timbre of the thirteen-year-old's voice was plummeting rapidly and discovered that the youngster's voice had changed so much that he was unable to sing the songs in the register in which the backing vocals had been recorded. Paul, chagrined, was forced to start again from scratch.

As it turned out, Paul and Motown could have saved themselves the trouble. *With a Song in My Heart* was a misadventure from the start. As many critics and music historians have since noted, the material through which Stevie was forced to hack on this album was tortuous at best. After spending nearly three years and no small amount of money to position Stevie as an incendiary rock 'n' soul lightning bolt from the ghetto, the minds at Motown elected to have their young sensation grapple with a ponderous array of songs that included "When You Wish Upon A Star," "Make Someone Happy," and "Put On a Happy Face." The only thing missing was Pat Boone and a glass of milk. The record was a spectacular disappointment after the splash made by *The 12 Year Old Genius* and went nowhere—and deservedly so.

(Still, there may have been some sort of Gordy logic at work here. Stevie wasn't the only Motown act forced to perform moldy standards and Disney songs; the Supremes and others, for a while, were under similar orders. Gordy may have been trying to position his artists for larger venues with more conservative audiences.)

Even at thirteen, Stevie realized that the material was horrendously off-target, even though he undertook the *Song in My Heart* sessions with his customary exuberance. Despite his blindness—or perhaps because of it—Stevie had exhibited a pronounced independent streak his entire life. It came as no surprise to anyone who knew him at all that his well-developed sense of self would come very much into play as he evolved as a musical artist.

But there were only inklings of that now. The challenge of the moment was to weather the voice change that had asserted itself at a crucial moment in Stevie's career, that all-important transition from one-hit wonder to certified star. In concert, Stevie disguised his vocal problems on the difficult ballads by singing duets with Paul.

Despite his struggles with his voice and material, Stevie continued to mature as a performer, and more than held his own against his more seasoned contemporaries. One evening in particular placed this reality in sharp relief: the infamous "battle" between Stevie and the great Marvin Gaye at the Graystone Ballroom in Detroit.

By 1963 Gordy had purchased the Graystone, one of the focal points of the Detroit music scene. The place had a powerful resonance for Gordy on several levels. His purchase of the venue not only marked his emerging prowess as a businessman, but also settled a private score. When Gordy was growing up, black patrons were allowed in the ballroom on Monday nights only—as was the case at all white-owned ballrooms in the city. So his ownership of the place was more than just a tangible testament to his own personal advancement; it spoke to the cultural changes beginning to take hold in Detroit and across the country. Gordy's decision to buy the ballroom also served as a powerful symbol to black Detroiters because it halted what had been a systematic demolition of traditional black cultural centers in the city. The New Bethel Baptist Church, pastored by the highly influential Reverend C. L. Franklin (father of singer Aretha Franklin), had been torn down. By the 1960s, most of the clubs and other places of business owned by African Americans in the Black Bottom and Paradise Valley neighborhoods were gone via city edict. The Chrysler Freeway, which began construction in 1960, obliterated Hastings Street, which was the lifeline of black nightlife in the city, with establishments such as Henry's Swing Club, which had given rise to performers such as bluesman John Lee Hooker.

So Gordy's salvaging of the Graystone—he even valiantly resisted attempts to change its name—stood as an anchor against the erosion of black culture in Detroit. Gordy also understood its value as a marketing tool to showcase Motown artists. In June 1963, just a few weeks after Gordy's purchase went through and not long after the release of "Fingertips—Pt 2," Gordy's first concert in the ballroom featured Little Stevie Wonder. The event drew seven thousand, was gauged a great success, and not only showed people that downtown Detroit was a viable entertainment alternative for black audiences, but also reaffirmed Gordy's conviction that he had found a highly effective way to increase the local visibility of his performers.

One of his marketing methods involved various "battles of the stars" at the Graystone. He had always been intrigued by the long-standing gimmick of a "battle of the bands," where musical groups would take turns performing songs and a winner was gauged according to audience response. Now that he had the Graystone, where patrons showed up to dance to the latest records, he began to occasionally promote "battle of the stars" nights, during which artists would square off during breaks in the music.

The battles were instant sellouts. Some of the matchups included the Temptations vs. the Contours, the Supremes vs. the Velvelettes, and Martha and the Vandellas vs. the Marvelettes. Everyone embraced the concept and fun was had by all—until the night Little Stevie Wonder was pitted against the silky Marvin Gaye.

By then Gaye, who was Gordy's brother-in-law, had become an established star. His most recent hit had been "Pride and Joy," a Gaye classic. Stevie by then had the considerable "Fingertips—Pt 2" in his pocket. Even so, Gordy figured that Gaye would easily be the crowd favorite that evening, simply because of his hits, his polish as a performer, and his immense popularity as a sex symbol with his female fans.

But Stevie, ever competitive, wasn't conceding anything. He was up first and came out blowing fire, unleashing a fervid version of "Workout Stevie, Workout." Gordy watched the house respond with a roar, and decided that Gaye might be in for a tougher time than he first believed.

But Gaye answered with a stirring rendition of "Hitch Hike," shimmying like a tornado and driving the ladies wild. On the third verse, he surprised the crowd by playing a hot interlude on a Melodica, an oversized harmonica that powered a keyboard. Gaye had practiced endlessly on the instrument for just this occasion, figuring it would inoculate him against Stevie's harmonica pyrotechnics. The audience lustily cheered its approval.

Stevie then countered with his first single, "I Call It Pretty Music (But the Old People Call It the Blues)," and the crowd swayed along. At song's end, however, he sent an electrical bolt through the hall with an exultant *Everybody say yeah!* that sent the place into an instant delirium, as everyone recognized the now-famous exhortation from "Fingertips—Pt 2." Stevie then proceeded to virtually run the table with his "Fingertips" shtick, leaving the crowd nearly spent with his blue-streak harp play.

Gaye had one more shot left and was determined to carry the day.

He sprang back onstage as the band struck up "Stubborn Kind of Fellow" but, amazingly, was greeted not only by the screams he expected from the ladies but also by *boos*. Confusion showed on his face, but he gamely jumped into the song, determined to turn the tide. Some from the audience yelled, Marvin, you ought to be ashamed, taking advantage of a little blind kid! The singer ignored it and pressed on. At the conclusion of the number, the boos rained even harder. Gaye clearly was hurt but motioned for the band to play "Pride and Joy." Still the boos came, and Gordy quickly decided to intervene, taking the stage and the mike from Gaye and announcing that the show was over.

Gordy caught up with Gaye backstage, who had his head in his hands. Enormously sensitive and ambivalent about performing anyway, Gaye was crushed by the nasty turn the crowd had taken. Stevie, who had, as usual, been enjoying himself to the hilt, also was perplexed and concerned about Gaye, whom he idolized.

Gordy was a firm believer in competition; he had no doubt that it fueled the success of Motown. But he also realized that he had erred in pitting his artists in direct confrontation with each other, even if it was meant to be all in fun, especially when one of the contestants was an immensely talented blind kid who elicited instant sympathy from the audience.

There were no more "battles of the stars" at the Graystone.

IN 1964, Gordy decided it was time for Stevie and his family to move out of the house on Breckenridge to a home more befitting one of his rising stars. It wasn't anything Gordy had to do, but Stevie had begun to finally turn a profit for Motown; it was the *right* thing to do. It also was no longer appropriate for the press and, for that matter, the neighbors to see Motown's Little Stevie Wonder living on a street for which "modest" was a very gracious description.

No, Motown was moving up in style—and it wouldn't do for one of its premier artists to live in a shabby, disadvantaged neighborhood.

And so Gordy purchased a home along Greenlawn Avenue on Detroit's northwest side, between Six Mile Road and Seven Mile Road, one of the city's classier neighborhoods, for $18,000—a nice, healthy sum at the time. The house had four large bedrooms, spacious hallways, an upstairs, a nice big yard. The neighborhood was almost totally white; when Lula's brood moved in, they became only the third black family in Greenlawn.

Lula was shocked and thrilled when Gordy surprised her with the news about her new home. To move into a spacious home on the sunny side of town was, to her, nothing short of rapture on Earth. If she had been dream-stricken the first time she had walked through the house on Breckenridge, she virtually levitated as she entered the foyer—the *foyer!*—at Greenlawn.

And the truth was, she needed the room. Her brood was growing. In addition to Milton, Calvin, and Stevie, there now was Larry, Timothy, and Renee, blessings all. And there was Timothy and Renee's father, Paul Lynch, Lula's second husband with whom she would have a long-standing but ultimately unsuccessful relationship.

So the big house came in handy. Lula couldn't remember when she had been happier. It was all too much to comprehend, really, when she tried to take it all in, everything that had happened—and so *fast.* Finally, she simply decided that yet another prayer had been answered.

And then she set about the work of queen of the manor, and the maid of the manor as well. She didn't mind; in fact, she didn't let a speck of dust hit the floor for a solid year.

STEVIE WAS SPENDING increasing amounts of time on tour with the Motown Revue and was becoming a seasoned road warrior. His presence on the concert circuit was a calculated effort by Motown to increase the sales of his records, which had flagged in the aftermath of *12 Year Old Genius.* His changing voice was a factor, as was the material Motown foisted upon him. His future in the business was by no means assured, and, as 1963 turned into 1964, there was increased pressure on the boy to find a way to jump-start a career that suddenly seemed moribund. His concert appearances were smashing successes—he never failed to please the paying customers—but his popularity onstage wasn't translating into more airplay and more sales. That reality led in turn to more desperate measures by Gordy, including what must stand as the strangest and most incongruous chapter of Stevie's career: the mercifully brief attempt to insinuate Stevie as a member of the California surfin', Jan-and-Dean crowd.

In January 1964, a beach-music single (with surf sound effects and all) called "Castles in the Sand" was released, with "Thank You (For Loving Me All the Way)," the first single he had ever recorded, as the B side. After reaching number 52 on the *Billboard* pop chart (there was no R&B singles chart from November 1963 until January 1965), "Castles in the Sand" quickly melted into the sea. That record was notable, however, as the last time Stevie would be identified on a record label as Little Stevie Wonder. It was time for the change; not only was Stevie's voice struggling for its adult range, but he was growing like a weed. He was beginning to develop that unmistakable gangling teenage physique now, no longer the precocious punk kid whose head everyone liked to rub.

A single called "Hey Harmonica Man," issued shortly after Stevie's fourteenth birthday in May 1964, did reach number 29. But the album from whence it came, *Stevie at the Beach*—released in June 1964 at the apex of the surf-music craze—failed to crack the Hot 100. Stevie's swing at beach-rock came as Gordy arranged for his appearance in two beach movies produced by the legendary B-movie studio American International Pictures, *Muscle Beach Party* and *Bikini*

Beach, both starring Annette Funicello and Frankie Avalon. Stevie performs at the end of both movies and acquits himself honorably enough, although it doesn't take much imagination to envision the thought bubble over his head as he bops about with an assortment of Hollywood-issue beach hunks and bunnies: *What am I doing here?*

Not that Stevie didn't enjoy Los Angeles. The weather was a revelation, people were friendly, and there was a great vibe, he felt, on the West Coast. It certainly was a thrill to be in the movies. But even Stevie was attuned to the fact that it didn't seem to make much sense to interject an urban black kid with an R&B background from the industrial Midwest into a vapid Hollywood beach movie populated by characters who could not be more distantly removed from what he was about. The entire experience gave rise to that very question: What, exactly, *was* he about? It was a common question for any increasingly introspective teenager, particularly one who spent most of his time around people twice his age and had already begun to travel the world. Stevie was beginning to absorb some of the socially aware music of the era, especially Bob Dylan, who seemed to be releasing beautiful, caustic, cutting-edge albums every six months.

Stevie also was absorbing the 1960s on his own as he traveled from city to city and stage to stage, from New York to the Deep South to overseas locales such as London and Paris. As he received an education about what it was like to be a traveling musician, he also received his schooling in what it meant to be black in America. In Birmingham, after a concert at a ballpark before a racially mixed crowd, a shot was fired into the tour bus—missing the gas tank by inches. On another occasion, a member of the Four Tops fired a pistol at a white man attempting to steal suitcases from the tour bus. On yet another occasion, in Macon, Georgia, the entourage arrived to find a huge rebel flag as a backdrop for the stage where they were to perform. A Motown representative told the venue manager that the flag would have to come down; the manager suggested that the rep might be hung from a tree if he kept complaining. Although his tutor and the rest of the Motown entourage tried to shield him from as many of the crude insults as they could, there was no protecting Stevie from the knowledge that hotels often "lost" reservations when they discovered that the performers were black, that often meals from restaurants had to be taken out the kitchen door. Stevie still was a youngster and still developing his political consciousness; the usual approach by the Motown entourage was to try to defuse the tension of such situations with dismissive humor. But when fellow performers like Marvin Gaye spoke bitterly of the inequities suffered by blacks and of dubious causes like the war in Vietnam, Stevie listened and absorbed.

But the road also was a curative for Stevie during a time when things in the recording studio seemed frustrating and at loggerheads. He was especially fond of Martha Reeves and Junior Walker, who regarded Stevie as their protégé and spent much time with him. Reeves taught Stevie all the latest dance steps, which Stevie learned quickly and unveiled in front of unsuspecting audiences. He and Reeves also would sit up late and experiment with songs and make tapes, a pursuit that Stevie loved and at which he could outlast anyone. It was on these first tours, with unceasing overnight travel that exhausted the adults (in 1964, the Motown Revue did no fewer than ninety one-night stands, in addition to other, more extended engagements) that Stevie learned to operate with little or no sleep, his rest patterns directed less by a setting sun that he couldn't detect than by his own energy reserve. Walker was among those on the bus who were always willing to listen in the middle of the night, when Stevie would prod him awake to listen to an idea for a song or a new harmonica riff.

Stevie felt a special connection with Walker, whose classic, organ-infused hit "Shotgun" was always a favorite at Motown shows. He could always pick Walker's voice from a crowd—I know the Roadrunner's in here somewhere . . . There's that old Junior Walker boy!

That old "Shotgun" boy! Walker, in turn, would tease Stevie about having to stay in his hotel room to do homework, stopping by to see the boy on his way out to a night on the town. He would tease Stevie about girls, about his tutor—in short, about *everything*. It was all part of the constant wordplay and gamesmanship that help people cope with the discomfort of being thrown together in close quarters for weeks at a time, and Stevie relished the attention. As Stevie and the other members of the Motown Revue got to know each other as only road companions do, the kid was hardly ever viewed as having a handicap. His coping instincts were a constant source of amazement to others. Backstage at some gargantuan hall like the Apollo in New York, it seemed as though it took only a few minutes for Stevie to learn his way around; soon he would be dashing up and down stairwells and generally having the run of the place, just like any sighted person.

Stevie was a high-spirited and happy-go-lucky presence on the road, his demeanor giving little indication of the professional pressures he was experiencing. In addition to carrying his share of the performing load on the road, Stevie faced the additional responsibility of his academic studies. Hull, the tutor who also essentially functioned as a personal manager until Stevie was nineteen, took his duties seriously. "School" for Stevie on tour would begin at about 10 A.M. each day, since the Revue usually would have been up until the wee hours the previous evening. About four hours each day was spent on Stevie's studies. Like any kid, Stevie would complain and try to wriggle out of his study time, or sometimes feign fatigue or illness (this after keeping the bus awake most of the night). But Hull was firm, and Stevie usually was cooperative.

When Stevie was back home in Detroit, Hull took special care to make sure that he attended school as much as possible, even though the agreement with the school board required Stevie to attend class only an average of two weeks out of every four. While the truth was that, academically, Stevie probably was far ahead of most of his classmates due to the intensive individual attention he was receiving, everyone realized that he needed social interaction with his peers. Of course, Stevie wasn't a typical student, and everyone knew it; he was constantly being solicited by other students to listen to a piece of music on one instrument or another, or to hear a song by a classmate who might have designs on being another Little Stevie Wonder. Stevie always listened patiently, offering advice and suggestions. As a rule, Stevie was less rambunctious at school than he was in the more familiar surroundings of Motown or the road, and was considered polite and religious by teachers and classmates.

The blind school had wonderful facilities and programs, and Stevie sampled as many as he could in his limited time there. He was on the wrestling team for a while, and ran track; he participated in swimming, boating, and skating activities. And, of course, music. While his extended absences reduced his ability to have a meaningful role in most aspects of school life, predictably he was always welcomed with open arms by the school choir. He sang tenor and almost always was featured in the choir's Christmas program; one year he gave a solo rendition of "White Christmas."

Hull also monitored Stevie's schedule in Detroit, often playing the role of the heavy when it came to calling an end to Stevie's day. Stevie had more energy than ten people and seemed to need less sleep than anyone on earth; still Hull—by his own lights but also with Lula's urging—insisted that Stevie leave the recording studio no later than eight o'clock each evening. There were exceptions, especially if some production deadline was approaching, but generally Hull succeeded in preventing Stevie from being totally sucked into the great Motown maw.

THE DREAM STARTED to haunt Lula shortly after Stevie's fifteenth birthday. She never mentioned it to Stevie or anyone else. What good would that do? It would just be dismissed as more of Mama's worrying. But she couldn't shake it; the images kept coming back to her as she slept, shaking her to her core. She might go months without The Dream, and she would begin to believe with a growing sense of relief that it was gone for good. But it would always return, the very same dream with few variations, a vivid and wrenching terror.

The Dream would begin with Stevie as a little boy. In the dream, he can see, and the knowledge of that gives Lula a sensation of joy. Stevie has a tricycle, a top-of-the-line model, luminously painted in bright hues, streamers flowing from the handlebars. It was the kind of tricycle Lula never could have afforded when Stevie was very young. He pedals furiously around the neighborhood and is doing well enough; but Lula hovers constantly over him, runs after him, never lets him from her sight.

Then The Dream shifts through some vague transition and suddenly it seems as though it is the future, and Lula realizes she is in the backseat of a speeding car. She looks out the window and sees that the vehicle is whizzing through unfamiliar terrain, a landscape that is very arid and dry, desertlike. As her surroundings become more distinct, she realizes that Stevie, now a young adult, is actually driving the car; she also realizes that, in contrast to the first part of her dream, her son is blind. Yet somehow Stevie is piloting the car, albeit in an extremely reckless manner, receiving occasional instructions from strangers seated next to him in the automobile.

In that frustrating, syrupy slow motion of dreams, Lula tries to admonish Stevie to slow down, telling him that he can't see, that he shouldn't be driving. Stevie doesn't seem to hear her at first. She continues to shout in an attempt to attract his attention, and finally he acknowledges her presence.

Mama, don't worry, he says, I know how to drive. I drive all the time. I know what I'm doing . . .

Lula continues to protest, but suddenly realizes that they no longer are in the desert but have sped into a deep woods with huge, ominous-looking trees that block out the sun. Stevie continues to drive the car at the speed of light, his front-seat companions cheering him on. Suddenly there is a terrifying, cataclysmic event. He has lost control of the car, and everyone is flung violently about as if a hurtling roller-coaster had abruptly lost its traction on the rails.

Next Lula realizes that she has regained consciousness and is standing in a clearing in the woods, an area filled with pale light. Her eyes focus and she sees that Stevie is lying prone on the ground in the middle of the clearing. He appears to be dead. He is encircled by strangers dressed in garb that looks like it is from the Middle Ages— robes and hoods and the like. She tries to run to Stevie, but her legs won't move. Finally her legs respond and she begins to move toward her son, but strangers hold her back. She struggles and struggles . . .

And then Lula would wake up, terrified. She never got beyond the stage of The Dream in which she was struggling to get next to her son.

Lula was not one to rationalize away such things. To her, The Dream was an unmistakable prophecy. Stevie was in the care of strangers who urged him to take risks and who gave him a false sense of confidence about his safety and well-being. She also recognized that The Dream was a result of a pronounced separation anxiety, although she would not have described it in such technical terms. But she believed that the nightmare was first and foremost a warning. She knew that she could not be with Stevie every moment of his life, by his side during every step of his journeys that now seemed destined to take him around the world. She had the rest of her family to take care of, a new man in her life, new children to care for. She determined that all she could do was love him to the greatest extent of her power when he was home, and pray for his safety while he was away. She would not burden Stevie or any of the others with The Dream; she would keep it locked away within, in hopes that it would dissipate under the assault of time and prayer.

• • •

BY 1965 MOTOWN had hit full stride. The Holland-Dozier-Holland songwriting and production team was on a tear, rolling out the hits that would make the Supremes and the Four Tops international sensations and Motown a very rich record company. A sampling of H-D-H songs for the Supremes during the mid-1960s included "Back in My Arms Again," "I Hear a Symphony," "My World Is Empty Without You," "You Can't Hurry Love," "Baby Love," and "Where Did Our Love Go." For the Four Tops they penned hits such as "I Can't Help Myself," "Reach Out I'll Be There," and "Standing in the Shadows of Love." The H-D-H method, however, didn't just involve writing lyrics and music and bowing out of the process. The writing team stipulated how the songs would be sung, and controlled almost every other aspect of the record-making process. Artists typically had no say. It was the H-D-H Way, or the highway. Of course, this was the Motown Way as well, and the results speak for themselves; the studio wasn't just producing hits, it was spinning out instant classics that were fabulously successful. But some artists felt that there was a case to be made that working with H-D-H was something akin to entering into a deal with the Devil. Yes, you were the recipient of hook-rich, radio-ready songs, but you also had no opportunity to develop your own identity as an artist.

Stevie, for one, had the presence of mind even as a fifteen-year-old to know that an artist who was fully involved in the creative process was an artist who held more control over his professional destiny. Stevie nurtured this belief even as his hit drought continued well into 1965. He and Clarence Paul collaborated closely on the arrangements of his material as he matured, and while that allowed Stevie to learn much about the rudiments of songwriting and producing, his records were having no impact. The single "Happy Street" was released in the fall of 1964 with the B side "Sad Boy"; it was greeted with a resolute lack of interest. Another planned single, "Pretty Little Angel," was canceled.

Gordy maintained faith in Stevie's career, but there were factions within Motown that argued that Stevie's contract not be renewed. The anti-Stevie argument: The kid was shaping up to be a one-hit Wonder. Maybe "Fingertips" was a stroke of pure luck, one of those crazy things that only the gods can explain and will never be replicated. Cut the losses now, the thinking went, and don't look back.

But Gordy held fast—in fact, the producer who had argued that Stevie and some other Motown acts be let go was fired himself. A contract binding Stevie to Motown until he was twenty-one was executed, much as before, although this without Lula's recalcitrance. Neither she nor anyone else could conceive of Stevie anywhere except in the Motown family, as imperfect as that family could be at times. In a shock to the Motown system, Mary Wells in 1964 had taken the occasion of her twenty-first birthday to disavow her contract and defect to Twentieth Century-Fox Records, claiming that Gordy wasn't doing enough for her career. But Stevie wasn't about to make such a leap; he signed the new contract, which carried terms similar to his original deal, and set about the task of resurrecting his career.

By the time Stevie was fifteen, his voice had begun to settle and Motown was thrilled with the results. His new voice still retained that purity of tone that first attracted notice five years ago, but now it was stronger, deeper, more malleable. Gordy, who had never been a total convert regarding Stevie's singing voice, now realized that Stevie's full-bodied voice was truly exceptional. The kid also was showing the benefits of what essentially had been five years of intensive music training at the "academy" of Motown. At fifteen, he was a seasoned pro, still supremely confident in his powers and willing to work harder than ever to break through again.

Gordy was extremely anxious that Stevie ring up another hit as quickly as possible. A hit record opened a huge door for an artist, but only for a very brief period of time. If you didn't keep propping that door open with more hits, it would slam closed. The listening public was fickle with a short attention span, always willing to transfer their allegiance in a heartbeat to other artists.

To buy some time—and to help the listening public adjust to the more fully developed voice of the "new" Stevie Wonder—the decision was made to put out another live record. And Gordy had just the cut: a version of "High Heel Sneakers" from a Motown Revue show in Paris that Gordy had taped in early 1965. The song had become Stevie's popular set closer on that European tour, when Stevie again had proven to be the Revue's most popular act. The recording that Gordy intended to release was in many ways quite similar to "Fingertips." At the top of the song Stevie once again exhorts "everybody to clap your hands" and tweets out a spare little harp solo until the band falls in for the rest of the way. The band was a pickup group of Parisian musicians with whom Stevie had never played, and so (again like "Fingertips") there was a very spontaneous quality to the song.

But this recording reflected a very different Stevie Wonder. With "Fingertips," Stevie had won over the Regal Theater audience and, subsequently, the record-buying public with sheer emotion and charisma, not to mention some prodigious harmonica playing. Those elements still were much in evidence on "High Heel Sneakers," but Stevie's performance was more contained, professional, and calculated. He demonstrated a new and impressive vocal range, singing in a subterranean register for much of the song; his harmonica was slicker and more sophisticated as well.

Gordy believed the record served two distinct purposes. One, it would remind listeners that Stevie Wonder still was around and remained the dynamic performing artist that had captured their attention two long years earlier. But "High Heel Sneakers" also would serve notice that Stevie now was a maturing artist who deserved reconsideration. The marketing strategy in a dozen words: If you thought Little Stevie Wonder was hot, then check *this* out.

The single was released in August 1965 and went to number 30 on the newly reinstituted *Billboard* R&B chart and to number 59 on the pop chart. Those results fell short of what Stevie and Gordy had hoped for, but the feeling was that at least the kid was back in the game despite being preceded by two singles and two albums that had failed to chart. Gordy figured the response to "High Heel Sneakers" gave them something to build on; that mercurial door was open once again.

This time, Stevie would walk right through it.

STEVIE WAS UNSHAKABLE in his belief that he could write songs, and Gordy and the producers at Motown generally agreed that he had that rare potential. Stevie was notorious for unearthing original snatches of songs or harmonica riffs, free-form creations with bite and promise. But he was not yet at a point in his development where he could cobble together these ideas into coherent, fully realized songs. He needed help and guidance.

While Clarence Paul had been a gigantic influence on Stevie, schooling the boy on the classic rudiments of music and providing him with rock-solid fundamentals, the truth was that Paul by now was limiting Stevie's progress. The Beatles were taking America by storm in 1965, and Stevie was among those who took note of their bold, hard-driving yet pop-friendly work. Paul was an old-school craftsman whose forte was sophisticated, big band–style arrangements that were more supper club than Top 40. Gordy decided that Stevie should start building relationships with some of the other writers and producers in the Motown stable. Paul would remain Stevie's musical director until 1967 and would continue to play a primary role in his career, but Paul's influence was on the wane—to Stevie's benefit.

It was with producer Henry Cosby and lyricist Sylvia Moy that

Stevie regained his footing and reestablished himself on the music scene. One of their first collaborations was "Uptight (Everything's Alright)," a bouncy, irresistible canter of a song that also bears the unmistakable stamp of Motown session bassist James Jamerson and Benny Benjamin, the spectacular Motown drummer. The germ of "Uptight" was a chorus that came to Stevie while he was riffing around in the studio; Cosby and Moy grew the idea from there and together the three of them quickly fleshed out the song.

The finished product was a brilliant advance for Stevie. While there is plenty of signature Motown orchestration—a scalding backbeat by Benjamin, trumpet fanfare—the track is pure, mostly unadorned Stevie. There is no harmonica. It is Stevie and Stevie alone making his case, wriggling free from the constraints of the overly layered Paul productions. His vocal is ebullient, joyful, affirming—the very standards by which his fans would judge every subsequent Stevie Wonder song. *In every pocket you can see I'm a poor man's son*, Stevie sings at one point in "Uptight," and while every listener had no doubt as to the honesty of that statement of whence Stevie came, it was just as apparent that this particular effort came from a wellspring of extraordinary emotional power.

"Uptight" was released in November 1965 and immediately shot to number 1 on the R&B chart and number 3 on the pop chart. The single's success not only rewarded Motown for its support of their young charge but, most important for Stevie's long-term prospects, also served notice that he could produce hits while operating on the periphery of the Motown formula.

Most of all, "Uptight" was a space shot that thundered into the heavens to tell the world that Stevie Wonder was *back*. This time, he intended to stay.

Twelve

PANIC IN DETROIT

"I'm glad I'm blind. I can see more of life this way."

—Stevie, in an interview with *Teenset* magazine, 1966

Well, the Motor City is burning,
Ain't a thing in the world that I can do,
Because you know the big D is burnin',
Ain't a thing in the world Johnny can do.
My hometown is burning to the ground,
Worster than Vietnam.

—John Lee Hooker, "Motor City Is Burning," 1967

WITH THE ROCKET fuel provided by "Uptight," Stevie's music continued to surge forward artistically and commercially; his mid- and late teens stand as the start of the most fertile phase of his career. Yet the ever-buoyant, increasingly idealistic tenor of his work began to run head-on against the widening social upheaval of the 1960s— and against Motown's own checkered, often reluctant role during that era of civil rights protests and the antiwar movement.

After some touring to promote "Uptight," Stevie got back to work in the studio in an effort to follow up on that record's success. It didn't take long. In March 1966, Motown released "Nothing's Too Good for My Baby," another "Uptight"-style, straight-ahead romp powered by James Jamerson's authoritative bass and Benny Benjamin's relentless drumming. While "Nothing's Too Good for My Baby" (*I'm the luckiest guy in the world/'Cause I've got one pearl of a girl*) did not have the relative lyrical sophistication of "Uptight," it was a more than adequate sequel and featured a rambunctious, no-holds-barred vocal performance by Stevie, who seemed to be gaining more strength and confidence with every chorus. By the song's finale Stevie almost seems to be taunting the listener, punctuating the closing strains with some spontaneous *ha-ha-ha*s.

"Nothing's Too Good for My Baby" went to number 4 on the R&B chart and number 20 on the pop chart. Two months later, *Up-tight Everything's Alright,* Stevie's seventh album, made its appearance, sporting the title cut and "Nothing's Too Good." But the album also contained another song that would serve as a breakthrough for Stevie: a cover of Bob Dylan's withering "Blowin' in the Wind," which had already become a countercultural rallying cry. Stevie had been performing the song onstage for several months—he and Clarence Paul had worked out a lively, country- and gospel-flavored arrangement, with Paul supplying marvelous backing vocals—and had pushed to record it. Gordy was reluctant; his prized laboratory experiment was finally back on the map, and now he wanted to ruffle feathers with a damn protest song? Finally he compromised, consenting to include the song on the album—but not to releasing it as a single.

Up-tight Everything's Alright went to number 2 on the R&B album chart and number 33 on the pop album chart. More important, there was a strongly positive buzz about "Blowin' in the Wind," so much so that Gordy relented about six weeks later and decided to clip it as a single. The song quickly hit number 1 on the R&B chart and reached number 9 on the pop chart. Stevie's version of "Blowin' in the Wind" did not contain the barbed edge of the original, and as a result may have made the song more palatable to a wider range of people. But Stevie's rendition was unyielding in its own right. His reading of Dylan's classic line, *Yes, and how many years can some people exist/Before they're allowed to be free?* seemed to capture the essential plaint of the civil rights movement.

"Blowin' in the Wind" moved Stevie into a more vital realm. He was only sixteen, but his clarion voice now was associated with those calling for change. He quickly followed with "A Place in the Sun," an expert ballad that carried some of the same sentiments (*Like a branch in a tree/I keep reaching to be free*), another Top 10 hit on both *Billboard* charts. Stevie now not only was a consistent hit maker, but also was becoming widely recognized as a social commentator.

As it happened, Stevie's rise from "twelve-year-old genius" to a mature and socially relevant artist mirrored the most riveting chapters of the civil rights movement, both across the country and at home in Detroit. In 1963, as he began to emerge into the world at large, the bombing of the Sixteenth Street Baptist Church in Birmingham, Alabama, that killed four young black girls horrified the nation and made a permanent impression on Stevie. As "Fingertips—Pt 2" hit the airwaves, the song and its subliminal message of breaking against the restraints of social norms (symbolized by Stevie's refusal to leave the stage) was part of the soundtrack for Detroit's Great March to Freedom, a seminal but mostly forgotten event in the history of civil rights. The march, a huge event in Detroit, raised funds for the efforts of the Southern Christian Leadership Conference (SCLC) in Birmingham, and featured the Reverend Martin Luther King Jr., who, for the first time, began to articulate elements of his "I Have a Dream" speech that later would provide the high-water mark of his crusade for equality.

King declared the Detroit march "the largest and greatest demonstration for freedom ever held in the United States." The march also was notable in Motown history because Gordy decided to record King's speech and release it as its first spoken-word recording, a precursor to its Black Forum series later in the decade. It was a bold maneuver by Gordy, who now seemed to be jostling for a front-row seat as the civil rights movement gained momentum.

Gordy reinforced that view when he spoke at a SCLC benefit in Atlanta to present King with a commemorative copy of the recorded speech. "Realizing that in years to come," Gordy told the audience, "the Negro revolt of 1963 will take its place historically with the American Revolution and the Hungarian uprising, we have elected to record the statements of some of the movement's leaders. . . . In his speech Reverend King intelligently and succinctly explains the Negro revolt, underlines its ramifications, and points the way to certain solutions. This album belongs in the home of every American and should be required listening for every American child, white or black."

By his own admission, Gordy was not always so in-your-face about race relations. He was a businessman, not a crusader. It was no accident that many of Motown's early albums were released without pictures of the artists on the covers; Gordy didn't want to discourage white record store owners from displaying Motown issues or white consumers from buying them. The Marvelettes' album *Please Mr. Postman* had a picture of a mailbox on the cover. The front of *Bye Bye Baby: I Don't Want to Take a Chance,* by Mary Wells, depicted a love letter. A cartoon of an ape appeared on the cover of *Doin' Mickey's Monkey,* by Smokey Robinson and the Miracles. An Isley Brothers album cover featured two white lovers at the beach.

As time went by, Gordy and Motown would build a mixed record as participant and commentator as the social divisions deepened in America. Some critics have charged that Motown did not do nearly enough, and in particular point to Gordy's decision to move the company to Los Angeles in 1972 as a callous betrayal of the city from which it took its name.

Until he was about sixteen, Stevie mostly was on the outskirts of the debates about race and war. He was a black, blind kid from the ghetto working gallantly to become a pop star. What did he have to contribute that was meaningful?

Plenty, as it turned out. In an interesting interpretation of the biblical notion that "a child shall lead them," young Stevie became the first Motown artist to make political statements on his records and in public, at first subtly and then less so. Stevie indisputably was influenced by some of the socially conscious music coming from artists such as Dylan, the Beatles, and others, but it also was clear by then that he had begun to develop his own worldly opinions about current events.

Stevie continued to make his voice heard in connection with the civil rights movement. In 1966, Stevie headlined a benefit concert for the SCLC at Soldier Field in Chicago. Later that year, *Down to Earth*, his eighth album, was the first Motown record to feature a ghetto landscape on the cover; Stevie is depicted sitting on some concrete steps and playing his harmonica in front of a graffiti-marred wall. At the end of 1966, he released a single, "Someday at Christmas," which also ruminated on the issues of the day, although its force was blunted by its holiday trappings.

Not all of Stevie's work was political, of course. In May 1967, the single "I Was Made to Love Her" was released and became an instant smash, going to number 1 on the R&B chart and number 2 on the pop chart. Stevie opens the song with a too-hot-to-touch harmonica solo—just in case anyone was thinking he had lost interest in *that* instrument—and then peels off a soaring, breathless vocal performance that is in such a wonderful, carefree hurry that it virtually dispenses with a chorus. It was, and is, an arguably perfect pop song: two minutes and forty seconds of carefully controlled rock 'n' soul chaos. The song was another result of his highly productive partnership with Henry Cosby and Sylvia Moy. Also receiving a songwriting credit was Lula, who often threw in suggestions while cooking for Stevie and his collaborators during brainstorming sessions at her home. Stevie said the song took about ten minutes to write.

Plans were made to release an album in August with "I Was Made to Love Her" as the title song. Before that could happen, however, Stevie was exposed to a seismic event in Detroit civil rights history that had a lasting effect on his music in particular and Motown in general: the riots of 1967. So much for the Summer of Love.

RACIAL TENSIONS HAD been escalating rapidly in Detroit in the summer of 1967. The sentiments that were building were encapsulated just a few weeks before the riots erupted when the fiery H. "Rap" Brown, chairman of the militant Student Nonviolent Coordinating Committee, spoke at the Second Annual Black Arts Convention at Detroit's Central United Church. During a volatile, fist-shaking speech, Brown famously warned, Let white America know that the name of the game is tit-for-tat, an eye for an eye, a tooth for a tooth, a life for a life. . . . Motown, if you don't come around, we are going to burn you down! (The "Motown" in this instance was the city, not the record company.)

The subsequent riots started innocuously enough. At about 3:45 A.M. on July 23, an undercover police officer gained entrance to a "blind pig" at 9125 Twelfth Street that had been in business for three years, where a jukebox thumped out "I Was Made to Love Her" and other Motown hits. "Blind pig" was the local term for illegal, after-hours drinking clubs that rose like mushrooms in Detroit during Prohibition, taking advantage of the plentiful liquor available across the river in Canada. After prohibition, blind pigs remained and became an integral part of black culture in Detroit, especially along the Hastings Street corridor that was the locus of African-American nightlife in the city until urban renewal efforts and the Chrysler Freeway eradicated it.

By the late 1960s, Twelfth Street had become the focal point that Hastings once had been, and several blind pigs operated in the area. The club at 9125 Twelfth Street was registered on the city books as the offices of the United Community League for Civic Action, essentially using its guise as a service organization as a cover. By 1967 the establishment was well known to police as a blind pig and had been raided nine times in the previous year alone.

Soon after the undercover officer entered the club, a police crew broke down the club door with a sledgehammer and rushed in. They were surprised by the size of the crowd, an estimated eighty-five people attending a party for two young men, one who had just returned from Vietnam and another who was about to leave for his tour of duty. Rather than simply arrest the club owners and let it go at that, the commanding officer decided that everyone there would be taken to jail.

Several paddy wagons were needed to transport the partygoers to the city lockup. There were delays, and a crowd of two hundred people eventually gathered outside the club to witness the proceedings. Many onlookers became upset at what they viewed as rough handling of those under arrest. According to eyewitnesses, someone yelled, "Let's get the bottles and bricks going," while someone else urged, "Let's have a riot!" Rocks, cans, bottles, and bricks began to pelt the street, and the rear window of the last police cruiser to leave the scene was shattered by a beer bottle.

From that small conflagration arose a massive, deadly revolt that would last for nearly a week. Eventually federal troops would be required to quell the violence. As the sun rose that Sunday morning, word of the troubles began to spread, and by midday the looting had grown exponentially, with thousands of people, black and white, showering police and fire personnel with debris. By Sunday evening, it seemed as if all Twelfth Street was ablaze, and the disturbance began to spread to other parts of the city. Rooftop snipers were reported—

two police precinct houses were said to be under fire—and it soon became clear that anarchy was in effect. The National Guard was brought in to no avail, and on Tuesday President Lyndon Johnson made the decision to send in federal forces to reassert law and order. Nonetheless, it still was rough going for days. Some people were shot on sight by police for being in the street during curfew. Some people were fatally wounded by crossfire while hiding in their homes. Federal paratroopers were employed in what had become a literal war zone. By Thursday, the rioting finally had been suppressed; federal troops did not leave the city until August 2, when future Secretary of State Cyrus Vance, leader of the federal assessment team, declared that "law and order have been restored in Detroit."

The final tally: 7,231 people arrested; 700 people injured; 43 people dead (33 blacks and 10 whites); $50 million in property damage. Compared to this, the 1943 Belle Island riots had been a mere alley fight.

Interestingly, the Motown studios, despite being a stone's throw from the heart of the rebellion on Twelfth Street, avoided damage. Whether this was due to dumb luck or some manner of consideration from the looters will never be known, since black-owned businesses in general were hardly spared in the rioting. Two of the more notable losses in that regard were Joe Von Battle's record store and the Chit Chat Lounge. Von Battle's establishment had long been a touchstone of Detroit's black community, dating back to its origins on Hastings Street before the city's so-called reclamation project forced a move to Twelfth Street. The store was black Detroit's primary source of R&B, gospel, and other types of music popular with African Americans, and it was widely viewed as a community gathering place and listening post. When the riots began, Von Battle placed a sign that read SOUL BROTHER in his window and stood guard with a handgun at the front door. But his shop was ransacked anyway, and he ultimately was forced out of business. As for the Chit Chat Lounge, its death by arson meant the end of a vibrant establishment where Motown's studio band, the Funk Brothers—Jamerson, Benjamin, keyboardist Earl Van Dyke, guitarist Robert White, and others—had moonlighted for years.

Yet neither Motown nor its artists went unscathed by the riots. The unrest and the death and destruction it spawned gave way to a great deal of introspection throughout Detroit. There was a very tangible sense of gloom, as if the entire city had fallen into a giant emotional depression after spending all its rage. Stevie, for his part, was determined that he not lose the optimistic and hopeful flavor of his music. Other artists at Motown, performers and writers alike, resolved that they would find ways to address the issues of the inner city in their work. Nonetheless, Motown was shaken to its core by the riots.

As the owner of the city's highest-profile black business, Gordy faced increasing pressure to take a leading civic role in the rebuilding efforts—and he did, volunteering the Supremes to be the spokespersons for a philanthropic campaign that raised millions of dollars for rebuilding efforts. When King was assassinated in April of the following year, Gordy and the Supremes attended his funeral and then dispatched a troupe of Motown stars and musicians, including Stevie, to star in a benefit concert that raised $25,000 for the impending Poor People's March on Washington, engineered by the SCLC. Gordy, Stevie, and the others then joined celebrities such as Sidney Poitier, Sammy Davis Jr., and Harry Belafonte Jr. to inaugurate the march. It was Motown's most blatantly political activity since the recording of King's "Great March" speech in Detroit five years before.

But Gordy always was ambivalent about letting activism into the studio. As committed as he may or may not have been to the various causes of the day, he was first and foremost a business entrepreneur who was reluctant to muddy a successful commercial enterprise with messages that some customers might find objectionable. From a distance, every risky or controversial move that Gordy undertook on the

behalf of civil rights seemed to carry with it a countermove that soft-
ened its impact. He recorded King's speech at the Great March, for
example, but didn't similarly preserve an important Detroit speech by
the decidedly more militant Malcolm X a few months later. He
recorded an album of "revolutionary" black poetry by Langston
Hughes and Margaret Danner in 1963, but he didn't release it until
1970, as the first offering of Motown's Black Forum series. The Black
Forum series, featuring spoken-word performances by black political
and cultural leaders, including Stokely Carmichael, Ossie Davis, and
Amiri Baraka (the former LeRoi Jones), was an invaluable contribu-
tion to the archive of black history. But despite Gordy's stated wish in
1963 that such works be heard "in every American home," the series
was poorly distributed and promoted, with the exception of a collection of King speeches after his assassination. As a result, Motown was
rarely associated with the Black Forum series in the public eye, which
in effect greatly reduced the likelihood of any backlash against the
record company's commercially successful music labels.

All this is not to say that Gordy was insincere in his efforts.
When record store owners balked at stocking the Black Forum
records, he often threatened to withhold shipments of Motown's hit
records until they acquiesced. But he had chosen a difficult strategy:
to attempt to add a voice to the forces of change while walling off his
profit-making interests from the inevitable damage that comes from
taking such a stand. It was a classic lose-lose situation, in that Gordy
could never do enough to appease the more radical elements of the
civil rights movement while still earning the enmity that came with a
successful black man—a *very* successful black man—in a white man's
world.

By 1968, however, Gordy and the rest of Motown began to follow Stevie's lead and started to experiment with more socially relevant music. This wasn't exactly by Gordy's design. In 1968, a bitter
dispute between Gordy and the Holland-Dozier-Holland song-

writing team over royalty issues led to a work slowdown of sorts by H-D-H. A divisive lawsuit against Gordy would follow, and Gordy was forced to assemble another team of writers for the Supremes, which at the time was far and away Motown's primary cash cow. The new writers—R. Dean Taylor, Deke Richards, Frank Wilson, and Pam Sawyer—were nicknamed "the Clan" by Gordy, and set to work. Right out of the gate came "Love Child," a "message" song if there ever was one, which would merely become one of the most popular records in the history of the Supremes.

The first words heard in "Love Child" are "tenement slum," and the lyrics go on to fashion a story about two young lovers struggling with the ancient divide between wanting to give in to their passion but wary of the consequences of unwed motherhood. Illegitimacy is treated as a shameful burden, and the lyrics quite conspicuously lobby for young people to exercise caution and responsibility in matters of physical ardor (*This love we're contemplating/Is worth the pain of waiting/We'll only end up hating/The child we may be creating*).

And yet "Love Child" wasn't just a pointed social fable—it was an unmitigated commercial gem. Diana Ross is spellbinding: the song scales crescendo after crescendo, and as a simple matter of pop craftsmanship has few equals. The record hit number 1 on the pop charts and seemed to float in that vicinity for an eternity.

This development was a dream come true for Gordy, who could not have failed to see the have-your-cake-and-eat-it-too symmetry to "Love Child." He still was a mighty believer in the quaint yet dynamic love songs of the H-D-H variety; Motown's bank account was testament to that approach. But "Love Child" demonstrated that songs with sociopolitical themes had real commercial potential, which helped neutralize his reticence toward such edgy undertakings. While he contemplated this new cultural data, Gordy immediately set out to ensure that the Supremes capitalized on this new tack. An album featuring "Love Child" was generated in short order, and the Supremes appeared on the cover dressed not in the slinky, elegant gowns of the past but in roughed-up jeans and sweatshirts, propped against a ghetto wall. The group wore similar "ghetto costumes" during an appearance on *The Ed Sullivan Show,* an affectation that looks bogus and ridiculous now, but at the time was a startling departure for a black performing act—especially one from *Motown,* of all places, which had always prided itself as a finishing school that expected its artists to look sharp or look out.

With "Love Child," the chains began to loosen at Motown regarding politically sensitive material. The Temptations chipped in songs like "Cloud Nine" and "Ball of Confusion (That's What the World Is Today)" that dealt with issues like drug use and race relations. One verse from "Ball of Confusion" went like this:

People movin' out
People movin' in
Why? Because of the color of skin.
Run run run, but you sure can't hide.
An eye for an eye, a tooth for a tooth,
Vote for me and I'll set you free,
Rap on, brother, rap on.

This was solar systems away from the

I've got sunshine
On a cloudy day
When it's cold outside
I've got the month of May

comforts of "My Girl." Producer Norman Whitfield, a recent arrival at Motown who had overseen the bold retooling of the Temptations, wanted to push the envelope even more. With Barrett Strong, Whitfield wrote "War!", a powerful anti–Vietnam War protest song, for the Temptations. But Gordy also assigned the song to the comparatively unknown Edwin Starr, who nailed "War!"—its jarring opening (*War! Huh! What is it good for? Absolutely nuthin'!*) remains one of the classic turns in rock. It became a big hit, and the Temptations ultimately recorded the song too. But none of that could dissuade Gordy and Motown from looking for eggshells whenever they found themselves treading along a controversial path.

The watershed moment in this internal struggle at Motown came in 1971, with Marvin Gaye's groundbreaking album, *What's Going On.* Gaye, one of the great soul balladeers of his era, had been with Motown since its earliest days, coming to Detroit from Chicago with songwriter-producer Harvey Fuqua (who also would become a Gordy brother-in-law). Gaye was a talented drummer and was a session musician on many of Motown's early records, but Gordy—ever with a nose for talent—thought Gaye could make it as a front man. By 1962, Gaye had a hit with "Stubborn Kind of Fellow," which was quickly followed by a succession of hits. He established an image as a sexy soul crooner and was especially well-suited for duets with female stars; he had hits with Mary Wells, Kim Weston, and, most notably, Tammi Terrell ("Ain't No Mountain High Enough").

But Gaye, though low-key and soft-spoken, was deeply introspective and highly opinionated about the issues of the day. As much as any artist at Motown, he chafed under the label's restrictions against political material. He said once that he was not a "cog in some machine," and that artists "must look beneath the surface and show that there is more to this world than meets the eye." He also said he "wondered what I was doing singing rock and roll in some dive instead of leading the marchers." Slowly, over the course of several years, Gaye began to put together a series of concepts that ultimately became *What's Going On.* A key element of the work was inspired by Gaye's brother, Frankie, who returned from Vietnam in 1966 and struggled to find work. He eventually accepted a job as a hotel doorman, which Marvin thought was a travesty considering the sacrifices he had made for his country. Gaye vowed to honor his brother's ordeal with a song, which led to "What's Happening Brother," one of the cornerstones of *What's Going On.* The album dealt not just with the war and its cost, but with violence, racism, and ecology. *What's Going On* was a veritable cornucopia of protest and social consciousness.

The album also broke new musical ground. The nine songs on the album segued thematically from one to the next, with a complex and lush layering of music and ambient sounds forming an uninterrupted bridge between them. Instead of nine songs standing alone, the album seemed of a whole piece—a radical innovation for Motown. It was, inarguably, a masterpiece.

Gordy, predictably, had some protests of his own as the scope and intent of the album became clear, and he discouraged Gaye from pursuing the project. He told Gaye that it wasn't commercial and would jeopardize his image as a sexy soul balladeer. Gaye replied that he didn't care about image, that he felt compelled to speak out through his music. And back and forth it went. Complicating matters was the fact that Gaye was by then having marital problems with his wife, Gordy's sister, Anna. Also at work was Gordy's intense territorialism that dictated that artists not be given so much creative freedom as to upset the producer-dominated, assembly-line apple cart that churned out lucrative formula hits. *What's Going On* threatened all of this; but the bottom line was that Gordy firmly believed the public would not embrace this bold departure by Marvin Gaye.

But Gaye persisted, and in the end Gordy had to concede that the album was an awesome artistic achievement—especially after Gaye swore he would never make another record for Motown if *What's Going On* wasn't released. During the early album sessions, Gordy had told Gaye that either the album wouldn't work and Gaye would learn something, or it would work and Gordy would learn something. As it turned out, Gordy learned something.

"What's Going On" was released as a single in January 1971. Before long it had reached number 2 on the pop chart and number 1 on the R&B chart and would go on to sell two million copies. The album was similarly well received, and critics hailed *What's Going On* as a masterwork that represented a quantum (and welcomed) leap away from the canned Motown "sound." Three decades later, *What's Going On* was lodged near the top of virtually every list of the most important albums of the twentieth century.

Bearing careful witness to these proceedings was Stevie, who was close to Gaye and listened to his complaints as he struggled against Gordy's opposition. The lessons were obvious and plentiful, not the least of which was that great artistic statements required complete creative control. That was much easier said than done at Motown, something that the *What's Going On* saga made eminently clear. This was valuable information for Stevie Wonder to have at his disposal in 1971 as he turned twenty-one and, for the first time, would begin to go about acquiring full authority over his career. Stevie wanted to make music like no one had ever heard before; he vowed that neither Berry Gordy nor anyone else would deny him that destiny.

STEVIE'S LATER WORK would, of course, contain an abundance of social messages, and throughout his life he would be associated with a number of causes, from fighting world hunger to campaigning for a national holiday in honor of Martin Luther King Jr. But his willingness to speak up as a young artist was always remembered by others in the civil rights movement. This was especially true in Detroit. In the aftermath of the riots, Stevie quickly was elevated to the rank of holy figure and remained there. Proof of his status came in 1972, when Motown announced plans to move to California—Gordy wanted to expand into TV and movie production—and a rumor spread that Gordy had remarked, "If a black disc jockey [in Detroit] never played one of my records, I wouldn't give a damn." The allegation probably was an urban myth; Gordy denied he ever said such a thing. But the rumor provided a window into the animosity on the street in the Motor City regarding Motown's move. Black radio stations in Detroit instigated a boycott against playing Motown records for months afterward; the only artist spared was Stevie Wonder.

Thirteen

LIVING FOR THE CITY

T HE WRITER DAVID RITZ recalls that Stevie was seventeen
when he first saw the kid in concert. It was in Rome, amid a
European tour mounted in support of the *I Was Made to Love Her*
album, and Stevie was a man possessed for three hours, carousing
about the stage to the extent that the audience feared for his safety. To
put it mildly, he blew the roof off the dump ("his voice an instrument
of fierce beauty, unmitigated joy"), and Ritz was mesmerized, not an
uncommon reaction to a live Stevie performance in those days.

After the show, Ritz ventured backstage for an interview and
encountered a young man still operating at full tilt. Showing no signs
of strain from a pyrotechnic show that had left his audience limp, Stevie was still rolling, energy radiating off him, goofing around with his
entourage and well-wishers, speaking to high comedic effect in mock
Italian (always the mimic, Stevie's practice was to slip into a fractured,
hilarious version of the local dialect, be it Paris or Little Rock), and
flirting with the women. (At one point he removed his sunglasses and
exclaimed, "Oh, baby, I've never seen anyone so fine!")

Ritz finally persuaded Stevie to focus on the interview and soon was answering more questions than Stevie. (You rarely interview Stevie; Stevie interviews you.) Stevie wanted to know about Dante's *The Divine Comedy*. He asked about Italian pop singers. When Ritz asked him what he was reading, Stevie pointed to a stack of books in Braille that included speeches by Martin Luther King Jr. and Malcolm X. Stevie and the writer then discussed racial politics until 4 A.M., Stevie's handlers snoring on a nearby sofa, navigating another impossibly late night. Stevie, according to Ritz, "bounced from idea to idea, inexhaustible, curious, brilliant."

And so it was with Stevie as he reached his late teens. His acute intellect was in full flower, due to a convergence of factors: his blindness, which increased his sensitivity; his budding relationships with other artists and thinkers; the very nature of his livelihood, which was to bring words and music to the world. Stevie was a gifted artist coming of age during one of the most tumultuous periods in American history, and his head exploded with visions of possibility as he hungrily imagined ways to match his music with the times. Stevie was an artist in the truest sense, in that he firmly believed—there was no question *about* it, to him—that his art manipulated him, not the other way around. A person of great faith who harbored deep thoughts about the notion of a higher power, Stevie considered himself a vessel for the new ideas and sounds that poured out of him. Somehow, for some reason, he had been chosen as a man of his times; along with the opportunities and privileges that life was bringing him came an inherent responsibility, as he saw it, to bring messages of love and unity to the world. That meant making music that described people and ideas and worlds that folks hadn't cared about before, or hadn't even *thought* about.

Marvin Gaye had said it best: To be an artist is a blessing and a privilege. Artists must never betray their true hearts. Artists must look beneath the surface and show that there is more to this world than meets the eye. Marvin also said: I always knew I was an artist...

and not the cog in some machine. That's what it came down to, in the end. Stevie wanted to talk about *art* and *meaning* and *human rights* and *how to change things*. He had a *vision*. And people still fumbling around for three-minute singles in a concept-album world . . . come on, Jack!

All this was lost on the foremen down at the Motown hit factory. And by this juncture, the assembly-line metaphor truly was apt. Care still was lavished on Motown recordings, but they were all beginning to sound alike. The Gordy formula was a certified success; no one could argue with that, and few did. All right, boys, you've got your blueprints—now let's get cranking! Problem was, Stevie wanted to mint Porsches, Ferraris . . . but the plant was geared up to churn out only Mustangs. How are you going to make Porsches in a Ford factory?

Not that Motown wasn't thinking *big* when it came to Stevie. Gene Kees, who had taken over for Clarence Paul as Stevie's musical director, shared some of the grand design Motown had in mind for Stevie in 1967: "By the time he's twenty-one, he will have become Stevie Wonder the entertainer, not just Stevie Wonder the maker of pop records. He has the potential to be another *Sammy Davis.*"

Another *Sammy Davis*? Well, *shit*, why didn't you just *say* so? Who wouldn't want to be another Sammy Davis? You know, hanging with the Pack in Vegas, babe, maybe get a permanent gig at the Sands, like, get together a groovy set list of finger-snapping standards . . . *Ladies and germs, let's have a lucky Las Vegas welcome for Big . . . Stevie . . . Wondeeeeeer! Earnest applause. A big band of old, hunched-over white guys, propped up in a bandstand sporting a large "SW" insignia, swings into "For Once in My Life." Stevie takes the stage with a gold-tipped cigarette in hand, clad in a tuxedo and draped in jewelry, and starts to sing: "For once in my life/I've got someone who needs me . . . yeah! And that someone is you, ladies and gentlemen! Give yourselves a hand! Thank you for coming! Just flew in from the coast—boy, are my arms tired! Anybody here from the Motor City?"*

Unsurprisingly, Stevie was a bit more expansive in his aspirations. He wasn't ungrateful to Motown; far from it. He knew as well as anyone that it was no less than some form of divine intervention that he had been plucked off the streets by a record company—a record company in his own *hometown,* mind you, far from the traditional coastal entertainment centers of New York and Los Angeles—and nurtured and trained and promoted until he had finally tapped his potential and become a star.

And perhaps you can't blame Motown too harshly for its Stevie-as-Sammy pipe dream. No one, not even Stevie, could picture what he would become, which meant that Gordy and Motown had a limited field of vision with which to work. What was so wrong about striving to become another Sammy Davis, for crying out loud? To Gordy's generation, Sammy was the epitome of the successful crossover artist—crossover as in crossing over from black audiences to white—and that was where the real money was, right? And while Sammy had his causes, he wasn't aggressive about it—you follow? People are put *off* by all that angry black man stuff. If you're always railing about how lousy the world is, people get tired of that. They'll get tired of *you.* Protest singers never last. Pay attention, Stevie, we're trying to *help* you here . . .

But what Motown never understood—or didn't understand until many years later—was that Stevie Wonder's activism wasn't about anger. He came from a different place than that . . . a place where anger kept a room, sure, but didn't collect the rent. In that respect he was different from the Rap Browns and Dick Gregorys and Malcolm Xs, the fiery shooting stars who used anger as jet fuel as they burned across the sky. He was different even from the Martin Luther Kings, who were more subdued but who unmistakably channeled the anger of a people. Somehow, even when he *was* angry, Stevie was able to have his say without people reacting *to* the anger. They refused to shoot the messenger, and, more often than not, they heard the message. Few but Stevie could record a song like the bitterly sarcastic "You Haven't Done Nothin'" (with background vocals by the Jackson 5) with the refrain

> *'Cause if you really want to hear our views,*
> *You haven't done nothing.*

aimed directly at posturing white liberal politicians and not be subjected to a tremendous amount of heat on a personal level. But Stevie wasn't vilified; people tended to get the point. Perhaps it was that natural goodwill people felt toward him due to his blindness, the same dynamic that Gordy used to muse about as he watched Little Stevie from the wings, that mysterious *something* that got Marvin Gaye booed off the stage at the Graystone Ballroom during that long-ago Battle of the Stars. Stevie could uncork "You Haven't Done Nothin'" and the targets he spewed with his ire didn't say, Oh yeah? Then screw you, you ungrateful son of a . . . They were more likely to say, That's how you really feel? Well—I need to get my head around that . . . Somehow, some way, Stevie had an immense line of credit that cut across all social barriers, a creditworthiness that almost always got him a hearing. Hell, Stevie had *cash on hand.*

In the final analysis, Stevie came not from anger, but from joy. It was that simple. In that respect, he was a true child of the 1960s. *It's all about love, brother. We've got to find ways to love each other.*

Still, it made the suits at Motown nervous, and by the time Stevie was eighteen and nineteen there were plenty of suits at Hitsville U.S.A. Stevie knew that he was being stifled, but Motown had been his home for nearly half his life and the roots ran deep. He was enough of a realist to understand that he wasn't going anywhere else until he was twenty-one; it was contractually impossible, or at least would require a spilling of blood to a magnitude that Stevie had no stomach for. Until then, he would simply have to finesse things. There would be some victories and some defeats. But the day he turned twenty-one, he told himself, all bets were off.

MOSTLY THERE WERE victories, even if the commercial results sometimes were mixed.

Not many recording artists can boast of a greatest-hits collection by the age of seventeen. Stevie could, and it was a Top 30 performer on both charts. But Stevie hardly was looking back, even though he was forced to suffer through the occasional half-baked musical scheme birthed by the Motown brass. One example: 1970's *Stevie Wonder Live,* which featured Stevie phoning in dirges such as "By the Time I Get to Phoenix" (the Sammy Davis master plan at work). Another example: The 1968 album *Eivets Rednow* ("Stevie Wonder" spelled backward), a Gordy-hatched series of Stevie harmonica instrumentals that included "Alfie" by Burt Bacharach and Hal David. The album is beautifully done, but at complete odds with the stylistic innovations at which Stevie was becoming proficient. That the album title cleverly disguised Stevie's participation seemed instructive.

Beyond those missteps—neither of which could be placed at Stevie's feet—the kid could do little wrong. In December 1968 came the album *For Once in My Life,* which led with the title track and also included exceptionally strong material such as the funked-up "You Met Your Match" and the fluid "Shoo-Be-Doo-Be-Doo-Da-Day." The title track, written by Ron Miller and Orlando Murden, had been recorded previously by several artists. But Stevie once again exhibited his ability to make someone else's song his very own, infusing it with his rollicking charm and sending it to number 2 on both the pop and soul charts.

The next year found Stevie exerting even more independence in his music and in his life. He not only released the hit *My Cherie Amour*—the title track having originally been the B side of the single "I Don't Know Why"—but also graduated from the Michigan School for the Blind and concluded his studies with Ted Hull. He was free now to devote his undivided attention to his career, and the results were immediate. Forthcoming was what was arguably his first great, classic album, *Signed Sealed & Delivered,* an outstanding collection that offered further evidence that Stevie was maturing into an artist of exceptional singularity. The title song alone made the album's case for greatness, two minutes and forty seconds of celebratory mirth that opens with a signature Stevie cry of joy and just cascades along from there. The songwriting credits also were significant in that Stevie was joined by Lula, his blind pal Lee Garrett, and his girlfriend Syreeta Wright, a Motown secretary and aspiring singer whom he would marry within the year.

But *Signed Sealed & Delivered* provided much more than an outstanding title song. "Never Had a Dream Come True" is a fabulous ballad. "Heaven Help Us All" (*Heaven help the roses/As the bombs begin to fall*) mixes a religious theme with social commentary. But the album's masterpiece may well be its cover of the Beatles' "We Can Work It Out," wherein Stevie makes the original version seem like the result of some backwater amateur hour. Stevie not only delivered a blistering turn on the lyrics and showed off harmonica acrobatics to die for, but also played all the other instruments and produced the track entirely by himself. The technical prowess of the cut—with its razor-sharp layering of background vocals that punctuate his lead vocal to perfection—was an almost frightening demonstration of Stevie's talent both in front of the microphone and at the mixing board. (He wasn't restricting that talent to his own work. Around this time he also wrote and produced a big hit for the Spinners, "It's a Shame," which undoubtedly could have been a hit for Stevie as well.)

By now, however, Stevie's interests had expanded beyond his career, although it seemed that all roads eventually led back to his music. He had had girlfriends over the years, and certainly was no stranger to sexual play out on the hustings. But there was something different about Syreeta Wright, with whom he seemed to have a rapport from the moment they met. That he was fond of her was easily apparent to friends like Lee Garrett, who would mock Stevie good-naturedly about his fondness for Syreeta. "Signed, Sealed, Delivered" was in fact the result of Stevie's crush on the secretary, who not only had musical talent of her own but was intelligent and deeply spiritual, a teacher of Transcendental Meditation who was among the first to expose Stevie to Eastern philosophy. They became very close and while in London in June 1970 announced their engagement. They married ten weeks later at the Burnette Baptist Church in Detroit. The marriage would end amicably a couple of years later, and Stevie would produce two modestly received albums for her.

At the time of his marriage, Stevie was twenty years old, not exactly an elder of the tribe, but he always had been older than his years. He was making important strides in his personal life, and he was anxious to take similar control with his music. Gordy and other executives like Motown president Ewart Abner were fully aware that Stevie was rebelling against the strictures at Motown, and certainly were aware that Stevie had the right to void his contract on his rapidly approaching twenty-first birthday. With that in mind, Gordy was in an uncharacteristically flexible mood when Stevie insisted that he be able to make his next album without interference. Gordy agreed, even though he had his doubts about the commercial viability of what Stevie had in mind: a concept album that would become *Where I'm Coming From*, which, with a few exceptions, was essentially an extended political statement about Vietnam and other social issues.

With Syreeta by his side, Stevie spent nearly a year on the LP, which would ultimately become the last Stevie Wonder album issued by Motown before he turned twenty-one.

The album was intensely personal, unmistakably strident, and only moderately successful in relation to his other recent efforts. Clearly influenced by late '60s rockers like Sly Stone and Jimi Hendrix, *Where I'm Coming From* did manage to reach number 7 on the R&B chart, but failed to crack the Top 50 on the pop charts. (Stevie always contended that Motown neither understood nor adequately promoted the album.) It yielded only one hit single, "If You Really Love Me," which was a departure in tone from the rest of the album. More typical was "Think of Me as Your Soldier," which expressed Stevie's sympathy toward and anger about American GIs subjected to a meaningless war, and "I Wanna Talk to You," which addressed the gaping political generation gap of the day.

That the record was a relative commercial failure was of little concern to Stevie. It was, for him, a treatise not only about the social landscape of the times but of the changes warring about within him as a creator of music. "I Wanna Talk to You" could just as easily have been an admonition to Motown—and one that Motown would have been well advised to heed.

ON THE EVE of Stevie's twenty-first birthday, May 13, 1971, Berry Gordy threw a party in Stevie's honor at the Gordy mansion in Detroit. Gordy was spending most of his time in Los Angeles by then but made a special trip back to his hometown to host the festivities. No mention was made of the legal significance of the occasion. Gordy certainly wasn't going to bring it up if Stevie wasn't.

But Stevie had already taken steps to declare his independence. He had hired an attorney and told him what he wanted to do: call an end to his current contract with Motown, get the money he had coming to him, and then renegotiate a new contract that not only placed him in the driver's seat financially but gave him absolute creative freedom. He wanted to be able to record whenever and wherever he wanted, with whomever he wanted and with whatever material he wanted. He would forever be in Gordy's debt, but he had no doubt that Motown had made a killing with his efforts to date. His conscience was clear.

Gordy flew back to Los Angeles the day after the party under the impression that no changes or demands were imminent regarding Stevie's situation. But waiting on his desk, he says, was a tersely worded letter from Stevie's attorney, notifying Motown that Stevie wished to void his contract and accept payment of the monies due him. Gordy was upset. What the hell? How could Stevie and Syreeta sit there last night, guests of honor at a party in his home, and not let him know this was coming?

Gordy called Stevie's number in Detroit. Syreeta, a favorite of Gordy's, answered and told Gordy that Stevie wasn't home. Gordy explained why he was calling and told Syreeta how hurt he was that Stevie hadn't talked with him personally about his contract—or hadn't at least let him know that he had hired counsel to negotiate on his behalf. (No one but Gordy and Syreeta know the true tenor of the conversation, but Gordy—one of the more astute businessmen ever to grace the planet—surely was savvy enough not to have been too wounded or shocked by this turn of events.) Syreeta told Gordy that she believed that Stevie would be unhappy to hear how his attorney had handled the situation. Sure enough, Gordy says, Stevie called back and apologetically told Gordy the same thing: He had not meant for his lawyer to be so aggressive. Stevie ultimately fired the attorney, but he held firm with Gordy and reiterated that he wanted out and that he wanted his money.

This was another in a series of jarring events for Gordy and Motown. Benny Benjamin, the gifted but troubled drummer, had died in an automobile accident, tearing a hole in the heart of the Funk Brothers, the Motown house band. Gordy's rift with the Holland-Dozier-Holland songwriting team had widened. His creative conflicts with Marvin Gaye had reached their apex. Martha and the Vandellas stopped touring due to illness. He was contemplating a lock, stock, and barrel move to California, which he knew would bring screams of protest. And now, Stevie—his most treasured creation at Motown along with the Supremes and the Jackson 5—was threatening to jump ship. What was fair about that?

But Stevie was adamant, and Gordy soon realized that he had no choice but to pay Stevie whatever he was owed and then attempt to sign him to a new contract, if he could. Any other approach—to fight Stevie over the money or his contract—would, he knew, be a public relations disaster. Stevie enjoyed enormous goodwill with the public, and Gordy knew better than to tamper with that. So Stevie ultimately was paid slightly less than one million dollars by Motown, and that was that.

Stevie professed not to be terribly concerned about the money. He had all he needed for what he intended to do: go to New York, live in a hotel room, and record an album at the state-of-the-art Electric Lady studios in Greenwich Village. Which is precisely what he did. He pitched camp at a Howard Johnson Motor Inn on the West Side, and booked time at Electric Lady. If Motown wanted him, they would have to come and get him.

IN NEW YORK, Stevie basically decided to withdraw for a while. His marriage to Syreeta was encountering difficulty, with much of the friction involving Stevie's obsession with the studio. Stevie felt as if he had been on a grinding recording schedule for half his life; he had spent the last ten years learning and touring and studying, all the while cranking out records that for the most part spoke well for his career, but also were generated under the duress of knowing they had to sound a certain way—the Motown way. It was time to absorb new influences, grow in new directions. It was time for Stevie to pursue his musical destiny, and that would take some time.

Electric Lady was the brainchild of the late Jimi Hendrix, who poured much of his fortune into the making of the studio. Hendrix, himself a renowned studio rat, was notorious for spending every waking hour in the studio when he was making a record, and he accumulated the latest equipment and technology at Electric Lady to make sure that he would be able to stretch every last tweak out of every last song. For Stevie, already ravenously curious about the machinations of studio technology, this was akin to a ticket to heaven. One of his most profound complaints about Motown was that its studios were sorely behind the curve in the realm of technology. Stevie wanted to push and massage and mold his sound, to shock and surprise himself with what he could accomplish; the studios at Motown simply did not have what it took to realize that aim. It was, in Stevie's view, a musty museum that still excelled at making a certain kind of record; he just wasn't making those kinds of records anymore.

So Stevie barricaded himself in the studio with a piano, drums, and Clavinet (a five-octave electronic instrument similar to an electric piano), and spent nearly a year recording the songs that would comprise *Music of My Mind.* He began with about forty songs that he quickly recorded in one fashion or another, then started to experiment with different instruments and techniques to find the sounds that matched the ideas resonating in his head.

While this process was underway—during which Stevie, like Hendrix before, virtually lived in the studio, running up a staggering $250,000 studio tab that came out of his own pocket—he attended a recording session for the mellifluent singer-guitarist Richie Havens. There he met Robert Margouleff and Malcolm Cecil, cutting-edge recording engineers who were major innovators with what was then the still-germinating synthesizer technology. Stevie, always an easy mark for the newest gadget, listened to an album of electronic music by Margouleff and Cecil (recorded under the name Tonto's Expanding Head Band) entitled *Zero Time* and loved what he heard. He promptly hired the pair to engineer his new record, an association that would prove to be a watershed event in Stevie's musical development. Although still a relative newcomer to the technology, Stevie rapidly assimilated synthesizers into his work on *Music of My Mind* and began to hone the sound that would be so identified with his later work.

The results were instantly apparent. On "Superwoman (Where Were You When I Needed You)," a song that seems to be a direct reflection of Stevie's struggles with Syreeta, a beautiful, jazzy, delightfully understated synthesizer backdrop carries the song effortlessly along, the way a gentle spring breeze might assist a butterfly. "Superwoman" is over eight minutes in length—something that Stevie never would have pulled off under the old Motown restictions—yet seems half as long. The lyrics are full of regret and finality, but there is a hypnotic, tranquil quality that brings a sense of closure at song's end.

"Superwoman"—as well as several other songs on the album—was by leaps and bounds more sophisticated and nuanced than anything Stevie had ever committed to record at Motown. Yet he wasn't taking full leave of the bread-and-butter love songs that he so expertly and almost casually tossed off in Detroit. "I Love Every Little Thing About You" is tapped ingeniously from that same vein, and its studiously lighter-than-air feel is impossible to resist. All in all, *Music of My Mind*, while not quite a masterpiece by Stevie's standards, was the pivotal album of his career; it served as a transitional stepping-stone from the crucial yet provincial influences of Motown to the sheer, tectonic plate–rattling innovation of what was to come.

But there still was the matter of a contract.

As it happened, Gordy prematurely celebrated Stevie's dismissal of the attorney who so unceremoniously served him notice that day in Los Angeles. Another by-product of Stevie's friendship with Richie Havens is that he made the acquaintance of Havens's contract attorney, a titanium-plated negotiator named Johanan Vigoda, who convinced Stevie (who didn't need much convincing anyway) that he was dealing from a decided position of strength. Vigoda argued that the time had come to play hardball with Motown, and Stevie agreed. Stevie shopped around at other labels, and there was plenty of interest; but, with Vigoda's help, he saw how the changes going on at Motown could be turned to his benefit.

Motown, which moved to Los Angeles when Stevie escaped to New York, was by necessity facing up to the reality that it needed to evolve to survive. The music world was changing; Gordy could see that. Although Motown was no longer the same place in which he had grown up, it still felt like home to Stevie. He knew the company. He knew the people. He felt no small allegiance to Gordy and the other folks there. And they knew *him;* they just didn't know him well enough to realize that he couldn't pogo-stick around and play "Fingertips" for the rest of his life. Part of the problem was that Gordy and the rest of them still seemed to perceive him as the rambunctious, practical-joking kid who once raced up and down the stairs at Hitsville; it was difficult for them to imagine him as an adult. Difficult for them to imagine, that is, until he freaked them to the core and took their money and went to New York. Now, though, it was pretty certain that they were convinced of Stevie's conviction to make his own way. The other side of that coin was that, more than any other record label, Motown truly understood the depth of his ability and potential. It was one thing to hear the finished record and marvel at what Stevie had wrought; it was another matter altogether to watch him concoct it all right in front of you. Lastly, Stevie certainly knew he could be a part of helping Motown achieve *its* destiny. Motown needed a kick in the rear. And he was just the twenty-one-year-old genius to apply that kick—if the price was right.

Gordy and Motown never really did get the number of the truck that hit them. Vigoda went in and laid his cards on the table: complete creative control, ownership of publishing rights, a generous percentage of the profits from his records.

Stevie got everything. When the chairs pushed back from the table for the last time, Stevie had the freedom to do what he wanted—essentially, Motown had no choice but to release whatever Stevie gave them, with no veto power—and he got the nice round guaranteed sum to go with it. (Four years later, he would parlay that contract into another, a $13-million deal with Motown, at that time the most valuable artist contract in the history of the recording industry. Gordy said later that he realized it was time for Stevie to fly.)

Stevie promptly turned over *Music of My Mind* to Motown. The suits searched in vain for the singles . . . *any* singles. How can you sell an album without any singles? Maybe we can cut "Superwoman" down from eight minutes . . . Vigoda pointed to the contract. *Music of My Mind* was released as was. It went to number 6 on the R&B chart, number 21 on the pop chart. Not a blockbuster, but not too shabby, either. Stevie didn't care. Notice had been served to the world; Stevie Wonder was on a new path, and the results just might be worth watching.

Stevie fled back to the studio to work on his next album. It would be called *Talking Book*, and it would feature a little song called "Superstition." But first . . .

A HUMID SUMMER night in Tuscaloosa, Alabama, 1972. Memorial Coliseum on the University of Alabama campus is swirling with the pungent fumes of marijuana and smuggled-in bourbon, a packed house awaiting an appearance by the Rolling Stones. The Stones, the original bad boys of rock and roll, are at the peak of their artistic game—the epic *Exile on Main Street* is their current album—and full-bore into the druggy debauchery that has become their calling card. Here, on this night and in this place, the Rolling Stones truly are the Greatest Rock and Roll Band in the World, and 17,000 long-haired, blue-jeaned, roaring-drunk or chemically altered white kids are here to see them prove it, and will hardly know it if they don't. If there is a black person in the crowd, he'd better be selling Cokes.

It's festival seating, of course, which means first-come, first-served, which has prompted thousands of people to wait outside the venue all day in the hot sun—some camped out overnight—in order to rush in like Olympic sprinters to claim good seats. It also means that concertgoers have been sitting around getting hammered for a good long while; as a matter of fact, they are pretty damned surly. It's the *Stones,* man . . . Why do they even need a warm-up band? They think this crowd isn't warmed up? This show was sold out *three months ago.* They should just cut the crap and get out there and *play* . . . Who's the opening act? Oh, yeah, Stevie Wonder . . . At least I *heard* of 'im . . . Pass that over here, willya brother? Peace . . . I guess Stevie Wonder's cool. But, c'mon, some black guy? We need some guy who can *rock* this place, get this place ready for the *Stones.* You follow me, Elrod? *Come on! Let's go! Boogieeeeee!*

And so on . . . Finally the lights go down and a great roar arises, lifting the crowd out of their seats, since almost everyone has forgotten that there *is* an opening act and believe within their bone marrow that this is the cue for the *Stones,* man! But it's not the Stones. Instead, here comes Stevie Wonder, his blind ass being led out on to the stage by two of the best-looking black women you've ever seen, his head rolling around on his neck like crazy. This dude is *freaky,* and he's throwing out a million-watt smile that brings a big warm laugh from the crowd, because what that smile says is, I may be blind, Jack, but even I know these chicks are hot! So Stevie's got the place half-won over before he even plays a note . . . and then he starts to jam. And he *rocks.* He tears the place *down.* He rips through "Fingertips," just to get everyone's attention, which he does, his harmonica riffs bouncing off the far walls of the cavernous concert hall, again forcing the stoned masses from their seats. And from there on, he simply bludgeons them, playing some hits, playing the bongos. People are standing in their *chairs* now, because, dammit, I wanna *see.* And then, with everyone in the palm of his hand, he's at the piano for a couple of ballads—"Superwoman," "Heaven Help Us All"—and Memorial Coliseum is quiet and appreciative. Then he rears back and smacks them between the eyes with "Shoo-Be-Doo-Be-Doo-Dah-Day" and "Signed, Sealed, Delivered," Stevie weaving at the piano like a human metronome on speed, emoting into the microphone, and all you can see is an arena full of people undulating and crashing together like swells off the ocean. And then the two gorgeous black chicks come to reclaim him, and he leaves the stage to a mighty outpouring of thanks. And much later, at the end of a very long night, people filing out of Memorial Coliseum not only are talking about the Stones, who were fabulous, but also about Stevie Wonder and how he grabbed the crowd by the throat and swung them about like a rag doll . . . in fact, they'll never forget it.

And that was how Stevie Wonder came to the heart of Dixie, not terribly far from where his mother had picked cotton thirty years before in the soft dirt of the sharecroppers' farm in Hurtsboro, and convinced seventeen thousand Southern white folk to dance in the aisles and beg for more.

THE TOUR WITH the Rolling Stones in 1972 was a marketing ploy by Stevie's new handlers to introduce the artist to a larger audience. Under the terms of his new contract, he was allowed to augment Motown's promotional team with outside people of his own choosing—and the New York public relations firm Wartoke Concern went to work, not only angling for a slot on the Stones' tour, but placing him on TV shows like *I've Got a Secret* and *What's My Line?* The thinking was that everybody knew that Stevie had a nice following, but despite his reputation as a crossover artist, his audience remained primarily black. If he was to mature into a blockbuster artist who justified his fat contract—and meet the expectations that came with it—he would have to expand his following.

Wartoke Concern shouldn't have worried so much. Stevie's next album, *Talking Book*, would resolve these issues—and then some.

The first inkling of the success in store for *Talking Book* came with the release of its first single, "Superstition," on October 24, 1972, three days before the album was released. From the very outset of the song—a fairly placid drum rhythm that is abruptly sucker-punched by a snarling Clavinet riff that is as vivid a definition of funk as exists anywhere—it is abundantly clear that this is a piece of music to be reckoned with. Stevie's voice breaks in:

Very superstitious
Writing's on the wall

Whirlwind trumpets and saxophones fall into the fray, and "Superstition" is off to the races. *When you believe in things you don't understand/Then you suffer* is the operative lyric; that certainly is enough to chew on from an intellectual point of view, but this is a visceral song that delivers right to the gut. "Superstition" still stands as the perfect intersection of rock, pop, funk, and soul, and the single shot to number 1 on both *Billboard* charts and propelled the album to number 1 on the R&B chart and number 3 on the pop chart.

Many have contended that "Superstition" represents Stevie's greatest musical achievement. It certainly was the most wildly popular record he ever made. Oddly enough, however, in a testament to the argument that even Stevie didn't always know what was in his best interests, he originally asked Motown to hold off on releasing the song as a single. It seems that Stevie had told Jeff Beck, the brilliant guitarist, that he could record the song—Beck, as it turned out, had lent some of his guitar work to *Talking Book,* and Stevie had offered to let Beck record "Superstition." But Stevie also recorded his own version—a cut that he had to ruefully admit was nothing less than dynamite. Stevie included the song on the master he delivered to Motown but told Gordy that he didn't want it to be the first single released since Beck would also be recording it. Gordy (and everyone else who heard it) was flabbergasted by the request. Without question, the song was one of the best efforts of Stevie's career to date, perhaps *the* best. It was one of those rare songs that you just immediately had to listen to again . . . and again; the suits at Motown couldn't keep it off the spindle. They began to lobby Stevie to agree to releasing the song as a single: "I told Motown it was going to cause a lot of static, but they said 'No, man,'" Stevie recalled. "They had control of releasing the singles."

Beck later recorded his own version of "Superstition" which did not compare with Stevie's hit. Though disappointed, Beck later observed that the decision to release the single was the right one.

But *Talking Book* wasn't some one-trick pony. The first song on the album, "You Are the Sunshine of My Life," also was a number 1 hit and would become one of the songs most closely identified with Stevie Wonder. The song, an immaculate piece of feathery, romantic pop, would be covered by Frank Sinatra and many others, not to mention countless lounge singers straining to be heard above the din of countless happy hours across the Milky Way. "You Are the Sunshine of My Life" has a back story, too; Stevie recorded it during the sessions for *Music of My Mind,* inspired by his new love, backup singer Gloria Barley, who appears on the track. But he didn't want to include it on the album because he felt the tone of the song matched neither his frame of mind in the wake of his breakup with Syreeta nor the overall mood of *Music of My Mind.* He saved it for *Talking Book,* and the song provided Stevie with consecutive number 1 singles for the first time in his career.

Talking Book pulled no political punches—the song "Big Brother" is evidence of that, a dressing-down of politicians inspired by Stevie's fascination with George Orwell's classic novel *1984.* But the album's sheer style and spirit made it irresistible to the listening public, and it became the first of a string of four groundbreaking albums over the course of four years—each of them pop classics—that comprise the most significant phase of Stevie's extraordinarily phase-packed career. After *Talking Book* came *Innervisions* ("Living for the City," "Higher Ground," "Don't You Worry 'Bout a Thing"), then *Fulfillingness' First Finale* ("You Haven't Done Nothin'," "Boogie On Reggae Woman"), then *Songs in the Key of Life,* a double LP that remains Stevie's personal favorite among his work ("Sir Duke," "I Wish," "Pasttime Paradise," "Isn't She Lovely," "As"). Each album hit number 1.

It was a remarkable run, arguably as impressive a streak as any artist has ever put together (save, perhaps, Joe DiMaggio). Again, these albums were not mere compilations of disparate singles offered for the convenience of the record-buying public; like Marvin Gaye's *What's Going On,* they were sophisticated, challenging works, each characterized by their thematic unity, musical short stories connected by a circulatory system of uncommon musical innovations and lyrical sentiments. With that quartet of albums, Stevie had grasped the Holy Grail long sought after by so many artists but captured by precious few: His work was commercial *and* relevant. And all this had been accomplished in the context of a murderously unforgiving business. Nearly a decade had intervened between the success of "Fingertips—Pt 2" and "Superstition," between *12 Year Old Genius* and *Talking*

Book, a passage of time equivalent to a millennium in the record industry. Musical trends can morph overnight, much less from 1963 to 1972. Stevie not only had stayed abreast of the times; he was shaping them.

Everything that Stevie's music was about—innovation, emotion, social consciousness—may have been consummated in his song "Living for the City" from *Innervisions.* The song, a seven-minute, twenty-three-second epic, spins the tale of how "a boy is born in hard-time Mississippi" and makes his way to New York in hopes of a better life, only to encounter the cycle of despair that dominates the urban ghetto. While this plot line does not literally represent Stevie's life story, it stands as his most autobiographical work in that it relates the experience of Lula (*His mother goes and scrubs the floors for many/You best believe she barely makes a penny*), other members of his family, and untold other African Americans who for generations made the migratory sojourn from the oppressive South to the unforgiving metropolises of the North. The song's protagonist, full of hope and awe as he arrives in the big city, soon runs afoul of a predatory legal system and winds up in prison. "Living for the City" had a special resonance when the single was released in late 1973, as decaying inner cities across the country grappled with the aftermath of the violent 1960s and drew new political battle lines. In Detroit, the song's release coincided with the election of the city's first black mayor, Coleman Young. Young campaigned against police brutality but also solicited the support of white business interests, presenting himself as a candidate who could begin a healing in the city's core. As more than one observer noted at the time, "Living for the City" seemed to sum up the tenor of the Young campaign and the fragile psyche of Stevie's hometown.

Stevland Morris, the blind kid from the Detroit projects whose teachers warned of a future of making rugs and potholders, was not only rich and famous but *influential*. It seemed as if there was nothing he could not accomplish. But, amid all the success and joy and good work and *meaning,* there was a dark cloud gathering about him, an omen of tragedy. Stevie could sense it now.

And Lula's fitful dreams continued.

Fourteen

HIGHER GROUND

*H*OVERING ALONG IN *the black forest of deep space, asleep and yet awake, still absorbing data at that subconscious remove out there just beyond arm's length . . . asleep, and yet hearing the bubble machine of voices and other murmuring sounds that swirl and gather and pirouette and scatter . . . asleep, and yet aware of the tires whirring on the asphalt, vibrations billowing from beneath the car . . . asleep, and dreaming, and yet those dreams, a blind man's visions, violent with faceless and shapeless and colorless portent, give away nothing of what is to come . . . only that something is to come . . . and in the dream-womb, finally, the resolution begins to draw near, the answer as to how and when and where, approaching like a dark, silent comet, racing, reaching, yearning, taking celestial aim . . . and then it is here. The air begins to growl with its presence, a low, slow-motion, dream-syrup roar, trying to find the right note, the perfect pitch, before letting the full howl rip . . . and then the comet, if that is what it is . . . bathed in fire and catapulting from the knowing heavens, knowing that this is the time and the place, having always known it and only now willing to share the circumstances of fate . . . the comet*

slams and shatters, and the world seems to shudder at the heart of its
very core, the howl piercing space exploding Mama-baby-love-cold-
fear-God-music-sex-beauty-knowledge-power—NOTHING . . .

AS STEVIE RECORDED *Innervisions* in 1973, a pervasive sense of
dread enveloped him. It was a vague foreboding that he tried to ignore
at first, attempted to dismiss as some sort of anxiety that would pass.
But it would not pass, and soon the feeling began to take shape as an
omen of some dark event or tragedy. This was extremely unsettling to
Stevie; he was a deeply religious person who gave little or no credence
to any sort of supernatural order of things. Still, he knew that there
was much that human beings did not know about themselves and
how they connected to the energy of the world around them. He
knew that some very perceptive people frequently had fuzzy premo-
nitions that proved to be true. He also knew that his blindness made
him more open to the silent language of the universe. Stevie wanted to
ignore it, to forget about it. But he simply couldn't shake it. Something was going to happen to him.

Of all people—particularly in his line of work, often marked by
excess—Stevie should have felt relatively safe and secure. Due to his
blindness and his particular station in life, he had a coterie of aides and
handlers who placed him in a protective cocoon in every waking (and
sleeping) hour of the day. He was healthy and in the prime of life; he
didn't abuse drugs or alcohol. He was happy and entertained no self-
destructive thoughts. He had goals. He was, after all, trying to change
the world.

But the dread persisted, and he began to make fatalistic remarks
in public and to the press. In the studio, he was a man possessed. Two
days before his twenty-third birthday, he produced the spiritual funk
anthem "Higher Ground"—the words, music, recording, every-

thing—in three hours, the fastest he had ever finished a song. It was as if time was running short. The lyrics pounded like surf at high tide:

Gonna keep on tryin'
Till I reach my highest ground,

As the events of the next few months unfolded, the eerie prescience of those words would become clear.

STEVIE WAS ASLEEP as the car sped north on Route 85 near Salisbury, North Carolina, in the predawn hours of August 6, 1973. *Innervisions* had been released three days earlier, and the supporting tour was under way. Stevie had staged a concert in Greenville, South Carolina, and now was traveling to the Duke University campus in Durham for a benefit performance. At the wheel was Stevie's cousin, John Harris.

Logging trucks were common in the densely forested region, and were a nuisance for travelers in a hurry; a driver could spend his life trying to get around the damn things, which pondered down the highway like drunken dinosaurs, their cargo jutting out from the truck bed. No one could say what happened next, exactly . . . but suddenly the car was entangled with one of the plodding trucks and there was a great, grinding screech as metal hit metal and, then, impossibly, as if in some lavishly produced Hollywood action movie, one of the great logs disencumbered itself of the truck and came smashing through the windshield, spearing Stevie square in the forehead. It was, as everyone agreed later, one hell of a shot—something you couldn't have replicated if you rigged it up and tried it a million times.

Everything scraped to a skidding, crumpling halt. Harris, in shock, reached over in the terrifying darkness for Stevie, and pulled back a hand wet with blood. It was bad . . . real bad.

Finally the ambulance arrived and transported Stevie, unconscious and still bleeding, to Rowan Memorial Hospital in Salisbury. After triage was performed there, he was immediately transferred to North Carolina Baptist Hospital in Winston-Salem, which had neurosurgical facilities. There, it was determined that Stevie had a broken skull and severe brain bruising. He was in a coma. It also was determined that he was extremely fortunate to have even survived.

LULA HEARD THE news on the radio in Detroit. She finally got someone on the phone and listened in disbelief as she learned about the events of the last few hours. She hung up the phone, and made arrangements to fly to North Carolina to be at her son's side. Then she felt her legs waver beneath her; she found a chair and sat down, trying to regain her equilibrium. It was then, as the awful reality of everything began to cave in on top of her—*Stevie's hurt, he might die*—that she remembered The Dream: Stevie's lifeless body in a clearing in the dark woods, surrounded by strangers.

THE DOCTORS TOLD the reporters who kept the deathwatch vigil out in the lobby that Stevie slowly was regaining consciousness, but the circle of family, friends, and aides who monitored every scant twitch couldn't tell it. He was motionless. He just lay there, all manner of wires and tubes shooting out of him like spaghetti noodles, his swollen head layered in gauze. First one visitor and then another would gingerly take his hand, lean over to his one exposed ear, and gently say: Stevie, you there? Can you hear me, brother? If you can hear me, we love you, Stevie . . . And on and on like so, people whispering around him in funeral parlor tones.

Lula arrived in a panic, rattled from the trip and the unbearable suspense that went with it. She immediately ran everyone out of the room. Baby, your Mama's here now . . . It was a difficult sight to take in. His head was three times its normal size; that was the worst of it, the part she couldn't bear. How could this happen? She realized, suddenly, that everything had pointed to this catastrophe, this test. You would think that the child's blindness was test enough . . . but it never was a test for him, not really. It had been a gift, in the end. But she knew the exalted carry a special burden, and that God often calls them home, much sooner than their earthly peers can accept or comprehend, so that their works can be conducted on a grander plane. She took Stevie's hand and knelt at the side of the hospital bed, and began to pray: *Our dear Heavenly Father, if Thy will is that this boy be summoned to join the angels and do Your bidding from on high, then Thy will be done . . . but, Father, if you choose to spare this angel here and now, to remain among us, I know that he will carry Thy torch into the far corners of the world . . .*

IRA TUCKER DIDN'T agree with all the tiptoeing around. Tucker, Stevie's publicist and all-around right-hand man, knew that Stevie liked things *loud.* He played music loud, the TV loud . . . hell, Stevie himself was the loudest dude on the planet. And everybody creeping around like they're afraid to wake him up—he needed to wake up! He was in there somewhere . . . he just needed to snap out of it. He needed something to grab on to, to pull him out of the water! He was probably in there right now, swimming around, looking for the way out. Besides, if the situation was reversed—if it was Ira in a coma, and Stevie hanging around—well, Stevie wouldn't be quiet. He'd be jabbering at the top of his lungs and telling Ira to wake *up,* Jack! He'd probably be playing music and raising hell, trying to roust the spirits . . .

But it was like a tomb in there.

So Tucker had a talk with the doctor. What if I get down right in his ear and try to call him out? Maybe even shout? You say he should be coming out of it . . . we gotta shake him out of this! . . . The doctor shrugged. Sure, why not? It won't hurt anything. Give it a try—but not too much, okay? Don't break his eardrum, for God's sake.

Tucker scurried back to Stevie's room. HEY, STEVIE! . . . STEVE! . . . Come on man, wake up! We're all here waiting on you, brother . . . STEVIE!

Nothing. Well, he'd try it again later, maybe tomorrow. He's hearing it—we just can't tell it yet, Ira would say.

Lula remained steadfast that he would be okay. The doctors were saying good things, but what did they know? And even if he did wake up, who was to say what sort of damage might have been done? He took a real jolt to the head, a near-fatal blow. What if he was some kind of vegetable? If it turned out that Stevie, the most verbal human being you could imagine, was impaired in some way, maybe couldn't talk or sing . . . that would almost be worse, for him, than dying. But she told herself not to think about such things. The outcome was in God's hands now. All the rest of them could do was wait.

Tucker was back the next day, still advancing his theory. Today, he announced, he would sing in Stevie's ear. Stevie needed music. The hospital wouldn't let them drag a stereo in, so Ira would have to sing. The others rolled their eyes and said, Why not? Go for it.

So Tucker started singing "Higher Ground."

Gonna keep on tryin'

Nothing.

Gonna keep on tryin'
Till I reach my highest ground.

Stevie's hand was resting on Tucker's arm. Tucker kept singing, and then there was a faint rustling . . . and Tucker looked down and saw Stevie's fingers begin slowly to move in time with the song. No joking . . . *they were moving.* Tucker felt an electrifying surge of elation. *Yeah!* he cried, his voice ringing down the corridor. *Yeah! This dude is gonna make it!*

SOON STEVIE WAS conscious and functioning. Everybody knew he was going to be all right when he started hitting on the nurses. Still, no one was sure about what side effects might remain. The shock to his system had been so severe, his senses of taste and smell had shut down (temporarily, as it turned out). Stevie kept telling everyone that he would recover, that he would be all right. But who really knew?

When Stevie regained some strength, he was transferred to the UCLA Medical Center in Los Angeles. After some more time went by, he announced he was ready to try to play an instrument again. Tucker brought in Stevie's Clavinet and set it up. But Stevie didn't try to play it right away . . . he seemed to be afraid to touch it. Tucker and the others began to worry: What if he can't do it? What if he . . . lost it? Finally he sat down and haltingly ran his fingers over the keys— and began to play. Nicely, fluidly, perfectly. Relief flooded Stevie's face. Everything was going to be all right, just like he had said.

FATE—OR WHATEVER you choose to call it—had given Stevie Wonder a pass. The inexplicable horror that seems to claim the lives of so many gifted and beloved people in the prime of their lives—the drugs, accidents, and misguided malevolence that took from us the Jimi Hendrixes and the Buddy Hollys and the John Lennons—came to pay Stevie a visit, but then decided to move on. Maybe he was blessed; maybe he was just lucky. But he knew that something momentous had occurred. And, as different as Stevie always had been from the rest of his seeing, uncomprehending species, his response was no different from many others who had encountered death and walked away from it: He understood that his time on earth is precious, ever-fleeting. And when you are attempting to change the world, every moment is more precious and fleeting still.

Lula never had The Dream again. All the portent had passed now; her son had survived the test. Looking back over all of it—from Hurtsboro to East Chicago to Saginaw to Detroit to, now, Los Angeles, California—it occurred to her that she had survived it, too.

THE LONG BLACK limousine eased to a stop in front of the Hollywood hotel where Stevie's entourage had encamped for the 1973 Grammy Awards, presented in March 1974. Soon Stevie emerged into the late afternoon sun in a shimmering black tux with a coterie of others, including Lula in a long red gown.

All were convinced that a big night was in store. There was palpable excitement inside the car. As always, he was fiercely competitive with his fellow musicians in a collegial way, admiring their work while doing his best to top them. Tonight, he hoped to top them all.

The limo glided on its way.

How you feeling, baby?

I'm good, Mama. It's gonna be a good night.

You gonna win?

I'll win something. We'll roll with it. But if I win, I want you up there with me, Mama.

I'm not gonna do that. Milton can take you up there.

Mama—I mean it, now.

I don't need to be up there in front of all those people. You don't worry about it.

The big car surged on, down Ventura Boulevard and onto the Hollywood Freeway. The sun was beginning to settle down into the blue-smoke haze that swaddled the brown hills that overlooked L.A.

Stevie and the others began to babble about the other nominees. So-and-so had put out a fine record, someone said. I *love* that record, Stevie said. But, someone else said, it just ain't in the same *class* with . . .

Lula pulled away from the conversation, and looked around her with new eyes: All these people, dressed in the finest clothes, stacked in a car so plush you could live in it, if you wanted to. And Stevie, her precious boy, still here. *And I'm still here,* she thought, shaking her head. *We're still here, both of us. We are lucky to be alive, and all thanks be to God.*

It had not been nearly as easy as people made it sound sometimes. The bones of the story had been told plenty of times by now; virtually any pop music fan could recite it. Young, poor, black, blind musical genius is plucked from the Detroit ghetto by Berry Gordy, signed to a contract at age ten, and goes on to sell tens of millions of records. Just as easy as that.

But nothing's easy, she thought, *and nothing's free.*

Sometimes she wondered what things would have been like if Stevie had never been discovered. She already had the house on Breckenridge in Detroit by then, and by then she had chased the evil out of their lives, and barely lived to tell the tale. She had the job at the fish market. They probably would have made out okay, she thought. Still struggling, but okay.

But Stevie's talent brought newer, more sophisticated kinds of evil to their door. And she fought it, for a while. But Stevie wanted to take his shot, he wanted it so bad . . . and, finally, she gave in. And then they took her little precious boy away from her, and there were times that she wondered if she would ever get him back.

But now here she was with him, riding in a long black car, wearing a dress that cost a year's wages for some folks. And Stevie, little blind Stevie, was lighting up the world.

The limo pulled up to the Shrine Auditorium, where the red carpet showed the way inside. People were stacked on top of each other on either side of the runway.

Come on, Mama, walk with me, Stevie said.

As they made their way inside, something akin to Beatlemania broke out, cheers and screams and emotion showering down from above, people yelling his name: Stevie, over here! Yeah, Big Stevie!

The ceremony was more than Stevie could have ever hoped for. He won five Grammys—Best R&B Vocal Performance, Male, and Best Rhythm & Blues Song prizes for "Superstition," Best Pop Vocal Performance, Male, for "You Are the Sunshine of My Life," and two Album of the Year awards (one as artist, one as producer) for *Innervisions.*

For the first four awards, Lula held fast to her refusal to go on stage with Stevie. But when the last was announced—for Album of the Year, the big one—Stevie grabbed her firmly by the arm. Come on, Mama, he said. This time it's you and me.

And so, arm in arm, as "Sunshine" resonated throughout the auditorium, Stevie and Lula made the trek to the podium, the cheers crashing around them. Stevie took the statuette and held it high in triumph, his trademark smile flashing like a searchlight. He then turned and presented the trophy to a stunned Lula.

It's for you, Mama, he told her; it's for you.

Stevie found the microphone and addressed the audience and the millions of viewers at home. Her strength has led us to this place, he said, clutching Lula. Then Lula spoke: Thank you all—for making the sunshine of my life.

The applause and cheers ignited again, as tears fled down Lula's face. Finally, they made their way backstage, where the press awaited.

My, my, Lula thought, looking at the wrestling throng of photographers, their flashbulbs bursting like fireworks, like . . . fireflies. *My, my, my.*

Epilogue

Los Angeles, California, 2002

*T*HE LIFE OF Stevie Wonder since his brush with death has been one of almost perpetual activity. He has been endlessly praised and feted and—in the surest sign of having achieved iconic status—parodied by the likes of comedic actor Eddie Murphy on *Saturday Night Live.* He was one of the most visible figures behind the difficult and arduous campaign to honor civil rights leader Martin Luther King Jr. with a national holiday. He also was one of the chief architects of USA for Africa, the project that in 1985 brought together an unprecedented lineup of musical superstars to record "We Are the World" to benefit famine victims. Shortly after the World Trade Center attack in 2001, Stevie was front and center for a benefit for the victims of that horrific disaster.

Today, in his early fifties, he continues to roam the world and is closely identified with a host of social causes and Democratic Party politics. It was Stevie who made a great show of his support for President Bill Clinton and First Lady Hillary Clinton in 1998 at a state dinner in the immediate aftermath of the revelation of Clinton's dalliance with White House intern Monica Lewinsky. At a time when

Clinton's status with longtime friends and supporters was very much under siege, Stevie affectionately bear-hugged the First Couple and said afterward that he "told the president a long time ago that I was his friend. And I am of the belief that when you say you are someone's friend, it doesn't mean you are a fair-weather friend. You're there all the time." Al Gore, in a recurring tribute to Stevie, frequently requested that "Sir Duke" be played as he took the stage during the 2000 presidential campaign. TV cameras caught Stevie in the audience as Gore delivered his pivotal nomination acceptance speech at the 2000 Democratic National Convention in Los Angeles. As the neck-and-neck 2000 campaign reached its frantic zenith, Stevie traveled virtually around the clock on Gore's behalf, and was the focal point of an Election Eve rally and concert in Miami that drew an estimated one hundred thousand people.

Although by some measures the white-hot peak of his popularity has passed, his music remains almost omnipresent; it seems to always be playing in stores, on the radio, on movie soundtracks. (Stevie was famously dissed in the 2000 movie *High Fidelity* by actor Jack Black during his portrayal of a hilariously volcanic music store clerk who verbally batters a customer searching for a copy of Stevie's croony ballad "I Just Called to Say I Love You." But the film kisses and makes up with Stevie later, affectionately playing "I Believe (When I Fall in Love It Will Be Forever)" as the credits roll.)

Most of his appearances these days are for causes of one kind or another. As the years between albums for the notoriously fastidious Wonder increase (at this writing, a new studio album and a long-promised gospel album are long overdue; his last studio album, *Conversation Peace,* appeared in 1995) so does the length of time between his concert tours. Even so, he continues to be held in almost ethereal esteem in the music world, and artists ranging from Prince to Garth Brooks to the Red Hot Chili Peppers continue to cite him as a seminal influence on their own work.

And yet, with the new millennium, it was clearer than ever that Stevie Wonder remained much more than an entertainer. He was, well, *Stevie Wonder*—an institution unto himself and the embodiment of an ideal, as well as a man who had transcended an overwhelming disability to win over the world. "He's the only person I know," syndicated sports radio host Jim Rome told his nationwide audience one morning in 1999, "who is welcome anywhere he goes."

IT IS TEMPTING to simply report that Lula Hardaway lived happily ever after. It would, for the most part, be true. In 1976, Stevie told her he would buy her a new house wherever she wanted: Detroit, New York, anywhere. Lula chose Los Angeles, where Stevie was spending (and still spends) much of his time. She still lives quietly in the sprawling, well-appointed ranch house in the San Fernando Valley foothills, a pool in the backyard, a Rolls-Royce and a Mercedes in the garage. She keeps tabs on her six children—including her most peripatetic one—via an incessantly ringing telephone. She has had some reversals in her love life over the years, relationships that didn't work out. Now, at seventy-one, she lives alone and seems to prefer it that way.

As she shared in Stevie's success and settled into a life of financial security, Lula strove over the years to bring her family together and let bygones be bygones. She reestablished contact with her mother, although with unrewarding results. She kept in touch with her father; he visited her once in Los Angeles, and she offers a dim Polaroid print as evidence. Aunt Ilona and Deacon Robert also were occasional visitors. After Robert died, Ilona visited annually until a few years before her death in 1990, a loss that Lula still feels deeply. Her parents are deceased now. The curse of a long life, Lula says, is that you must stay behind while your loved ones go on to their rewards.

Everyone turned out for Mr. Judkins's funeral in 1976, including Lula. The program from the memorial service contains his picture, that of a handsome rake wearing a wide-brimmed hat at the pro-scribed jaunty angle. Stevie bought his father a new Cadillac while he was still alive, and Judkins spent his later years trolling around in the sleek, gleaming automobile, big-dogging it to the end. "I still say he's the best-looking devil God ever put on this earth," Lula says, shaking her head.

In September 2002, Lula and her family were forced to deal with the shocking and tragic death of her son Larry, forty-eight. High blood pressure, a series of respiratory ailments, and other health problems have also slowed Lula recently, but her dogged tenacity and keen anticipation of the publication of this book recounting her struggles and victories have kept her in good spirits. She has been to the dark side of life and back; her chief motivation in telling her story, she says, is her hope that young women who feel trapped and power-less can shake off their chains, as did she. Before Berry Gordy ever met little Stevland Judkins, Lula had escaped an abusive relationship, learned to support herself, purchased a home, and had taken control of her life and her family. With inner fortitude and God's help, she says, other despairing women can do the same.

Lula recently was admitted to St. Joseph's Hospital in Burbank with a severe heart irregularity; the condition later was corrected with medication, but her situation seemed touch-and-go for a while. As she recovered, Stevie made a long-scheduled appearance a few blocks away on *The Tonight Show with Jay Leno*. Stevie told Leno of his mother's close call, then turned toward the camera and said, "Mama, I'm not ready to lose you yet!"

That goes for all of us.